Reducing Reoffending

Published by

Willan Publishing
Culmcott House
Mill Street, Uffculme
Cullompton, Devon
EX15 3AT, UK
Tel: +44(0)1884 840337
Fax: +44(0)1884 840251
e-mail: info@willanpublishing.co.uk
website: www.willanpublishing.co.uk

Published simultaneously in the USA and Canada by

Willan Publishing
c/o ISBS, 920 NE 58th Ave, Suite 300,
Portland, Oregon 97213-3786, USA
Tel: +001(0)503 287 3093
Fax: +001(0)503 280 8832
e-mail: info@isbs.com
website: www.isbs.com

First published 2007

Reprinted 2008

Paperback
ISBN: 978-1-84392-218-6

British Library Cataloguing-in-Publication Data

A catalogue record for this book is available from the British Library

Project managed by Deer Park Productions, Tavistock, Devon
Typeset by TW Typesetting, Plymouth, Devon
Printed and bound by TJ International Ltd, Trecerus Industrial Estate, Padstow, Cornwall

Reducing Reoffending

Social work and community justice in Scotland

Fergus McNeill and Bill Whyte

WILLAN
PUBLISHING

Contents

Figures and tables

Acknowledgements

We owe many debts in relation to this book; probably more than we remember and certainly more than we can repay, other than with our thanks.

The support of colleagues in the Criminal Justice Social Work Development Centre, the Glasgow School of Social Work and the Scottish Centre for Crime and Justice Research has been critical both in enabling us to develop our research and scholarship in general and to commit time to the task of writing this book in particular. Similarly, without the benefit of the innumerable ideas and insights that we owe, directly and indirectly, to the many academic colleagues, students, policy-makers, managers, practitioners and service users who have helped us over the years, this book would have been very much the poorer.

We are also indebted to the various friends and colleagues who have commented on (and sometimes contributed to) different parts of the book, including Monica Barry, Susan Batchelor, Ros Burnett, Stephen Farrall, Beth Fawcett, Trish McCulloch, Gill McIvor, Shadd Maruna, Paulo Mazzoncini, Mike Nellis, Gwen Robinson and others. As ever, the responsibility for any errors and omissions is ours alone.

Finally, we want to thank Brian Willan, not only for his patience and equanimity in the face of chronic deadline drift, but also for having the vision to commission a book about social work and community justice in Scotland in the first place.

He admitted that he was not an innocent man unjustly punished. He had committed an excessive and blameworthy act . . . To attempt to take society by the throat, vulnerable creature that he was, and to suppose that he could escape from poverty through theft, had been an act of folly. In any case, the road leading to infamy was a bad road of escape. He admitted all of this – in short, that he had done wrong.

But then he asked questions.

Was he the only one at fault in this fateful business? Was it not a serious matter that a man willing to work should have been without work and without food? And, admitting the offence, had not the punishment been ferocious and outrageous? Was not the law more at fault in the penalty it inflicted than he had been in the crime he committed? . . .

He asked himself whether human society had the right to impose upon its members, on the one hand its mindless improvidence and, on the other hand, its merciless providence; to grind a poor man between the millstones of need and excess – need of work and excess of punishment . . .

He asked these questions and, having answered them, passed judgement on society.

He condemned it to his hatred. He held it responsible for what he was undergoing and resolved that, if the chance occurred, he would not hesitate to call it to account. He concluded that there was no true balance between the wrong that he had done and the wrong that was inflicted upon him, and that although the punishment might not technically be an injustice it was beyond question an iniquity (Victor Hugo, *Les Miserables*, Hugo, 1862/1982: 96–7).

For Morag, Caitie and Calum

FM

For Noel

BW

Introduction: challenging times

For scholars, students and practitioners of criminal justice alike, Scotland is an intriguing place to be and an intriguing place to study – now more so than ever. Despite her close proximity to and historical ties with the other UK jurisdictions, Scotland has had a distinctive and proud legal tradition and justice system since before the Act of Union in 1707. It is a tradition based primarily on common law (rather than statute) and in which the exercise of discretion by both prosecutors (or 'procurators fiscal' as they are known) and sentencers plays a pivotal role (Young 1997). Moreover, it is a system which, since the advent of devolution and the establishment of the Scottish Parliament in 1999, has faced intense political scrutiny and an unprecedented plethora of policy and practice initiatives (Croall 2006; McIvor and McNeill 2007).

Within this broader context, Scotland's arrangements for the supervision of offenders in the community are, in our view, particularly fascinating. Recently, several distinguished penologists have argued that the UK, the USA and other English-speaking jurisdictions have witnessed very significant 'penal transformations'; that is, fundamental reconfigurations of the field of punishment. David Garland has written of the 'eclipse of penal welfarism' by an emerging 'culture of control' (Garland 2001). Malcolm Feeley and Jonathan Simon have charted the rise to prominence of a new penology characterised by and expressed in a risk-based 'actuarial regime' (Feeley and Simon 1992, 1994; Simon and Feeley 1995). John Pratt and others have analysed the emergence and significance of 'the new punitiveness' (Pratt 2000; Pratt *et al.* 2004). And yet, against the typically dark shadows portrayed in these analyses, Scotland (at least at first sight) seems to stand out as a penal anachronism, unlike the rest of the UK and most other English-speaking countries, in that here it remains the legal duty of generically trained social workers (not probation officers), employed by local authorities (not correctional services), to 'promote social welfare' in their dealings with offenders.

However, though Chapter 1 provides some analysis both of the genesis of these unique arrangements and of their continual adaptation to changing social, political and penal conditions, it is not the purpose of this book to explore whether criminal justice social work in Scotland really is a twenty-first century penal anachronism or whether it is better understood as an institution that is in fact transforming, albeit perhaps more slowly and more subtly than has allegedly been the case elsewhere (but see Hutchinson 2006; O'Malley 2004). Rather, our purpose is both more practical, and arguably more urgent, precisely because both social work *and* community justice in Scotland are facing some very significant and very tangible changes. However, before providing an account of these changes, it makes sense first to briefly recall the relatively recent emergence of criminal justice social work, so that we can properly locate and contextualise current developments.

Criminal justice social work

As we will see in Chapter 1, although probation in Scotland has a long history, criminal justice social work only emerged as a distinct specialism as a result of the Law Reform (Miscellaneous Provisions) (Scotland) Act, 1990. This Act provided for the development not only of National Objectives and Standards (SWSG 1991a) (hereafter NOS) and ring-fenced funding from central government for criminal justice services, it also enabled the emergence of renewed professional identity *within* social work supported by specialist qualifications (specifically the MSc in Advanced Social Work Studies in Criminal Justice and Advanced Award developed and delivered by the Universities of Edinburgh and Stirling).

The policy direction for criminal justice social work was (and continues to be) provided by the NOS which challenged social work to demonstrate its credentials in promoting social welfare (the welfare of the community *and* of individuals within it) under section 12 of the Social Work (Scotland) Act 1968, through its contribution to reducing custody, reducing reoffending and improving community safety. The duty to promote social welfare (under section 12) continues to belong to the local authority *as a whole* rather than to social work departments or sections within it. Similarly, under section 27 of the 1968 Act, it is the local authority which is charged with providing services to the criminal justice system as part of its unified responsibilities.

The thinking behind the 1968 Act can be misunderstood as a mere reconfiguration within the dialectic of traditional notions of justice and welfare rather than as a serious attempt at a distinctive approach rooted in Scotland's European traditions (see Smith and Whyte, forthcoming). At the time, Bruce (1975, 1985) reported it as nothing less than a paradigm shift, transferring responsibility for community safety from the justice system directly to the community. Intriguingly (as we will see at the conclusion of this book), this is somewhat reflective of current debates on the nature of community justice and on the comparative effectiveness of a *criminal justice paradigm* characterised by crime, conviction and punishment as opposed to a *social justice or social educational paradigm* characterised by prevention, change (or development) and inclusion (or integration).

The 1968 Act remained sympathetic to the original concept of probation as holding back from punishment for a period of time through a legal device or 'bond' to the court, making the person (with their agreement) subject to supervision in the community. In Scotland (unlike in England and Wales), the principles behind this concept are maintained in the Criminal Procedure (Scotland) Act 1995 wherein probation is ordered *'instead of* sentencing' (section 228, emphasis added). Though, as we will see in subsequent chapters, the emphasis on social justice and welfare in 'advising, assisting, and befriending' has been rather downplayed of late, it is still reflected in the stress on inclusion and integration within Scotland's most recent criminal justice plan:

> Our goal is ... a co-ordinated service which manages offenders *throughout their sentence to their reintegration* into a law-abiding lifestyle. (Minister of Justice in Scottish Executive 2004a: 7–13, emphasis added)

The policy objectives in the original NOS for criminal justice social work (which have never been formally supplanted) were identified by Malcolm Rifkind, then Secretary of State for Scotland, in his 1988 Kenneth Younger Memorial Lecture. In essence, the policy was based on a tacit acknowledgement that 'prison doesn't work' and should be 'used sparingly'. The lecture outlined what has been referred to as a 'twin track' (or bifurcated) approach to criminal justice social work:

> While the use of imprisonment *may be inescapable when dealing with violent offenders and those who commit the most serious crimes*, we must question to what extent *short sentences* of imprisonment and periods of *custody for fine default* are appropriate means of dealing with offenders. (Rifkind 1989: 85, emphasis added)

In effect, Rifkind identified two (overlapping) priority target groups for adult provision – the 'non-violent' offender and those committing 'less serious offences', particularly those who become subject to 'short sentences' or 'custody for fine default'. The subsequent NOS also indicate that young people, whatever the category of offending, ought to be a priority for criminal justice social work provision. It is important to stress that Rifkind's twin track was never intended to be a *sentencing* policy. Rather, it was and remains the framework for efficient and effective use of social work resources in the criminal justice system.

The operational implications of the policy framework were that criminal justice social work should be able to make a range of *community disposals* available to the courts, specifically for non-violent offenders and less serious offenders, so as to avoid the expensive use of custodial provision. It was envisaged that serious and violent offenders were likely to face custody unless credible *alternatives to custody* were made available should the court

3

decide to use them. The NOS also placed emphasis on the importance of reparation and recognised that criminal justice social work services were intended to operate *on behalf of* victims by helping the offender to change, thereby effectively protecting the community. The Association of Directors of Social Work's subsequent statement of values (ADSW 1996: para. 2) stressed that a victim perspective should form a core part of the content of criminal justice social work supervision. While the initial target outlined for criminal justice social work related to reducing the unnecessary use of custody, the emphasis within NOS was always on social work's contribution to changing behaviour; or in contemporary discourse, on supporting desistance. Moreover, in ethical terms, it was the offending that legitimated social work intervention in the life of the individual through the criminal justice process, as opposed to through other more voluntary 'welfare' routes.

The introduction of 'ring-fenced' funding in 1990 meant to some degree that provision was no longer an autonomous responsibility of local authorities. NOS were developed nationally; core funding levels were set nationally; and the service was inspected nationally. It could be argued therefore that the local authority had become at best a partner and at worst a servant of central government (Huntingford 1992). As we will see below, the provisions within the recent Management of Offenders (Scotland) Act 2005 have taken these developments a stage further with the establishment of Community Justice Authorities operating within a national strategy. In principle, this allows for the best of both worlds; a service with nationally agreed strategic objectives but which is nonetheless integrated and delivered locally, in response to local needs and local priorities through various forms of partnership provision. Thus, if the twin track policy is still to be taken seriously (as we would argue that it should be), the new Community Justice Authorities will need to be able to identify patterns of need locally through audits analysing, for example, local crime data, social enquiry report data and standardised assessments of risks and needs. Such data should enable *local* providers to develop services and resources that are fit for purpose.

We have already mentioned the National Objectives and Standards (NOS) on several occasions and, given their significance as, in effect, a founding document for criminal justice social work services, it makes sense to describe them in more detail here before moving on to more recent developments. The NOS were devised in partnership between government, local authorities, the judiciary and other interested parties. They aimed to provide detailed benchmarks for social work services. As we will see in Chapter 1, their introduction was considered an essential prerequisite for restoring the confidence of the courts, particularly in the use of probation as an effective community-based disposal.

The risk in providing detailed 'national standards', as they have become known, is that they tend to be seen as entailing merely procedural compliance or efficient processing of cases. It is important to note that the document also provided national *objectives*. These objectives continue to have clear implications for the nature of the professional services required and for the ways in which its quality and effectiveness should be assessed. The statement of objectives set out in the 'General Issues' section of the NOS applied to social work provision of all types at every stage in the criminal justice process. The objectives were identified as being:

- to enable a *reduction in the incidence of custody*, whether on remand, at sentence, or in default of financial penalty, where it is used for lack of a suitable, available community-based social work disposal;

- to *promote* and enhance the range and quality of *community-based social work disposals* available to the courts and ensure that they are managed and supervised in such a manner that they have the confidence of courts, the police, and the public at large;

- to ensure that social work disposals are provided to the courts or other agencies in such a way that the *full range of disposals* is available when required so that the most appropriate one can be used, particularly with the *persistent offender*;

- to give *priority* to the development of *community-based social work disposals* and other services to *young adult offenders*;

- to promote the development of schemes to enable the courts to grant *bail* in an increased number of cases;

- to provide and facilitate *services for prisoners*, and their *families*, to help them prepare for *release from custody*, and to assist them to *resettle in the community*;

- to help offenders *tackle their offending behaviour*, assist them to live socially responsible lives within the law, whenever appropriate, through the involvement and support of their families, friends, and other resources in their community;

- to *assist the families of offenders* where family life suffers as a consequence of offending behaviour;

- to promote, provide, and facilitate the development of schemes for *diverting accused persons* from prosecution to social work in those cases where there is sufficient evidence to prosecute but it is not deemed necessary to do so in the public interest;

- to *promote* and assist the development of *services to the victims* of crime;

- to promote and assist action to *reduce and prevent crime*. (SWSG 1991a, emphases added)

Importantly, a supplement entitled *Towards Effective Policy and Practice* (SWSG 1991b) was added to the document after its initial publication to reinforce the policy framework and stress the importance of performance and outcomes, to promote the importance of effective practice and to identify a set of operational principles derived from research on effective intervention, summarised under the following headings:

- Identifying and managing risk of reoffending and risk of custody
- Focusing on offending behaviour.
- Tackling behaviour associated with offending
- Addressing underlying problems
- Reintegrating offenders with the community
- Using authority positively
- Ensuring diversity of practice

The supplement identifies the components of effective practice diagrammatically in a 'triangle' illustrating the nature and scope of offence-focused intervention within the context of provision aimed not only at reducing reoffending but at better social integration. Although, as we outline in Chapter 1, criminal justice social work has faced many challenges and has developed significantly since 1991 (see also McIvor and McNeill 2007), both the framework provided by the 'twin track' policy and enshrined in the NOS and the commitment to the development of effective practice in pursuit of that policy have proved enduring. However, current changes both in social work as a profession and in community justice suggest that criminal justice social work is experiencing, or is about to experience, a very significant reconfiguration.

Current challenges in social work and community justice

First, in relation to social work, for over 25 years (following the implementation of Social Work (Scotland) Act 1968) the responsibilities and boundaries of social work *departments* themselves generally defined, for practical purposes, the range and roles of social work *services*. However, since reform of local government in Scotland in 1996, there have been changes in both political and organisational arrangements for delivering social work, with a greater emphasis on providing these services in partnership with others working in the spheres of education, health and justice and in the public, private and voluntary sectors.

Scotland's parliament is now fully responsible for social work and the Scottish Executive is only beginning to exercise its law making powers.

Though there have been a raft of social work related initiatives, the most fundamental contemporary challenges for social work in Scotland arise from the recent *Report of the 21st Century Review Group* (Scottish Executive 2006a). The review was ordered in 2004 by Scottish ministers after several very high-profile social work 'failures'. It focused primarily on the central purpose and role of the social worker and of the social work profession in the modern world (see www.socialworkscotland.org.uk). The main recommendations of the review's report were that social work in Scotland needed to develop so as to:

- deliver services designed around the needs of service users, carers and communities;
- contribute to building the capacities of users, carers and communities to meet their own needs;
- play an active part in prevention and earlier intervention;
- become part of a public sector-wide approach to supporting vulnerable people and promoting their wellbeing;
- recognise and effectively manage the mixed economy of care in the delivery of services;
- develop new approaches to the management of risk which ensure the delivery of safe, effective and innovative practice;
- enable and support staff to practise accountably and to exercise professional autonomy;
- develop a learning culture that commits all individuals and organisations to lifelong learning and development; and,
- deliver services through effective teams with the right mix of skills and expertise and operating with delegated authority and responsibilities. (Scottish Executive 2006a)

Although there is little direct discussion of criminal justice social work in the report, a literature review about the professional skills required to reduce reoffending was commissioned in the review process (McNeill *et al.* 2005). That review concluded that:

What is required is a complex mix of skills which require significant personal qualities as well as a high degree of training across a range of ... disciplines in order that one worker is able to draw together approaches that address various areas of an offender's life so as to coherently and consistently support the change process. It seems to us that, within the criminal justice context at least, *social work almost exclusively encapsulates this broad skill base with its holistic attention to the full spectrum of an individual's needs in his or her social context.* The development of effective services to reduce re-offending in Scotland therefore requires political and professional investment in equipping the relevant frontline staff with the key skills required for effective practice and in creating the contexts for practice that provide them with realistic opportunities to exercise these skills. (McNeill *et al.* 2005: 41, emphasis added)

Whether or not this conclusion was accepted by the review group (or by the Executive), there is certainly no sign in the final report of the review that criminal justice social work could or should be removed from the wider profession. The recommendations above therefore should be read as applying as much to criminal justice social work as to any other aspect of social work.

This is significant because, as we will see in Chapter 1, the immediate history of the current reforms around community justice in Scotland date back to the Scottish parliamentary election campaign in 2003. The Scottish Labour Party's manifesto for that campaign (in May 2003, eight months ahead of the publication of the Carter Report (2004) in England and Wales) promised the creation of a single agency or 'Correctional Service for Scotland' – staffed by professionals and covering prison and community-based sentences to 'maximise the impact of punishment, rehabilitation and protection offered by our justice system' (Scottish Labour 2003). If enacted, this would have entailed the removal of criminal justice social work from local authority control and perhaps, in professional and disciplinary terms, from social work itself. The Partnership Agreement between Scottish Labour and the Scottish Liberal Democrats, published following the elections, moderated Labour's position slightly by undertaking to 'publish *proposals for consultation* for a single agency to deliver custodial and non-custodial sentences in Scotland with the aim of reducing reoffending rates' (Scottish Executive 2003a, emphasis added).

COSLA (Convention of Scottish Local Authorities) and ADSW (Association of Directors of Social Work) responded to the Labour manifesto commitment by pledging to fight 'tooth and nail' against the proposed measures, arguing that there was no justification for such changes and no evidence that they would work to cut reoffending (*The Scotsman*, 9 May 2003). Following the election they commissioned a report from the International Centre for Prison Studies to explore whether the available international evidence supported the proposed organisational changes. The resulting report was submitted as a response to the related Consultation on Reducing Reoffending (Scottish Executive 2004b) which reiterated the First Minister's previously stated position that 'the status quo is not an option' (McConnell 2003: 21). However, in a conference speech towards the end of 2003, the report's author, Professor Andrew Coyle, concluded that 'there is no evidence that particular organisational arrangements for the delivery of criminal justice provision in any one country lead to higher or lower use of imprisonment or affect reoffending rates' (Coyle 2003: 12).

In the introduction to the Reducing Reoffending consultation the Justice Minister acknowledged that 'the answer to reducing reoffending does not simply lie in more imprisonment ... The prison population continues to expand, in many cases with offenders who might actually be suitable for non-custodial penalties' (Scottish Executive 2004b: 4–5). Neither, however, was the answer seen to lie in increasing the availability and use of community-based disposals, since the growth in the prison population had paralleled an increased use of alternatives such as community service and probation.

Rather, despite Coyle's (2003) conclusions, organisational change *was* proposed as the potential solution, but it was not to be the radical change that Scottish Labour's manifesto had first mooted. The analysis of responses to the Reducing Reoffending consultation highlighted widespread lack of support among consultees for the bringing together of the Scottish Prison Service and criminal justice social work services under a single correctional agency structure (Scottish Executive 2004c). Concerns were voiced that a single agency would not necessarily be any more effective in tackling reoffending, that it would fail to address the complex needs of offenders and that it would reduce the ability of relevant agencies to manage risk. At an organisational level, the proposed arrangements were thought unlikely to reconcile differences between some organisations while excluding others and resulting in a loss of accountability, responsiveness and independence at the local level. Some of those consulted believed that the proposals could impact adversely on the status, skills and professional recognition of social work staff and that the associated bureaucracy and disruption could divert resources from front-line service provision (Scottish Executive 2004c).

In the face of strong opposition to the establishment of a single agency, the Criminal Justice Plan, published in December 2004, set out proposals for the creation, instead, of Community Justice Authorities (hereafter CJAs) (Scottish Executive 2004a). Following a consultation which sought views on their functions, structure and constitution, and on the role of partner organisations (Scottish Executive 2005a), the Justice Minister announced that eight CJAs would be established to facilitate strategic planning across areas and between partner agencies, with some agencies (including the police, courts, prosecution, prisons, Victim Support Scotland, Health Boards and relevant voluntary agencies) becoming statutory partners within the CJAs. It is intended that the CJAs will redesign services around the following offender groups: less serious/first-time offenders; offenders with mental health problems; offenders with substance misuse problems; persistent offenders, including young offenders coming through from the youth system; prisoners needing resettlement and rehabilitation services; violent, serious and sex offenders; and women offenders. The Community Justice Authorities (Establishment, Constitutions and Proceedings (Scotland)) Order, contained in the Management of Offenders (Scotland) Act 2005, provided for the creation of the CJAs, which came into effect on 3 April 2006 (Scottish Executive 2006b). In the first year their primary responsibility will be to produce a strategic plan for their area in consultation with statutory and non-statutory partner bodies. Thereafter their responsibilities will include the allocation of resources across and monitoring of criminal justice social work services.

The Management of Offenders (Scotland) Act 2005 also established a National Advisory Body on Offender Management, chaired by the Justice Minister, which began work in March 2006. Described as a 'new body to tackle Scotland's high reoffending rates' (Scottish Executive 2006c) and with a membership consisting of representatives from the Convention of Scottish Local Authorities, the Association of Directors of Social Work, the voluntary sector, Victim Support Scotland, the Association of Chief Police Officers in Scotland, the Parole Board, the Risk Management Authority and a range of experts, its roles are to develop and review the national strategy for managing offenders, provide advice to enhance offender management practice and support the work of the new Community Justice Authorities. The first National Strategy for the Management of Offenders (Scottish Executive 2006d) was published in May 2006, aimed at encouraging a set of common aims and expected outcomes centred on increased public protection and delivering a consistent approach to managing offenders in prison and in the community (Scottish Executive 2006d).

The purpose and structure of this book

In the context of these critical and potentially far-reaching reforms, the purpose of this book is twofold. First, we want to make a timely contribution to these developments by gathering together, for the first time in one book, an up-to-date (but historically grounded) analysis of the challenges faced by those supervising offenders in the community in Scotland; an authoritative account of the legal contexts for such supervision; and some critical commentary on how CJAs might best travel towards effective practice. Our hope is that this book might play a part in ensuring that we carry the best of our penal past into this new future. Second, for those from further afield (whether scholars, students or practitioners) who nonetheless share our fascination with questions of community justice and with Scottish answers to those questions, we hope to provide an accessible but critical introduction.

The title of this book, *Reducing Reoffending: Social Work and Community Justice in Scotland*, might be read as an empirical claim (that community-based supervision does reduce reoffending) or as an aspiration that reductions in reoffending can and should be delivered as part of a broader enterprise of advancing community *justice* (a term which we explain in the conclusion). We mean the latter – though this should not be read as suggesting that we think that criminal justice social work services are or have been particularly ineffective in the past (see Chapter 2). Indeed, by the end of the book, we hope to persuade the reader not only that it is necessary to reduce reoffending in the interests of justice, but that it is at least as necessary to advance community justice in order to reduce reoffending.

Part I aims to provide an analysis of the challenges currently faced in community justice in Scotland. However, in order to avoid the 'forced forgetting' of the past that often accompanies major organisational change (Nellis 2001), Chapter 1 seeks to locate these challenges within their historical context – exploring the emergence of probation in Scotland and the peculiarities that have characterised Scottish probation since its inception in 1905. We expose historical continuities and discontinuities over the course of the last century and, in particular, show how the current developments represent yet another permutation of the distinctive organisational arrangements and constructions of practice through which social work services have adapted and survived in response to changing socio-political contexts of and public sensibilities about crime and punishment in Scotland. Chapter 2 explores the contemporary challenge of reducing reoffending. In order to think clearly about how that objective might be most effectively pursued, it explores two key questions. First, what do we know about the performance of community supervision in Scotland to date? Second, and equally important, we seek to contextualise the successes and failures of community supervision by exploring the scale, nature and extent of the problems that offenders themselves face in changing their behaviour. The answers to these two questions lead on to a very brief examination of some criminological perspectives on how best to explain and understand offending and reoffending. This analysis leads on to a discussion of what might constitute reasonable expectations in relation to the outcomes of community-based supervision. Chapter 3 takes the analysis further by reviewing the available evidence about when, how and why people stop offending; about desistance from crime. This analysis exposes not only the complexities of desistance processes, but also the many difficulties that offenders face in making the related transition. It also explores emerging evidence about what types of intervention might best support desistance processes and, in so doing, sets the scene for Part III of the book.

Recognising that such interventions are not constructed merely (nor indeed primarily) on the basis of research evidence, Part II provides an account of the legal contexts of criminal justice social work services in Scotland. In Chapter 4 we analyse the role that social work plays in the sentencing process through the provision of social enquiry reports. Chapter 5 explores the legal basis for the provision of community disposals including probation, community services and other measures. Chapter 6 describes the arrangements for social work services to prisoners and ex-prisoners throughout their time spent in custody and post-release and includes some discussion of the current proposals for major changes to the release arrangements for sentenced prisoners in Scotland.

In Part III we return to the question of how the practice of supervising offenders in the community might be best developed so as to support desistance, better social integration and reduce reoffending. Chapter 7 discusses the issue of 'offender management' or 'case management', although we suggest that a better term might be 'change management'. The discussion covers the key phases of intervention, from engagement and relationship building, through assessment to research-based planning and delivery. We also discuss different models of case management and some critical questions that these models pose in the Scottish context. Chapter 8 discusses how services might best support offenders in the development of their human capital (that is, their attributes, knowledge, skills and personal resources). In doing so, it discusses motivation and 'readiness to change' as well as the part that programmes can play in developing thinking and problem-solving skills. However, in reviewing the recent experience of probation services in England and Wales, Chapter 8 concludes that while the development of human capital through programmes may (sometimes) be a necessary part of supervision, it is (usually) not sufficient in supporting individualised processes of desistance and social integration. This leads us, in Chapter 9, to a discussion of how services might enable the development of social capital (meaning the resources that inhere in our social networks and that shape our opportunities). A review of the evidence about the links between social capital, offending and desistance, and of the emerging literature on what probation services might do to foster offenders' social capital, leads on to a concluding discussion which raises questions not only about the importance of working with families, but also of engaging with and developing communities.

It is this discussion that leads us to our conclusion, based primarily on empirical evidence rather than normative arguments, that in order for the current changes in Scotland to realise their potential in terms of reducing reoffending, the agenda needs to move beyond crime reduction and towards Scottish community justice. We close therefore by sketching out some of the related wider issues, questions and challenges with which twenty-first century social work and the new Community Justice Authorities can and must engage.

Part I
Analysing the Challenge

1. The history of social work with offenders in Scotland[1]

Probation has been described as a process of social reconstruction under the guidance of the Court and the Probation Officer. It is much more than a gesture of leniency. Properly applied the conditions of Probation differ in sufficient degree to meet individual needs. It means supervision, firm and friendly understanding and guidance of one human being by another. (City of Glasgow 1955: 8)

'... Now listen Joe, I'm here to be trusted
But mess me about and your probation's busted!'
As time passed by, we began to talk
My days were over of running amok ...
('The Social Worker', Joe, HMP Barlinnie 1996)

Introduction

This chapter provides a brief outline of the history of social work with adult offenders in Scotland. Though it might seem irrelevant or even indulgent to reflect upon the origins of the service in the context of the important contemporary changes that are occurring within criminal justice social work in Scotland, we would argue that it is precisely these changes that make analysis of the past essential. In similar vein, Nellis (2001) has recently warned us of the dangers of the 'forced forgetting' of the past that often accompanies centralised modernisation. Commenting on developments in England and Wales around the time of the establishment of the National Probation Service, Nellis wrote:

> In the midst of these changes, someone, somewhere should ensure that the probation contribution to the penal heritage is properly remembered ... [probation history] needs to be remembered because conscious acts of remembrance and reflection – proper analytical history – could

remind the contemporary service of its roots and achievements, its turning points, its lost opportunities, its past ambitions and its un-realised possibilities. In short, a historically tutored memory may help us to realise that the centralised, highly managerial, and potentially short-lived future into which the service is being drawn is not the only – or the brightest – future that it might have had. (Nellis 2001: 35)

This chapter lays no claim to being a 'proper analytical history' but it is intended as a conscious act of remembrance of probation's origins. Though the links between probation, juvenile justice and the child-saving movement would allow us to begin this history in the nineteenth or even the eighteenth centuries, our focus on social work services for *adult* offenders allows to begin with the advent of probation in Scotland in 1905. The subsequent history of probation is then divided into three periods: early probation (1905–1945), post-war probation (1945–1968) and probation in the social work depart-ments (1969 to the present day). We then move on to discuss the contempor-ary shift towards 'offender management', exploring to what extent these developments represent significant continuities or discontinuities with the past. As a preface, however, it is necessary to make some comments about probation histories themselves.

Revising probation histories

The history of probation in England and Wales has attracted significant recent attention. In particular, Maurice Vanstone, by building on the critical work of Bill McWilliams (1983, 1985, 1986, 1987) and focusing on practice-related discourses, has significantly challenged and revised the traditional story of probation's origins as an essentially altruistic endeavour, character-ised by humanitarian impulses linked to religious ideals. As Vanstone (2004) notes, Young's (1976) earlier account of the history of probation stressed the role of charity in confirming middle-class ideas about society. Charity maintained the position of the middle classes by confirming that where unfortunates failed to capitalise on the opportunities that charitable endeav-ours provided, they confirmed their own intractable individual degeneracy, deflecting attention from broader economic or political analyses of social problems. Among a broader range of philanthropic activities, probation emerges in this account as a class-based activity that justifies the existing social order and defends it through its mechanisms of persuasion, supervi-sion and control.

Probation's charitable roots, however, form only part of the story of its origins. Vanstone suggests that:

although the evangelical humanitarian mission is an important element in the story of early probation, the emergence of the study of individual psychology, the shift from individualism to individualization in the application of punishment, and political and societal concerns about the maintenance of social order have been neglected or at least underplayed. (Vanstone 2004: 34)

Vanstone (2004) draws on the work of Rose (1985, 1996), which describes the emergence of psychiatry (in the broadest sense) as a political science and its increasing influence in the penal realm. Though earlier ideas of Christian charity endured, probation became progressively more closely aligned to this new science. In effect, probation officers became the caseworkers of these new ways of understanding or diagnosing the aetiologies (or causes) of offending and of how best to 'treat' offenders.

The emergence of this more scientific discourse and its role in the professionalisation of probation was not entirely benign. For example, Vanstone (2004) notes the 'silences' in traditional histories concerning the less palatable aspects of the new science, including the fondness for eugenics evidenced by some of probation's early patrons and practitioners. However, Vanstone also draws attention to a perhaps more significant silence in traditional histories concerning the role of probation in *justifying* the use of imprisonment. Although, as we see below, probation seems always to have been about diversion from custody, the process of selecting 'suitable' cases necessarily provided rationalisations for punishment as well as leniency. Thus, just as in the missionary era the precursors of probation officers discursively constructed some as deserving and some as undeserving of 'mercy', so in the scientific era probation officers differentiated amenable from incorrigible offenders by deploying narratives of suitability for 'treatment'.

Most accounts of probation's early history, whether traditional or revisionist, draw primarily on policy discourses as their main sources. The originality of Vanstone's recent work rests in his determination to seek, wherever possible, evidence of practitioners' views about the modes of penality that they were constructing or enacting and of how these constructions shifted over time. Thus he aims to move beyond official accounts of penal purposes and practices and to expose areas of consonance and dissonance in the parallel histories of policy and of practice. Frustratingly, the prospects for producing such a rich analysis within the Scottish context seem bleak. There are very few sources for a Scottish history of probation. First, there is no established traditional history to revise by contextualising it within broader social and cultural changes. Second, there is no comprehensive account of the development of probation policy in Scotland. Third, even if these traditional or official histories did exist, there are precious few surviving accounts from early practitioners with which those histories might be compared. In this chapter, all that can be offered is the exploration of a few sources to sketch out some preliminary analysis of some interesting or distinctive features of social work with adult offenders in Scotland.

17

Early probation: punishment, supervision and treatment

Glasgow was among the first parts of Scotland (and of the UK) to establish a recognisable probation service delivered by a state as opposed to a charitable agency (Scottish Office 1947). The Glasgow service was established as early as 1905 and a very brief history of its first 50 years was published by the City of Glasgow Probation Area Committee in 1955 (City of Glasgow 1955). This document suggests that the origins of probation in Glasgow were linked to public concern about the excessive use of custody for fine-defaulters. The authors note that a report on judicial statistics for Scotland revealed that 43,000 people were received into prison on these grounds in 1904 (16,000 from Glasgow alone) at the rate of 800 per week and that in Scotland at that time one person in 75 of the population was sent to prison compared to one person in 145 in England and Wales (City of Glasgow 1955: 9).

Probation emerged in Glasgow as a response to this penal crisis largely because of the efforts of Bailie John Bruce Murray, a local councillor who had taken a 'great interest in the treatment of offenders and who had studied the workings of the Probation Service in various parts of the United States of America' (City of Glasgow 1955: 9). Murray persuaded the Glasgow Corporation (or Council) to appoint a special committee (in June 1905) to investigate establishing a trial for a system of probation. On 14 December 1905, the committee submitted a report, which was approved by the Corporation, recommending that the chief constable be invited to select police officers for each District Police Court to act, in plain clothes, as probation officers of the court. Their duties were to include daily attendance at the courts to receive instruction from magistrates in cases that they deemed suitable for probation; to make enquiries as to the offenders' circumstances and their offence, for the guidance of the courts; to observe and supervise the probationer in line with the method suggested by the magistrate during the period fixed for continuation, caution or otherwise;[2] and to make reports to the magistrate. Six police officers of the rank of detective sergeant were subsequently appointed. Shortly afterwards, three women were appointed as probation officers to work with child offenders. By 1919, there were eleven (male) police officers working as probation officers and five women probation officers.

Perhaps partly because it was located at the outset within the police service the initial emphasis in practice seems to have been on delivering supervision, albeit of a caring sort, rather than 'treatment'. Mahood (2002) captures the paternalistic tone of supervision well in discussing the early use of probation with juveniles:

> Ideally the probation officer would be a Sunday school teacher, or someone connected with the Boy Scouts or some other youth club, 'so

that the officer may have his ward as much as possible under his care, and give him the best possible attention'. (Mahood 2002: 445)

The Glasgow history, despite the praise that it reserves for some of the early police-probation officers, implicitly characterises this model of practice as being limited, noting that it was the Probation of Offenders (Scotland) Act 1931 that (following the report of a departmental committee set up by the Secretary of State to review the Protection and Training of Children and Young Offenders) 'completely revolutionised the Probation Service in Glasgow and the idea of treatment, training and reformation of Probationers superseded that of supervision' (City of Glasgow 1955: 11).

As well as effectively creating a comprehensive set of local services by establishing probation committees in each local authority, the 1931 Act created a Central Probation Council to advise the Secretary of State. In terms of the governance of practice, however, one of the most intriguing provisions of the 1931 Act was that it expressly prohibited the appointment of serving or former police officers as probation staff, indicating that this may have been a common practice in Scotland beyond Glasgow and that it had fallen out of favour. This change in staffing arrangements seems closely associated with the transition from supervision to treatment. The significance of the new 'science' for the authors of the Glasgow history is evidenced, for example, in the assertion that 'treatment', although evidently combining social and medical notions, nonetheless required an individual process following on from some kind of selection (if not diagnosis). Their discussion of selection reflects the assumption that only some offenders are 'reclaimable'; probation 'should be applied only to those in whom wrong-doing is not habitual and whose age, record, or home circumstances, give reasonable hope of reformation' (City of Glasgow 1955: 7). The discourse of scientific practice continues in the description of the officer as someone who through interviewing and home visiting,

> *studies* the habits and surroundings of the Probationer and, by the impact of his personality, ever-ready advice and the force of example, tries to *influence* the offender towards the *normal* in life and conduct. The Probationer is helped to sustain *natural* relations with his fellows – relationships of employment, of friendships and of home ties. (City of Glasgow 1955: 8, emphases added)

In the development of a treatment approach to probation practice, it is likely that women officers played a pivotal role. Though their work was initially limited to juvenile offenders, it seems significant that, in Glasgow, the five women officers recruited in the police-probation era were the only survivors of the 1931 Act's proscription of police-probation officers. The Glasgow history acknowledges that 'the knowledge and experience of these women were of great help in setting the stumbling feet of the newcomers [one women and six men] on the right road' (City of Glasgow 1955: 13). In the light of other sources, this role as experienced staff in a reconfigured service after 1931 may have given these women (and others like them throughout Scotland), the opportunity to advance the treatment ideal; an ideal that had been developing in and through their work with juveniles even before the 1931 Act:

> According to Mary Hill, JP, the first female probation officer in Scotland, the probation system 'introduced a new era in penal treatment, because it recognizes man as an intelligence to be reformed by methods directed to the inner self, rather than a machine to be tinkered at externally'. (Mahood 1995: 58–9)

Indeed, Mahood (1995) locates the emerging probation service primarily among a range of evolving institutions associated with the child-saving movement. She draws on the accounts of early probation officers and their contemporaries to describe the role that probation played in extending the reach of the state into families' lives:

> According to one probation officer in 1925, 'It often happens that a child is put on probation and the probation officer had to shoulder the whole family'. Thus under the probation system, surveillance clearly did not stop with the offender. 'There is frequently a reacting benefit to the other members of the household and a higher sense of responsibility introduced into the home. It is frequently found that there is a laxity of parental control in the home and the visits of the probation officer tend to strengthen the control.' (Mahood 1995: 59–60)

Moreover, in some circumstances probation officers were themselves seen as being responsible for 'rescuing' children from 'vicious homes':

> [Mary Hill, the first female probation officer] claimed that '[a] good probation officer . . . is the best sort of person to look after the child who has gone wrong, not the parents who might "make light" of the offence' . . . It was acknowledged that when the probation system broke down, which was often the case, blame lay on the 'continued failure of parents'. In these cases a residential school was the best place 'to send on probation children from vicious homes'. (Mahood 1995: 68–9)

It is clear from these quotes that, particularly in relation to juveniles, it would be misleading to interpret probation (even as treatment) simply as an *alternative* to institutional or punitive measures; rather, it could be used both as a prelude to or an adjunct of both institutionalisation and punishment. For example, some of the early police-probation officers may have shared the view of the chief constable of Edinburgh, who suggested in evidence to the

Young Offenders (Scotland) Committee in 1925 that 'birching' should be an extension of the probation officer's role as surrogate parent: '[In] cases where boys on probation were neglected by their parents "Whipping should also be ordered as an additional penalty in cases of serious misbehaviour or repeated convictions"' (Mahood 2002: 446).

That said, by the 1930s, perhaps as a result of the influence of women staff, it seems to have been more common for probation to be cast as an alternative to such measures:[3]

> A boy gets into trouble because he has not learnt to adapt himself to the life of the community. What is needed is that he should be re-educated, and the probation system was devised for this purpose. A brief experience of pain cannot alter a boy's point of view or teach him how to direct his energy or control his impulses. All it can do, and unfortunately often does, is to make the boy a 'swank' and prove to his friends that he is 'tough'. Vanity makes him repeat his offence. (Winifred Elkin, Howard League for Penal Reform, *Glasgow Herald*, 28 October 1937, quoted in Mahood 2002: 453)

Post-war probation: treatment and welfare

Probation's slow but steady development as a measure for both adults and juveniles suffered as a result of World War Two. The transition to peace and the lifting of wartime restrictions and disciplines gave rise to concerns about increases in criminal activity. The Glasgow history describes the service faced with these challenges as being 'undermanned and rather war-weary' (City of Glasgow 1955: 15), at least until experienced officers returned from war service and new staff were recruited. The Criminal Justice (Scotland) Act 1949 created new duties for the service and its officers, including the provision of 'social reports' on those aged 17–21 and pre-trial reports on children (previously provided by education authorities). Notably, the 1949 Act introduced the requirement for sentencers to consider reports before imposing any sentence of detention on those aged under 21 and stipulated that such sentences must be a measure of last resort.

In discussing the nature and purpose of these social reports, the Glasgow history notes that:

> To assist the Court in coming to a decision as to the best method of *treating* an offender ... it is necessary that the Court should be in possession of the full facts regarding the accused and his place in the Community ... The Court must have a real, true and balanced picture of the accused person's social background and of any factors which may have *caused* him to transgress the Law if it is to impose a form of

treatment which will serve best the accused person and the Community. (City of Glasgow 1955: 21, emphases added)

Here, the description of social enquiry and of the significance of quasi-diagnostic reports again reflects the 'scientific' discourse of offender-oriented treatment, presaging the Streatfeild Report's (1961) high tide of optimism about the supposed potential of social science in informing a more effective and rational approach to sentencing.

Though the statistics provided in the Glasgow history reveal significant increases in the business of the service between 1932 and 1954 (with the number of orders rising from 1,313 to 2,019), closer analysis of the data reveals that the increase in the numbers placed on probation by 1954 is accounted for entirely by an increase in the number of juveniles under supervision. That this problem was not limited to Glasgow is well evidenced in a Scottish Office booklet, *The Probation Service in Scotland: Its Objects and its Organisation*, which was published in 1947 to promote the use of probation. The then Secretary of State for Scotland's foreword notes (with breathtaking confidence):

> The value of probation as a means of dealing with offenders, both adult and juvenile, has been proved beyond doubt; and great progress has been made in recent years in the development of the probation service in Scotland. But the principles and practice of probation, and the assistance which the probation service can give to the courts, are still too little understood. (Scottish Office 1947: Foreword)

The Scottish Office (1947) booklet notes that in 1932 in courts of summary jurisdiction, probation orders accounted for 950 out of the 9,173 disposals made in respect of children and young people (10.35 per cent) but only 1,117 out of 71,073 disposals involving adults (1.57 per cent). In 1945, the use of probation with juveniles had risen to 2,557 of 18,983 cases (13.47 per cent) but the use of probation for adults had fallen to 513 of 58,764 cases (0.87 per cent). Striking variations in sentencing in different localities were also noted; indeed in 1945 no adult probation orders at all were made in 19 of the 51 Scottish probation areas.

The authors of the Glasgow history, like their colleagues in the Scottish Office, were clearly vexed by this decline in the use of probation with adults; a decline which they attributed directly to the numbers of the adult male population engaged in military service during the war years when probation for adult offenders 'had fallen into disuse' (City of Glasgow 1955: 20). In addition to its provisions concerning young offenders, the Criminal Justice (Scotland) Act 1949 gave the courts new powers to make wider use of probation with adult offenders and the Glasgow history suggests that the numbers of adults on probation orders were once again increasing by 1954. However, that the reluctance to use probation as a disposal for adult offenders was an enduring problem in Scotland was evident in the Morison Report (1962) which related it to what the committee members considered to be a stubborn misconception that 'a person placed on probation has been "let off"' (Morison Report 1962: 3). The committee linked this misconception to the tendency to lay too much stress on juxtaposing probation and punishment. As they noted: 'From the probationer's viewpoint, there is ... a punitive element in the requirement to submit to supervision' (Morison Report 1962: 3). This may imply that some observers felt that the treatment ideal had softened probation's image and perhaps reduced its appeal to sentencers – at least as a measure for adults. However, in affirming an earlier definition[4] of 'the object of the probation order' as 'the ultimate re-establishment of the probationer in the community' (Morison Report 1962: 5), they nonetheless stressed an essentially benevolent and offender-centred view of rehabilitation as restoration to full citizenship.

The later versions of *The Probation Service in Scotland* revised and reissued in 1955 and 1961 (Scottish Office 1955, 1961), clearly represent efforts to continue to promote the use of probation, especially with adult offenders. In contrast to the Secretary of State's robust confidence in 1947, the later documents had a more measured tone, noting both the probation service's successes and the room for improvement that existed. The documents offer greater guidance to sentencers on the kinds of cases for which probation might be appropriate, clearly seeking to promote the use of probation in the middle ground between 'minor offences committed by those with clean records and good home backgrounds, and grave offences where there would be an undue risk in allowing the offender to remain at liberty' (Scottish Office 1955: 6, 1961: 6). Aside from issues of gravity and seriousness, the two documents also focus on the character, previous record and attitudes of offenders and what these factors suggest in terms of prospects for successful supervision. Interestingly, in this regard they suggest that adults may fare better than children on probation because they may be more cooperative and can look ahead and stand a better chance of surviving the 'difficult first three months'. The significance of home background is also noted, particularly where the officer may seem likely to be able to resolve disharmonious relationships with parents or spouses. With respect to 'a deep form of maladjustment', 'susceptibility to treatment' is identified as critical. In other cases, there may be evidence that supervision and advice can offer practical help to the offender to sort out his or her 'personal affairs' (Scottish Office 1955: 6, 1961: 6).

All three versions of *The Probation Service in Scotland* reveal an increasingly modern and recognisable preoccupation with performance. That said, the data that is presented relates primarily to the use made of probation by the courts rather than to the outcomes of supervision. Though the absolute numbers of orders rose unevenly from 3,666 in 1951 to 4,558 in 1959, probation's share of the increasing number of court disposals in the same period declined from 3.76 per cent to 2.87 per cent. Probation continued to be a much more popular disposal option for juveniles than adults; the proportion of juvenile cases involving crimes (as opposed to offences) leading to probation orders fluctuated between 26.7 per cent and 34.5 per cent during 1951–1959, the corresponding figures for adults varied between 4.3 per cent and 8.0 per cent.

Ultimately, the difficulty in advancing the use of probation among adult offenders may have been the undoing of the probation service in Scotland. The publication of the Kilbrandon Report (1964) revolutionised juvenile justice in Scotland through its determination to remove disposal decisions about children in trouble (whether for offending behaviour or on grounds of care and protection) from the criminal courts. Though Kilbrandon's most significant and enduring legacy is the Scottish Children's Hearings system, the 'Kilbrandon philosophy', which established the pre-eminence of a welfare-based approach predicated on social education principles, also affected the ideology and organisation of adult criminal justice in Scotland (Moore and Whyte 1998). Most significantly in this context, the report led to the integration of probation and aftercare services in generic social work departments. Offenders were thus placed alongside others deemed to be in need of social work services, the common duty of which was to 'promote social welfare' (Social Work (Scotland) Act 1968: s.12).

Though this may have represented the 'paradigm shift' from criminal justice to community justice referred to in the Introduction, there were also more pragmatic reasons for the ultimate demise of the service. First, the limited use of probation with adults meant that in some areas caseloads (once work with juveniles had been moved into the social work departments) would have been insufficient to sustain an independent service. This was despite considerable expansion in the 1960s and the advent of new responsibilities for fines supervision in 1964, for the aftercare of prisoners in 1965 (following the Criminal Justice Act 1963) and for parole supervision in 1968 (Murphy 1992). Second, and equally important, in the 1960s probation officers were better trained than most other social workers. Training requirements had been in place since the Probation (Scotland) Rules of 1951 but the Morison Report's (1961) recommendation that 'The probation service is now a profession requiring professional training and skill' (recommendation 14) had given probation training further impetus. By 1968, two-thirds of Scotland's 336[5] probation officers had at least a year's pre-service training with the remainder acquiring certificates of recognition of experience (Murphy 1992). Therefore, the knowledge and skills of probation staff were seen as vital resources for the new social work departments.

A further reason for the integration of probation within social work may have been that since the 1949 Act the local probation committee structure in Scotland had been based on local authorities rather than courts (unlike in England and Wales) (Murphy 1992). Though the Morison Report (1961) suggested that this arrangement had weakened probation in Scotland by distancing it from the courts and advocated change, these recommendations were not enacted in Scotland, perhaps partly because of an influential 'dissenting note' written by one Scottish committee member, Councillor John Mains. He argued that the existing structures had not weakened probation, noting that 'success rates' were the same in Scotland as in England and Wales. He also emphasised that the strength of the service (and of any social service) depended on its effectiveness as a *community* service linked to its localities. Moreover, he rejected the idea of specialism when, as he argued, the trend in social work was towards generic training. Murphy (1992) suggests that these arguments were to prove highly influential later in the decade in the debates concerning the Social Work (Scotland) Act 1968.

The Glasgow service seems to have been, at best, ambivalent about the developments that the 1968 Act heralded:

> It might be said that, having almost attained our targets in development, organisation and specialised service to the community, the Social Work (Scotland) Act comes as a 'death blow' and that our demise as a separate Service will mean the fragmentation and dissipation of our skills and knowledge. We do not propose to write an obituary, nor do we accept that unification with the other Social Services will in any way reduce our effectiveness in serving those who require our help. In contrast, we shall grasp this opportunity, this challenge, firmly, in the certain knowledge that our potential effectiveness in the field of social work will increase, as will that of those serving with us. (City of Glasgow 1968: 9)

Probation in the social work departments: welfare, responsibility and public protection

Despite the somewhat barbed optimism evident in the preceding quotation, by the late 1970s commentators in academic and professional journals were expressing concerns about the viability of probation and after-care services when subsumed within the social welfare functions of the social work departments (Marsland 1977; Moore 1978; Nelson 1977). Even in the context of such anxieties, the 1970s did witness the emergence of community service and it was in relation to community service that, in the 1980s, mechanisms emerged to address this very neglect. Community service began in 1977 through a pilot scheme in five areas where requirements concerning unpaid work were added to some probation orders. The Community Service by Offenders (Scotland) Act of 1978 allowed community service to be imposed as a 'stand alone' disposal for adults in relation to offences punishable by imprisonment. By 1986 community service was available in 50 sheriff courts, with partial funding from the Scottish Office. However, wide variations in practice across the country and the limited available funding were seen to be preventing the further expansion of community service schemes and it was to address these issues that the Scottish Office, in 1989, assumed full responsibility for the funding of community service and introduced the associated national objectives and standards (SWSG 1989; McIvor and Williams 1999).

As we have already seen, national objectives and standards (and 100 per cent funding) soon followed for all social work services in the criminal justice system (SWSG 1991a). Some contemporary commentators interpreted this as recognition that such services had indeed fallen into a state of comparative neglect during the generic era (Huntingford 1992; Moore and Whyte 1998). Correcting this neglect was a prerequisite of the policy of penal reductionism which was re-articulated as 'The Way Ahead' for Scottish penal policy in the late 1980s (Rifkind 1989). At this point, criminal justice social work looked set to follow the 'alternatives to custody' model which had already taken root in England and Wales. Indeed, the first objective delineated in the new standards (SWSG 1991a) was 'to enable a reduction in the incidence of custody ... where it is used for lack of a suitable, available community based social work disposal' (SWSG 1991a: s.12.1). Though probation in Scotland was never required to negotiate the ideological traverse towards punishment in the community, a focus on reducing reoffending, informed from the outset by emerging research evidence (McIvor 1990; SWSG 1991b), was nonetheless seen as being critical to the enhanced credibility of community penalties on which reduction in the use of custody was thought to depend. Linked with this emerging focus on effectiveness and credibility, the standards (SWSG 1991a) also signalled a shift in the ideology of the service. Paterson and Tombs (1998) have argued that the standards bridged the gap between social work and criminal justice perspectives by promoting a hybrid model of practice combining elements of the welfare and justice models (Parsloe 1976):

> ... the responsibility model recognises both that offenders make active choices in their behaviour and that choice is always situated within a person's social and personal context ... [in the supplement to the Standards (SWSG 1991b) we find a practice model] premised on the view that, through social work intervention which promotes individual responsibility for behaviour together with social responsibility for alleviating adverse circumstance, offending will be discouraged. (Paterson and Tombs 1998: 9)

By the mid to late 1990s, however, a growing emphasis on public protection on both sides of the border coincided with the introduction of significantly higher risk populations of offenders to probation caseloads. In Scotland, legislative changes in the early 1990s required prisoners serving sentences in excess of four years to undertake compulsory community supervision on release (Prisoners and Criminal Proceedings (Scotland) Act 1993). Subsequently, advances in both the rhetoric and the practice of public protection were rapid. Although it did not appear as an explicit objective in the original standards (SWSG 1991a), by the time of the publication of *Community*

Penalties: The Tough Option (Scottish Office 1998) the then Minister responsible was declaring both that 'Our paramount aim is public safety' (Scottish Office 1998: s.1.2) and that the pursuit of reductions in the use of custody 'must be consistent with the wider objective of promoting public and community safety' (s.1.2.3). Revisions to the Scottish Standards on throughcare services (SWSG 1996) and court reports (Scottish Executive 2000a), as well as other central reports and guidance (SWSI 1997, 1998) both presaged and reflected this shift in emphasis (for a more detailed discussion of the emergence and pre-eminence of public protection in official discourses and in practitioners' accounts on both sides of the border, see Robinson and McNeill 2004).

Towards 'offender management'

We described in the Introduction the debates and organisational changes that have followed the 2003 Scottish parliamentary election campaign. However, it is worth adding here that although the changes that were initially proposed in Scottish Labour's (2003) manifesto were clearly in the 'correctional' direction, the First Minister's vision for the future of criminal justice in Scotland interestingly retained rehabilitation among its three 'R's (respect, responsibility and rehabilitation). In an important speech which followed the election, McConnell argued that:

> There is a balance to be struck. A balance between protection and punishment – and the chance for those who have done wrong to change their behaviour and re-engage with the community as full and productive members. If we don't get that balance right then the system will fail through lack of confidence and trust. Our justice service depends absolutely on ordinary people ... we need them to be tolerant of the offender who returns to the community because they believe the person truly has been punished and has made amends and they are now ready to give him or her their second chance. (McConnell 2003: 11)

As we have noted above, this determination to stress the responsibilisation of the offender but to balance it explicitly (though usually more quietly and discreetly) with notions of tolerance and inclusion has been evident in Scottish penal policy since the introduction of the national standards (SWSG 1991a). The same theme, for example, underpinned the *Criminal Justice Social Work Services: National Priorities for 2001–2002 and onwards*, the third of which was to 'Promote the social inclusion of offenders through rehabilitation, so reducing the level of offending' (Justice Department 2001: 3). In this context, rehabilitation was cast as the means of progressing towards two compatible and interdependent ends: not only the reduction of reoffending but also the social inclusion of offenders. Importantly, this implies that rehabilitation is seen as a *social process* rather than a *medical process*. These interpretations of rehabilitation remain entirely consistent with the social welfare philosophy underlying the Social Work (Scotland) Act 1968, which implicitly recognised both the *intrinsic* worth of promoting the social inclusion of offenders and its *instrumentality* in reducing offending and promoting the community's social welfare.

Moreover, although McConnell's speech seems to suggest that punishment is a morally necessary prelude to reintegration, in Scotland (unlike England and Wales) there is evidence of a continuing, if somewhat more qualified, commitment to penal reductionism or 'anti-custodialism' (Nellis 1995). This was reflected in the second of the National Priorities, which was to 'Reduce the use of unnecessary custody by providing effective community disposals' (Justice Department 2001: 3). Though these priorities concerning the social inclusion of offenders and limiting the unnecessary use of custody have been increasingly subordinated to the first priority of contributing to 'increased community safety and public protection' by reducing reoffending (Justice Department 2001: 3), it is helpful to conceptualise these three intended outcomes (public protection through reduced reoffending, reducing the unnecessary use of custody and the social inclusion of rehabilitated offenders) as the three points of a triangle (see Figure 1.1). Although protecting the public by reducing reoffending has moved to the apex of the triangle as the super-ordinate purpose of contemporary criminal justice social work, Scottish policy and practice has continued to recognise the interdependence of the three priorities. This is why, for example, the Executive's Criminal Justice Plan, *Supporting Safer, Stronger Communities* (Scottish Executive 2004a), recognises that short-term prison sentences which fail to rehabilitate prisoners are counterproductive; indeed, in often making prisoners' situations and problems worse, they increase social exclusion and with it the likelihood of reoffending. Put another way, they fail to protect the public.

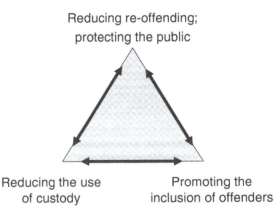

Figure 1.1 The interdependence of the intended outcomes of CJSW (Source: McNeill *et al.* 2005)

Conclusion

How should we understand this history and, in particular, what sense can we make of the ways in which social work with offenders has evolved over the last 100 years? In this chapter we have used the terms punishment, supervision, treatment, welfare, responsibility, public protection and offender management, to try to capture ways in which the character of the service has adapted and developed throughout its history. That said, we have also tried to suggest that these shifts in emphasis and approach have been gradual and that, through each of these transitions, much of the 'old' survived alongside the 'new'.

Recent research on practitioners' perspectives allows us to highlight some of the subtleties of how these transitions are navigated by social workers. Reflecting on in-depth interviews conducted in one Scottish authority in 2001, Robinson and McNeill (2004) found clear and consistent evidence that public protection was regarded as a legitimate policy purpose by all of those interviewed. More specifically, almost all of those interviewed described *their own views* of criminal justice social work's purpose in a manner consistent with the following 'formula': *to reduce reoffending by assisting people so as to protect the community and enhance its welfare.*

However, despite this consensus about public protection as a legitimate purpose, perhaps even a 'paramount' purpose (Scottish Office 1998), closer examination of the workers' views about the interpretation and oper-ationalisation of public protection revealed interesting variations. Concerning the interpretation of public protection, two main positions emerged when workers were questioned more closely. Some workers clearly regarded assisting individuals as an *intrinsic* good, an end in itself, albeit one the pursuit of which should also serve to protect the interests of the wider public. Others were clear that the provision of assistance was an *instrumental* good, a means to the end of reducing reoffending and thus protecting the public. Although it might be tempting to designate the first interpretation as a 'traditional' social work or welfare response and the second as representative of a more criminal justice oriented perspective, it was clear that none of the workers, including those who adopted the latter view, owned punishment as an objective. Indeed the only worker who mentioned punishment, despite being one who viewed assisting offenders as a means and not an end in itself, did so to disavow it:

Practitioner: I don't and never have seen it as a sort of punishment . . . maybe [because of the] grounding of social work I have . . . clearly that has influenced my work on a personal level and it obviously influences my value stands and the way I see things and how I probably *fit and shape* things to suit that as I go on about my daily business. (Robinson and McNeill 2004: 291, emphasis added)

The business of fitting and shaping things, of operationalising purposes, related to three main ways in which the welfare or social work tradition continued to find expression, despite the paramountcy afforded to public protection. First, as is already obvious, workers argued that helping communities *requires* helping offenders and used this to lend renewed legitimacy to 'welfare' activities. Second, workers characterised the social work *relationship* as the key vehicle for change. Third, workers stressed the broader *social contexts* of offending behaviour and of their efforts to bring about change. These ways of linking public protection and social welfare concerns – through highlighting mutual social interests, social work relationships as vehicles of change and the social contexts of change efforts – perhaps reflect contemporary Scottish policy in suggesting a broader concept of rehabilitation (as reintegration) connected with social inclusion agendas. However, they also illustrate how, at the front line, ideological transitions can be negotiated, mediated and managed in practice by individual penal professionals finding differing ways to re-inscribe existing purposes and practices with evolving policy imperatives and vice versa. The Scottish workers related the necessity for such manoeuvres to the perceived legitimacy of criminal justice social work in the eyes of its external audiences in the justice system and in society at large.

So while there are clear recurring themes in the century of probation in Scotland, we find these themes continually reframed in 'new' discourses and practices. On one level, the story is simple. From 1905 to 2005 most informed observers have recognised that the Scottish courts send disproportionate and unacceptable numbers of the population to jail. Though penal politics, public sensibilities and sentencing practices have all changed in various ways over the last 100 years, the problem of securing reductions in the financial and human costs associated with imprisonment endures. To address this problem, probation's various changes of identity – from supervision to treatment to welfare to responsibility to public protection to offender management – might be best understood primarily as a series of distinctive discursive constructs seeking to appeal to changing penal cultures and sentiments. This is not to say that these changing identities were or are mere artefacts; far from it, they represent shifting attempts to realise new and better penal practices in the interests of offenders, in the interests of communities and, ultimately, in the interests of justice. It is in this tradition that we would wish to locate this book and it is to the construction of these 'better' practices that we will turn, in due course. First, however, it is necessary to turn our attention to an exploration of the problem that 'offender management' services are increasingly charged with addressing: that of reducing reoffending.

Notes

1   This chapter draws heavily on an article previously published in *Probation Journal* (McNeill 2005). We are grateful to the publishers of that journal for permission to reuse the material here.
2   Under Scots law, continuations can be used both for administrative reasons and as purposeful deferrals of sentence to a specific future date. In the latter case, the offender can be required to be of good behaviour in the intervening period. A caution (pronounced 'kay-shun') requires the accused to lodge a sum of money with the court for a fixed period. The sum is forfeit in the event of further offending. The linking of these disposals to supervision by a probation officer could presumably have been done simply by inserting appropriate additional conditions to the continuation or caution, thus having a similar effect to the probation orders introduced in the 1907 Act. The main difference might be that there would be no mechanism for dealing with breach of the conditions until the continuation or caution expired.
3   Birching was formally abolished in the Criminal Justice Act 1948, section 2, which applied in Scotland as well as elsewhere in the UK.
4   This definition appeared at paragraph 83 of the report of the Departmental Committee on the Social Services in Courts of Summary Jurisdiction (1936, Cmnd 5122).
5   There had been only 78 probation officers in Scotland in 1951 (Murphy 1992).

2. Reoffending: understanding the 'problem'

> *Criminal Justice in Scotland is now set on a different path . . . above all a path that reduces reoffending, tackling those offenders who offend again and again, destroying not just their own lives but those of their families and all around them.*
>
> *We are set on transforming how we tackle crime and offending, wherever it occurs.*
>
> *Our common purpose is to protect our people.*
>
> *Our common task is to reduce reoffending.*
>
> *And, our common tool is effective offender management.* (Cathy Jamieson, Scotland's Minister for Justice, in Scottish Executive 2006d: Foreword)

Introduction

In order to think clearly about how the reduction of reoffending might be most effectively pursued, it is necessary first to think about the starting points for any effort to improve or enhance community supervision. This chapter explores two key questions in this regard. First, we address what we know about the performance of such supervision in Scotland to date. Second, and equally important, we seek to contextualise the successes and failures of supervision by exploring the scale, nature and extent of the problems that offenders themselves face in changing their behaviour. The answers to these two questions lead on to a very brief examination of some criminological perspectives on how we might best explain offending and reoffending. In conclusion, drawing on the evidence that this chapter reviews, we consider what might constitute reasonable expectations in relation to the outcomes of community supervision.

Community disposals, custody and reconviction

We discussed briefly in Chapter 1 the ways in which the purposes and practices of criminal justice social work have been progressively reframed and reconfigured during its 100-year history in Scotland. As we argued above, the twin objectives of reducing the use of custody and reducing reoffending have been linked in Scottish policy since 1991 (SWSG 1991a: s.10), in that achieving a reduction in the use of custody was seen as being dependent on delivering a credible service to the courts and, in turn, credibility was seen as being largely dependent on delivering reductions in reoffending (McIvor and Williams 1999; Paterson and Tombs 1998). However, there has been a very significant shift in the last decade away from an emphasis on reducing the use of custody towards an emphasis on reducing reoffending. This shift in emphasis has been strongly underlined most recently in the publication of *Reducing Reoffending: National Strategy for the Management of Offenders* (Scottish Executive 2006d).

The new national strategy states that the 'shared aim' of offender management services is 'to reduce both the amount of offending and the amount of serious harm caused by those already known to the criminal justice system' (Scottish Executive 2006d: 3). Moreover, the specific target for such services is defined as a 2 per cent reduction in reconviction rates in all types of sentence by March 2008. Interestingly, the strategy sets out to explain its focus on reoffending in some detail and it is worth quoting the relevant section in full here:

> All offending matters. But the community has a specific right to expect public agencies to use their contact with known offenders to reduce the risk that they will offend again, particularly in those cases which raise the most serious concerns about public protection. At the moment, most offending is reoffending. Of those convicted of a crime or offence in 2002, two-thirds had at least one previous conviction.
>
> This has an impact not only on individual victims and hard-pressed communities but also on offenders and their families. This is why a central theme of the overall strategy and a key component of our drive to reduce reoffending is Closing the Opportunity Gap and tackling social exclusion and poverty. The strategy will therefore depend for much of its success on helping offenders and their families access the services they need, such as advice on financial services, benefits and sustainable support, and also for these services to recognise offenders and their families as groups who should have equal access to their services. (Scottish Executive 2006d: 3–4)

Though this line of argument reveals some significant continuities with the distinctively Scottish historical priorities discussed in Chapter 1, specifically in its recognition of the linkages between protecting the public by reducing reoffending and helping offenders to achieve social inclusion, the strategy is surprisingly silent on the issue of reducing the prison population. In this regard, and in contrast to the penal reductionism that has been at the heart of probation's history in Scotland, the new strategy has little to say about the role of sentencing itself in reducing reoffending and about the well-documented and enduring problems in Scotland around the expensive and ineffective use of short-term prison sentences (SCCCJ 2005).

To the extent that community disposals, post-1991, were intended to encourage reductions in the use of custody, any impartial observer would have to conclude that they have failed in that task. While the data contained in Figure 2.1 reveal that the use of community disposals has increased very significantly in the period following the implementation of the national objectives and standards (SWSG 1991a), it also suggests that this increase has not been primarily at the expense of custodial sentences. Indeed, in the same period, such sentences, in general, have become more common and longer (Tombs 2004). The increase in the use of community sentences appears to have been mainly at the expense of the fine (McIvor and Williams 1999; Eley

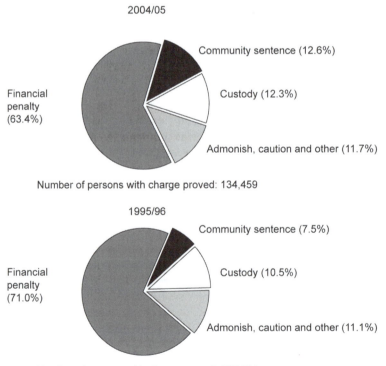

Figure 2.1 Penalties imposed in Scottish courts in 1995/96 and in 2004/05 (Source: Scottish Executive 2006e)

et al. 2005). In this respect, the rapid expansion of criminal justice social work since the 1990s, rather than heralding a less punitive and less intrusive justice system, arguably has produced a 'dispersal of discipline' in which increasing numbers of particular sections of the population find themselves subject to the 'carceral reach' of the state (Cohen 1985).

Recent research on the Scottish prison population reveals that this 'carceral reach', at least in respect of imprisonment, is much more evident in already disadvantaged communities. Houchin (2005) discovered that half of the population in Scottish prisons on the night of 30 June 2003 came from home addresses in just 155 of the 1,222 local government wards in Scotland; that although the overall imprisonment rate for men in Scotland at that time was 237 per 100,000, for men from the 27 most deprived wards the rate was 953 per 100,000; and that about one in nine young men from the most deprived communities would spend time in prison before they were 23. Though no comparable study of the geographical distribution of community disposals has yet been carried out, it seems highly likely that the correlations between social exclusion, crime, criminalisation and punishment would produce a similarly uneven distribution.

Though both the increasing use of custody and its very uneven distribution should concern us greatly, the more contemporary preoccupation with reconviction rates also requires some closer examination. In the consultation process following the Executive's announcement of its intention to create a single agency combining prisons and criminal justice social work services (Scottish Executive 2004b), particular stress was placed on the supposedly poor performance of criminal sanctions in terms of the subsequent reconviction of sentenced offenders. The consultation documents reported that 60 per cent of prisoners discharged from a custodial sentence in 1999 had been reconvicted within two years (for a more comprehensive account of these findings see Scottish Executive 2005b). For those who received probation orders in 1999, the figure was 58 per cent; for those who received community service orders it was 42 per cent; and for those who were subject to monetary penalties, it was 40 per cent. Bemoaning both these apparently high reconviction rates and the increasing use of prison, the consultation documents argued that something had to be done.

In fact, similar (and indeed worse) reconviction rates have been evidenced in other jurisdictions with significantly different and arguably more 'correctional' systems (including those using a single agency model). Thus, for example, the New Zealand Department of Corrections/Ara Poutama Aotearoa,[1] in reviewing international evidence from the UK, North America and Australasia, suggests that, across these diverse jurisdictions, about 60 per cent of those sentenced to community sentences are reconvicted within two years and that the equivalent figure for custodial sentences is about 70 per cent. In New Zealand/Aotearoa itself the reconviction figures for community sentences and custodial sentences are 64 per cent and 67 per cent respectively. In this comparative context, the Scottish figures do not look quite so disappointing.

More recent analysis of reconviction data[2] (Scottish Executive 2006f) shows that rates of reconviction have been fairly stable in recent years. Comparing the rates of reconviction for those released from custody or given a non-custodial sentence since 1995 reveals the following: the percentage of offenders reconvicted within two years of a custodial sentence varies between 61 and 65 per cent; the equivalent figure for probation varies between 59 and 64 per cent; the figure for community service shows a steady decline from 49 to 42 per cent. Moreover, the study notes that when the figures were adjusted to take account of 'pseudo-reconvictions' (that is, those convictions which follow the disposal in question but relate to offences committed *before* its imposition and therefore over which it could exercise no influence), the 'real reconviction' rates for the most recent cohort (2002/03) are 56 per cent for those released from custody, 51 per cent for those placed on probation and 33 per cent for those placed on community service. These figures for community penalties are much more in line with the data on the proportion of such orders which are completed successfully; for probation orders this figure is about 60 per cent, for community service it is over 70 per cent (Scottish Executive 2006g).

Reconviction data are, of course, notoriously unreliable and problematic measures of the impact of criminal justice sanctions, as the recent national strategy document concedes (Scottish Executive 2006d). Leaving aside the problem of pseudo-reconvictions referred to above, the nature, seriousness and frequency of any reconvictions would need to be examined to reach a more measured view about the impact of any sentence (Mair 1997). For example, in what sense is it a failure of supervision if a highly persistent recidivist house-breaker commits a single offence of shoplifting within two years of release or during two years of supervision? In this sense, the meaning of reconviction is relative to the nature of the offending history that precedes it. One approach which aims to take this criticism into account involves comparing *predicted* rates of reconviction with *actual* rates of reconviction during or after the imposition of different sanctions (Lloyd *et al.* 1994). To some extent, this approach allows differences in the characteristics and offending histories of the populations receiving different sentences (for example, the more significant criminal histories and greater criminogenic needs of prisoners in comparison with probationers) to be excluded from the analysis of their impacts.

Questions can also be raised about when to start counting reconvictions. Pease (1999), for example, has suggested that comparisons between custodial sentences and community penalties are only fair if the counting starts at the point of sentence, thus taking account of custody's incapacitating effects, as well as any post-release effect. Others might argue, by the same token, that both custodial *and* community disposals should not be judged until *after* they have run their course and the relevant interventions might reasonably be expected to have taken their effect, precisely so that community disposals do not suffer in comparisons because of their inability to incapacitate.

However, more fundamentally, reconviction data represent a poor measure of the impact of sentences because they measure only the justice system's *response* to reported, detected and prosecuted offending and not actual changes in the behaviour of offenders. The weight of criminological research suggests that this is, in fact, a very serious and double-edged problem. On the one hand, we know that relatively few offences lead to conviction; indeed, this is very clear from the most recently available Scottish data included in Figure 2.2. In Scotland in 2004–05, less than 13 per cent of recorded crimes and offences led to convictions and, of course, many other crimes and

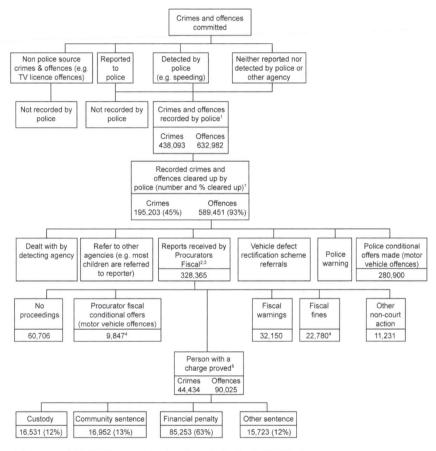

1 Crimes recorded in 2004/05 may not be cleared up or dealt with until 2005/06 or later.
2 A report to the procurator fiscal may involve more than one crime or offence and more than one alleged offender.
3 The total number of reports to the fiscal includes reports on non-criminal matters such as sudden deaths.
4 Figures relate to offers which were accepted.
5 Figures for persons with a charge proved count the number of occasions on which a person is convicted.

A number of outcomes may result in subsequent prosecutions or referrals to other agencies, for example if a condition such as payment of a fixed penalty is not complied with. For simplicity, these pathways are not shown in the diagram.

Figure 2.2 Overview of action within the Scottish criminal justice system, 2004/05 (Source: Scottish Executive 2006e)

offences will never have come to the attention of the police. On the other hand, we also know that the process of criminalisation (through which some acts come to be sanctioned through the law and others do not) is a very uneven one and that, more particularly, 'known offenders' (and those from more socio-economically disadvantaged areas) are more heavily policed than the general population and therefore disproportionately vulnerable to further criminalisation and penalisation (McAra and McVie 2005).

Thus we can conclude that while reconviction provides only a deeply flawed measure of the impact of sanctions, if it means anything at all, the international evidence suggests that it certainly does *not* mean that Scottish reconviction rates should be seen as being alarming, unacceptable or unexpected. Indeed, as we will see in the next section, a closer examination of the needs and characteristics of those subject to supervision in the community suggests that it might make more sense to ask why reconviction rates are not much higher than they are.

Offenders under supervision

Offenders under supervision in the community in Scotland are predominant-ly young, male and unemployed. Criminal justice social work statistics for 2004/05 (Scottish Executive 2006g) suggest that women offenders accounted for only 18 per cent of probation orders, 12 per cent of community service orders, 17 per cent of supervised attendance orders, 17 per cent of drug treatment and testing orders (DTTOs), and 8 per cent of restriction of liberty orders. Of those subject to probation orders, 70 per cent were unemployed; the equivalent figure for those on community service was 60 per cent and for those on DTTOs 79 per cent.

More detailed information on the needs, deeds and demographic charac-teristics of offenders subject to community supervision can be found in recent studies of probationers and parolees. One of the most comprehensive of such studies is Mair and May's (1997) *Offenders on Probation*. Their sample of 1,986 offenders was generally representative of all persons on probation in England and Wales in the mid-1990s; for example, 82 per cent of their sample was male and just over 40 per cent fell into the 16 to 24 age range. In terms of ethnic origin, 93 per cent was white and, of the rest, most defined themselves as black (5 per cent). Only one in five probationers was employed or self-employed (similar to the figure in Scotland reported above) and, of those who were employed, 79 per cent were in manual occupations. About a third of female probationers were living alone with dependent children and state benefits were the main source of household income for two-thirds of all respondents. About 40 per cent had experienced problems relating to debt.

Also of significance, a sizeable minority of the sample had spent time in some form of local authority care as a child; probationers were ten times more likely to have been in care than the general population. Of the probationers in the study, 19 per cent had lived in children's homes and 14 per cent in a borstal or young offenders unit. A similar proportion had been brought up in a one-parent family. Forty-two per cent of the sample had left school before the age of 16, while 49 per cent left at age 16. Only 12 per cent of male probationers had qualifications at O level or equivalent. Forty-nine per cent of the sample had health problems or disabilities and 30 per cent said that this restricted the work that they could do. Forty-eight per cent of offenders admitted some form of illicit drug use in the past 12 months and 10 per cent were identified as having a problem relating to their alcohol consumption.

In terms of their current offence, male probationers were most likely to have been convicted of burglary (23 per cent), violence (19 per cent), drink driving (14 per cent), other driving offences (14 per cent), other theft/handling offences (13 per cent) and theft of, and from, a motor vehicle (12 per cent). Women were most likely to have been convicted of other theft/handling offences (35 per cent), fraud, forgery and deception (29 per cent) and violence (16 per cent). Four-fifths of the sample had previous criminal convictions, with males more likely than females to have become involved in crime before the age of 18 (76 per cent and 59 per cent respectively).

In relation to prisoners, there is a wealth of research into the backgrounds, characteristics and needs of prisoners which demonstrates their serious and chronic disadvantage and social exclusion and, more significantly in the context of this chapter, its association with reconviction. Indeed, Coyle (2003), commenting on the Scottish reconviction data in the context of the debate about organisational changes, noted:

> It is disingenuous to suggest that this level of reoffending is a result of failures within the criminal justice agencies which are responsible for dealing with offenders. The reasons are more to do with factors which take us far beyond criminal justice. (Coyle 2003: 3)

Coyle cites the Social Exclusion Unit's (2002) report *Reducing Reoffending by Ex-prisoners*, which revealed that, compared to the general population, prisoners were 13 times more likely to have been in care as a child; ten times more likely to have been a regular truant from school; 13 times more likely to be unemployed; two and half times more likely to have a family member who has been convicted of a criminal offence; six times more likely to have been a young father; and 15 times more likely to be HIV positive. In respect of their basic skills, 80 per cent had the writing skills of an 11 year old; 65 per cent had the numeracy skills of an 11 year old; 50 per cent had the reading skills of an 11 year old; 70 per cent had used drugs before coming to prison; 70 per cent suffered from at least two mental disorders; 20 per cent of male prisoners had previously attempted suicide; and 37 per cent of women prisoners have attempted suicide. For younger prisoners aged 18–20 these problems are even more intense: their basic skills, rates of unemployment and previous levels of school exclusion are a third worse even than those of older prisoners (Social Exclusion Unit 2002: 6).

Providing further evidence for Coyle's (2003) position, the associations between some of these kinds of social factors and reconviction rates were explored in an important study by May (1999). Drawing on 1993 data concerning over 7,000 offenders from six probation areas (in England), May (1999) demonstrated that problems with drug use, employment and accommodation were related to reconviction in all six areas, that there was a simple relationship between financial problems and reconviction in some areas, and that offenders with multiple problems were more likely to be reconvicted.

A more recent analysis comparing the criminogenic needs (that is, needs associated with their offending histories) of offenders sentenced to community disposals and custodial disposals can be found in Harper et al. (2004). Drawing on recent data from the Offender Assessment System (OASys) in England and Wales, Harper and her colleagues reported that, on average, offenders are assessed as having four criminogenic needs. Although, as we have seen above, offenders in custody generally have a greater number of needs than offenders in the community, the similarities between the two populations are striking. Their findings are reproduced in Table 2.1.[3]

Table 2.1 Factors associated with offending

Section of OASys	Percentage of offenders assessed as having a problem	
	Community sentences	Custodial sentences
1 & 2 Offending information*	50%	66%
3 Accommodation	31%	43%
4 Education, training and employment	53%	65%
5 Financial management and income	22%	29%
6 Relationships	36%	42%
7 Lifestyle and associates	35%	52%
8 Drug misuse	27%	39%
9 Alcohol misuse	34%	33%
10 Emotional well-being	40%	38%
11 Thinking and behaviour	50%	59%
12 Attitudes**	21%	32%
No. of criminogenic needs	3.99	4.97
No. of criminogenic needs excluding sections 1 & 2	3.50	4.31

*Offending information includes the current offence and criminal history.
**The percentages with attitudes needs are likely to rise when an amendment is made to the OASys scoring system, effective from early 2005.
(Source: Harper et al. 2004: x)

Scottish research studies reveal broadly similar patterns in the needs and characteristics of offenders under supervision. McIvor and Barry's (1998a) study involved a sample of 155 probationers drawn from four study areas across Scotland. Eighty-two per cent were male and 48 per cent were between 16 and 20 years of age; 86 per cent had one or more previous conviction (the average number of previous convictions was 8.1); and 30 per cent had served at least one previous custodial sentence. Most received their current probation order for offences involving dishonesty (68 per cent). Offenders in their throughcare sample (McIvor and Barry 1998b) tended to be older – the majority were aged 21 or over – and their criminal histories were more significant. Seventy-nine per cent had previous convictions and 55 per cent had previously served a custodial sentence. Only two of the 60 ex-prisoners were women.

Problems relating to family relationships, drugs and alcohol use featured prominently in probationers' social enquiry reports (SERs) and workers most often attributed offending to alcohol or drug use. That said, there were some important differences identified between different types of offender. Compared with male probationers, for example, women's offending was more likely to be described as financially motivated or a response to emotional stress, while young offenders were more often described as impulsive or opportunistic and as influenced by negative peer pressure. The reasons put forward by social workers when recommending probation to the courts were the potential offered by probation to address or monitor offending (or behaviour associated with offending, including drug and/or alcohol use); the potential to provide help with practical problems such as employment or education; support of a more general kind (for example, help with relationship problems, social skills, etc.); and to build upon the offender's motivation to change.

Of course, while it is important to acknowledge the common characteristics and high levels of need within the offender population as a whole, it is equally important to acknowledge the variations in the needs, deeds and characteristics of different individual offenders, of those who have different patterns of offending and of offenders subject to different court disposals. To give one example, the literature on women who offend shows that while male and female offenders share a set of universal needs, there are also key differences in terms of behavioural issues, domestic expectations and risk factors (Carlen 2002; McIvor 2004; Zaplin 1998). What we can say with confidence is that offenders subject to community disposals or supervision on release from custody have very high levels of need, and that so long as these needs remain unmet they will increase the likelihood of them being reconvicted.

Explaining (re)offending

Against the sort of backdrop provided by this evidence about offenders' backgrounds, characteristics and needs, the rates of reconviction reported above begin to look more readily intelligible. Because criminal justice social work (and prison) services are dealing with a chronically disadvantaged, marginalised and excluded population who have learned offending behaviour partly as a response to such adversity, it is clearly unreasonable to expect that significant changes in well-established patterns of offending can be secured swiftly and without any recurrence of these learned behaviours. The challenges of supporting such changes will be discussed in more detail in the next chapter and in Part III of this book.

However, before moving on to consider the change process, it makes sense to briefly consider not just the associations between involvement in (re)offending and the needs and characteristics referred to above, but also to ask *how* these associations can be best explained. In other words, before exploring how to explain and understand desistance from offending, we should consider how to explain *persistence* in offending. Though there is considerable evidence that most people engage in some level of offending, particularly in their youth, the vast majority of young people are 'temporary delinquents' (Millham 1993) for whom offending is 'a transitory phenomenon linked to their social development' (Jamieson *et al*. 1999: 156). The prevalence of youth offending is demonstrated by self-report research studies involving young people. In their study of 14–25 year olds in England and Wales, for example, Graham and Bowling (1995) found that 55 per cent of males and 31 per cent of females admitted that they had committed a crime at some time. Two-thirds of the young people in Anderson *et al*.'s (1994) Scottish study said that they had committed an offence, compared to 94 per cent of boys and 82 per cent of girls in Jamieson *et al*.'s more recent Scottish research (1999).[4] Such studies suggest that the vast majority of people have committed a crime at some time in their lives, albeit of a relatively minor nature, such as stealing from school, vandalism, shoplifting and fighting. Lesser offending may therefore be considered a typical rather than an unusual form of behaviour, particularly for young men who offend more often and until an older age (Graham and Bowling 1995; Rutter *et al*. 1998; Flood-Page *et al*. 2000).

That said, there are undoubtedly some people for whom offending is not simply part of 'ordinary' youthful activity but is more enduring and more problematic. In Scotland, of the 49,300 individuals who were convicted of crimes and relevant offences[5] in 2004–05 (and for whom data was available), 65 per cent had been previously convicted at least once in the preceding ten years, but 13 per cent had been convicted more than ten times in the same period (Scottish Executive 2006f). Thus although the *aggregate-level* 'age-crime curve' (reproduced in Figure 2.3) shows that rates of offending overall peak in late adolescence and decline thereafter (though at different rates for males and females), the trajectories of the criminal careers of *individual offenders* who continue to offend are markedly different.

Seeking to explain these longer and more problematic criminal careers poses a somewhat different question from criminology's broader concern with seeking to explain crime and criminality in general; an endeavour that

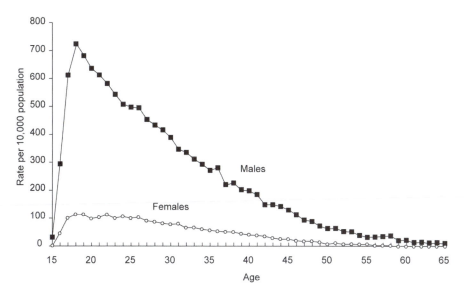

Figure 2.3 Individual offenders with one or more charge proved for a crime or relevant offence in Scottish courts per 10,000 population

has spawned a range of theories that explore and seek to account for crime in terms of biology, psychology, sociology and environment, as well as an important and more recent critical tradition drawing on Marxist and feminist perspectives (for useful brief overviews, see Gelsthorpe 2003 and Whyte 2004). Recently, among those that still seek to develop general theories of offending – an enterprise which some have argued is fundamentally misguided given the diversity of behaviours that come to be defined as 'criminal' (see Gelsthorpe 2003) – the trend has been towards multi-factorial models. Thus, for example, Farrington (2002) claims that his theory of male offending and anti-social behaviour is integrative, drawing on strain theories, control theories, social learning theories, rational choice theories and labelling theories in seeking to account for both the development of 'anti-social tendencies' and the occurrence of anti-social acts. In sum, Farrington (2002) suggests that offending is the result of a four-stage process involving *energising* (in which motivations develop which may lead to offending); *directing* (in which 'criminal' methods for satisfying those motivations may come to be habitually chosen); *inhibiting* (in which beliefs, values and socialisation may take effect to inhibit offending); and *decision-making* (in which situational opportunities, calculations about costs and benefits, the subjective probabilities of different outcomes of offending, and social factors inform decisions about offending). The consequences of offending may then reinforce anti-social tendencies, and the stigmatisation and labelling that often accompany criminalisation may also encourage further offending by diminishing the individual's prospects of satisfying their needs and wants by legal means.

Though Farrington's (2002) theory provides resources with which to understand reoffending and persistent offending – as a consequence of a particularly adverse combination of energising, directing, inhibiting and decision-making factors – Moffitt's (1993, 1997) 'theory of offender types' (reviewed in Smith 2002) is also highly pertinent. Moffitt famously distinguishes between 'adolescence-limited' and 'life-course persistent' offenders. Smith (2002) clarifies the distinction thus:

> According to this taxonomy, life-course persistent anti-social behaviour starts very early and continues throughout life, but the forms in which it is expressed and the ways it is perceived and described, and the social reactions to it, change at different stages of the life cycle. By contrast, adolescence-limited anti-social behaviour increases rapidly in early adolescence, then declines rapidly after the peak age at around eighteen. (Smith 2002: 734)

Though the two 'types' are hard to distinguish during adolescence in terms of their offending patterns, they are different in their earlier offending histories and in their adult behaviour; life-course persistent offenders start offending earlier and continue offending long after adolescent-limited offenders have stopped. Essentially, therefore, Moffitt's theory seeks to account for stability in the offending patterns of one group (the life-course persistent offenders) and change in the other. Importantly, as Smith (2002) points out, it is not Moffitt's contention that early offending 'locks' some young people into a cycle of reoffending; rather it is that the early onset of offending in some children is *indicative* of a range of other characteristics that adversely influence their development and their behaviour.

Reviewing the available empirical evidence, Smith (2002) concludes that Moffitt's broad account of the different offending patterns of the two groups is sustainable; however, the evidence for her related claim that the *causes* of offending in the two groups are different is more contestable. Moffitt's view is that a range of constitutional, personality, cognitive and family factors explain persistent offending but that the causes of short periods of offending in the transition from childhood to adolescence and adulthood are entirely different. Smith's (2002) view, in contrast, is that some studies suggest that adolescence-limited offenders may evidence some of the same sorts of factors that account for persistent offending but to a much lesser degree, so that the distinction between the two types is not as clear-cut as it appears.

Though the work of developmental criminologists and those who advocate a life-course perspective has provided very significant insights into criminal careers with some important policy and practice implications, critical criminologists would tend to suggest that the search for 'risk factors' and 'offender types' is fundamentally misconceived in that it tends to pathologise offending by focusing on the individual offender as the main unit of analysis. Thus, although developmental perspectives have underscored the significance of various social-structural factors, they misdirect our attention towards the individual-level impact of these factors, rather than emphasising that crime, criminality and criminalisation are social constructs that are governed by wider economic, structural, cultural and political forces. It is interesting to note therefore that Laub and Sampson (2003), two pre-eminent figures *within* the field of developmental criminology, have recently argued very convincingly that the 'risk factor paradigm' needs to be reconsidered. By analysing life-history interviews and other data concerning a cohort of men aged 70 on whom data has been collected since they were aged seven, Laub and Sampson illustrate the 'inherent difficulties in predicting crime prospectively over the life course' (2003: 290). Essentially, their analysis shows that boys with very similar risk profiles turned out to have very divergent lives.

Conclusion

In this chapter we have attempted to analyse and problematise some aspects of the recent debates about reconviction rates and reoffending in Scotland. We have argued that the last decade has witnessed a significant increase in the 'carceral reach' of the state: that rather than community disposals displacing custodial sentences and reducing the prison population, the numbers of people subject to both custodial sentences and supervision in the community have increased markedly. Moreover, this 'dispersal of discipline' is not evenly spread across the Scottish population; rather, the emerging evidence suggests that it is highly concentrated in the most deprived areas.

We have also outlined some of the significant limitations of using reconviction as a measure for the impact of penal sanctions and, in exploring the available Scottish data in international context, we have suggested that Scottish reconviction rates are neither surprising nor alarming and that they cannot be read simply as being indicative of an under-performing justice system. Rather, we have argued that reconviction is strongly associated with the chronic and serious problems of disadvantage, marginalisation and exclusion that commonly characterise the lives of both prisoners and those subject to community disposals. Indeed, the evidence that we have reviewed about the backgrounds and needs of those subject to such sentences in the UK in some respects raises the question of why reconviction rates are not higher.

Turning finally to attempts to explain offending and reoffending, we have briefly reviewed some important insights from developmental criminology – in particular concerning why (only) some offenders develop lasting criminal careers. As we have seen, such theories tend to be multi-factorial. With regard to persistent offenders, whether they are in some sense 'different in kind' from other (re)offenders remains a topic of debate, but there is no doubt that they tend in general to have more complex clusters of intense needs than other offenders (see McNeill and Batchelor 2004). However, seeking to *predict* who will reoffend and to what extent on the basis of their historical or current clusters of needs is fraught with difficulty.

The overall conclusion of this chapter must be that although the extent of the problem of reconviction may have been overstated, the challenges of reducing reoffending in practice are very considerable. Indeed, the scale, complexity and intensity of the needs that provoke offending, especially for those persistent property offenders who form the core group with which criminal justice social workers must engage, should caution us about the potential difficulties that services face in seeking to reduce reoffending and should season our expectations about what these services can deliver. As Maruna (2001) puts it in a memorable chapter in his book *Making Good*, in many respects and for many offenders, the prognosis is 'dire' – not because of their deficiencies (as some would have us believe) but because of the commonly desperate and dismal nature of their social circumstances and life prospects.

Yet, as we have seen above, most offenders, including many persistent offenders, *do* give up crime, despite the many needs that they have and the many obstacles that they face. Rather than dwelling further on contextualising and explaining (re)offending, therefore, the focus of the next chapter is on what we know about the process of 'desistance' from offending and about how this knowledge might better inform policies and practices which aim to reduce reoffending.

Notes

1 http://www.corrections.govt.nz/public/research/bestuse/reconviction.html, accessed 13 July 2006.
2 The data also show that reconviction rates overall are lower for women and higher for both younger offenders and for property offenders.
3 These figures are based on 10,000 OASys assessments drawn from 19 areas in England and Wales. However, Harper *et al.* (2004: 19) note that the sample is not randomly drawn from the population of offenders serving custodial or community sentences and is therefore not nationally representative.
4 The sample size and age ranges of these studies were as follows. Graham and Bowling (1995): 1,721 young people aged between 14 and 25; Anderson *et al.* (1994): 1,150 young people aged 11–15 years; Jamieson *et al.* (1999): 1,274 13–16 year olds.
5 'Relevant offences' are defined as common assault, breach of the peace, racially aggravated conduct or harassment, firearms offences and social security offences.

3. Ending offending: supporting desistance

I am finding out a great deal about myself. I am making new relationships and living in a world totally unknown to me. I love it yet there are times when I hate it. I am torn between two worlds – alienated from the old one and a stranger in this new one. (Boyle 1985: 80)

Change is the word that troubles me; I'm reluctant to use it in my case. It conjures up a new identity, something merely adopted, a fictional character. (Collins 1998: 171)

Introduction

The opening quotes above, which capture in different ways the discomfiting nature of change processes, come from two men who were among Scotland's most infamous offenders but who are now among her most celebrated desisters from crime. Both Jimmy Boyle and Hugh Collins acquired long histories of serious offending, both were convicted of murder, both served life sentences, both acquired additional convictions in prison and represented major management problems for prison authorities, and both experienced some kind of change in identity and direction while in Barlinnie's special unit. Their two-volume autobiographies (Boyle 1983, 1985; Collins 1998, 2000) make for interesting and challenging reading for anyone who wants to contribute to the termination of criminal careers and the harms that they cause.

Though most criminal justice social workers will spend the bulk of their time dealing with people whose offending histories are more mundane and less serious, this in no way diminishes the importance of getting to grips with how to understand the change processes involved in ending offending – increasingly known as processes of 'desistance'. Until recently, the desistance literature has tended to address 'the wider social processes by which people *themselves* come to stop offending' (Rex 1999: 366). Thus, it has not been necessarily or indeed primarily a literature about criminal justice interventions. Indeed, Maruna (2000) points out that much of the research focuses on 'spontaneous desistance', which is achieved without 'assistance' from or through the criminal justice system. However, he also argues that, in theory and in practice, the boundaries between 'natural' processes of desistance and rehabilitative interventions blur. *Processes of change towards desistance may share similarities whether they are sponta-neous or professionally assisted.* Knowledge about such processes therefore becomes critical to our understandings not just of 'what works?' in terms of interventions but also of *when and how and why* ex-offenders come to change their behaviours. This chapter therefore aims to build an understanding of the human processes and social contexts within which rehabilitative interven-tions are (or should be) embedded. It begins with a brief review of related theoretical perspectives before exploring some of the relationships between desistance, age, gender, attitudes, motivation and narratives, before proceed-ing to explore more directly the implications of desistance research for the construction of social work with offenders.

Understanding desistance

The implications of embedding interventions with offenders in understand-ings of desistance are potentially significant and far-reaching. Maruna *et al.* (2004) draw a parallel with a related shift in the field of addictions away from the notion of treatment and towards the idea of recovery, quoting an influential essay by William White (2000):

> Treatment was birthed as an adjunct to recovery, but, as treatment grew in size and status, it defined recovery as an adjunct of itself. The original perspective needs to be recaptured. Treatment institutions need to once again become servants of the larger recovery process and the community in which that recovery is nested and sustained . . . (White 2000, cited in Maruna *et al.* 2004: 9)

Although the language of recovery may be inappropriate in relation to offenders, given both that it implies a medical model and that it suggests a prior state of well-being that may never have existed for many, the analogy is telling nonetheless. Put simply, the implication is that criminal justice social work services need to think of themselves less as providers of correctional treatment (that belongs to the expert) and more as supporters of desistance processes (that belong to the desister). It follows that choices about the kinds of interventions to be used with and for offenders should be based on understandings of *their* individual change processes and how professionals can best support these processes, rather than offenders fitting in with pre-designed interventions that professionals prescribe for 'types' of offenders.

In seeking to build bridges between the desistance research and the literature on rehabilitative interventions, Maruna (2000) argues that the 'what works?' research (discussed in Chapter 8 below):

> ... tells us little about individual differences among client experiences in the process ... Every individual encounters and interprets unique social interactions within a program setting ... every intervention consists of thousands of different micro-mechanisms of change ... By concentrating almost exclusively on the question of 'what works', offender rehabilitation research has largely ignored questions about *how* rehabilitation works, *why* it works with some clients and why it fails with others. (Maruna 2000: 12)

Maruna argues that desistance research can and should redress these deficits in the 'what works?' research by identifying processes of reform and helping in the design of interventions that can enhance or complement spontaneous change efforts. Such research could assist practitioners with the challenge of helping people progress towards the point of being ready and able to make changes, perhaps by accelerating processes that appear to have slowed or stalled for a variety of reasons. Recognising the limitations of each form of research (desistance and treatment/rehabilitation) on its own, Maruna proposes a marriage of the two; with the desistance research's focus on the success stories of those that desist offering an 'individual-level view' that, in partnership with the treatment literature's identification of general practices that seem successful, can better inform understandings of the change processes involved.

So how should this 'individual-level view' concerning processes of desistance be understood and theorised? Maruna (2001) identifies three broad theoretical perspectives in the desistance literature: maturational reform, social bonds theory and narrative theory. Maturational reform (or 'ontogenic') theories have the longest history and are based on the established links between age and certain criminal behaviours, particularly street crime. Social bonds (or 'sociogenic') theories suggest that ties to family, employment or educational programmes in early adulthood explain changes in criminal behaviour across the life course. Where these ties exist, they create a stake in conformity, a reason to 'go straight'. Where they are absent, people who offend have less to lose from continuing to offend. Narrative theories have emerged from more qualitative research which stresses the significance of subjective changes in the person's sense of self and identity, reflected in changing motivations, greater concern for others and more consideration of the future.

Bringing these perspectives together, Farrall (2002) stresses the significance of the relationships between 'objective' changes in the offender's life and his or her 'subjective' assessment of the value or significance of these changes:

> ... the desistance literature has pointed to a range of factors associated with the ending of active involvement in offending. Most of these factors are related to acquiring 'something' (most commonly employment, a life partner or a family) which the desister values in some way and which initiates a re-evaluation of his or her own life ... (Farrall 2002: 11)

Thus, desistance resides somewhere in the interfaces between developing personal maturity, changing social bonds associated with certain life transitions, and the individual subjective narrative constructions which offenders build around these key events and changes. It is not just the events and changes that matter; it is what these events and changes *mean* to the people involved.

Clearly this understanding implies that desistance itself is not an event (like being cured of a disease) but a *process*. Desistance is necessarily about ceasing offending and then refraining from further offending over an extended period (for more detailed discussions see Farrall 2002; Farrall and Calverley 2006; Laub and Sampson 2003; Maruna 2001). Maruna and Farrall (2004) suggest that it is helpful to distinguish *primary desistance* (the achievement of an offence-free period) from *secondary desistance* (an underlying change in self-identity wherein the ex-offender labels him or herself as such). Though they do not use the term 'secondary desistance', Giordano *et al.*'s (2002) compelling and important exploration of desistance by women offenders suggests a four-part 'theory of cognitive transformation' involving openness to change; exposure to 'hooks for change' or turning points, the envisioning of an appealing or conventional 'replacement self'; and a transformation in the way in which the person views their (former) behaviour.

Although Bottoms *et al.* (2004) have raised some doubts about the value of the distinction between primary and secondary desistance on the grounds that it may exaggerate the importance of cognitive and/or identity changes which need not *always* accompany desistance, it does seem likely that where practitioners are working with (formerly) persistent offenders, the distinction may be useful; indeed, in those kinds of cases their role might be constructed as prompting, supporting and sustaining secondary desistance wherever this is possible. Similarly, Laub and Sampson (2003) claim to find little evidence in their landmark study of active cognitive transformation or identify changes, stressing instead a sort of 'desistance by default' tied to more 'structural turning points' occasioned by marriage or work or military service. However, we might wonder whether this conclusion is not the result of looking in the wrong places; that is, in the *retrospective* accounts of older men about long past processes of desistance which may, through the course of their life histories, have taken on the appearance of inevitability (see also Vaughan 2006).

There is significant empirical support for the suggestion that interactions *between* life transitions, social bonds and changes in identity are often associated with processes of desistance. In the next two sections of this chapter, we review some of this evidence, focusing first on age and gender and second on attitudes, motivation and narratives of desistance.

Age, gender and desistance

In a relatively recent Scottish study, Jamieson *et al.* (1999) explored desistance and persistence among three groups of young people aged 14–15 (the peak age for recruitment into offending for boys), 18–19 (the peak age of offending) and 22–25 (the age by which many would be expected to grow out of crime). They paid particular attention to gender differences in their study, which was based on interviews with a total of 75 'desisters' (43 male and 32 female) and 109 young people (59 male and 50 female) who were still offending or had done so recently.

The researchers discovered some significant age-related differences concerning desistance. In the youngest age group, desistance for both boys and girls was associated with the real or potential consequences of offending and with growing recognition that offending was pointless or wrong. Young people in the middle age group similarly related their changing behaviour to increasing maturity. This was often linked to the transition to adulthood and related events like securing a job or a place at college or university, or entering into a relationship with a partner or leaving home. For the oldest group, 'desistance was encouraged by the assumption of family responsibilities, especially among young women, or by a conscious lifestyle change' (McIvor *et al.* 2000: 9).

Although age and, in particular, the transitions associated with it, seemed to be a more important determinant of desistance than gender, Jamieson *et al.* (1999) did note some gender differences. The young women in their sample tended to offer moral as opposed to pragmatic rationales for stopping offending and were more likely to emphasise the importance of relational aspects of the process. Some young women linked their decisions to desist to the assumption of parental responsibilities. In general, young men focused more on personal choice and agency. Among persisters, girls and young women were more often keen to be seen as desisters, perhaps reflecting societal disapproval of female offending. Drawing on the same empirical study, McIvor *et al.* (2000) speculate that:

Assigning the offending to the past rather than acknowledging it as a current or future reality may enable young women to better cope with the tensions that may arise when, on the one hand, society encourages gender equality and, on the other, continues to double condemn young women who step beyond their traditional gender roles. (McIvor *et al.* 2000: 9)

51

In a more recent article, drawing on Giordano *et al.*'s (2002) study referred to above, Rumgay (2004) has suggested that women's desistance from crime is best understood as a process initiated by the *perception of an opportunity* to claim a pro-social identity during a period of *readiness to reform*, which is subsequently sustained by the deployment of strategies of resilience and survival in conditions of adversity.

The development of this 'readiness to reform' seems to be slower, in general, for young men. Graham and Bowling's (1995) earlier study of young people aged 14–25 noted a clear association between the life transition from adolescence to adulthood and desistance from offending among young women. Young men, in contrast, were less likely to achieve independence and those that did leave home, formed partnerships and had children, were no more likely to desist than those that did not. Failure to desist among young men seemed to be best explained by three sets of risk factors: a high frequency of prior offending, continued contact with delinquent peers and heavy drinking and controlled drug use. Graham and Bowling speculate that life transitions, 'only provide *opportunities* for change to occur; its realisation is mediated by individual contingencies. Males may be less inclined [than females] to grasp or be able to take advantage of such opportunities' (Graham and Bowling 1995: 65).

More recent studies have revised this conclusion to some extent, suggesting that similar processes of change do indeed occur for (some) males but that they seem to take longer to 'kick-in'; the assumption of responsibilities (for example, in and through intimate relationships and employment) does make a difference but this difference is more notable in men aged 25 and over (Farrall and Bowling 1999; Flood-Page *et al.* 2000; Uggen and Kruttschnitt 1998). Thus, it seems that young men take longer to perceive and to grasp the opportunities for change that these life transitions provide.

In Graham and Bowling's (1995) study, only two factors seemed to be positively associated with desistance for males in the 16–25 age range: first, their perception that their school work was above average, and second, continuing to live at home. It may be that continuing to live at home was associated with desistance because of relatively positive relationships with parents and, as a result, spending less time with delinquent peers.

Barry's (2004, 2006) recent study provides another key reference point for exploring how themes of identity and transition play out specifically for younger people desisting from offending. Through in-depth interviews with 20 young women and 20 young men, Barry explored why they started and stopped offending and what influenced or inhibited them in that behaviour as they grew older. The young people revealed that their decisions about offending and desisting were related to their need to feel included in their social world, through friendships in childhood and through wider commitments in adulthood. The resolve displayed by the young people in desisting from offending seemed remarkable to Barry, particularly given that they were from disadvantaged backgrounds and were limited in their access to mainstream opportunities (employment, housing and social status) both because of their age and because of their social class. Barry recognises crucially that:

> Because of their transitional situation, many young people lack the status and opportunities of full citizens and thus have limited capacity for social recognition in terms of durable and legitimate means of both accumulating and expending capital through taking on responsibility and generativity . . . Accumulation of capital requires, to a certain extent, both responsibilities and access to opportunities; however, children and young people rarely have such opportunities because of their status as 'liminal entities' . . . not least those from a working class background. (Barry 2004: 328–9)

We might ask whether other offenders might not, in some circumstances (such as leaving prison), also experience similar sorts of disabling liminality. Indeed, it may be that *most* (re)offenders suffer the consequences of the liminality that arises from their stigmatised social position and the limitations that are placed on them as conditional citizens whose rights are somehow suspended or attenuated (see Vaughan 2000 and Uggen *et al.* 2006).

Taken together, this evidence about age, gender and desistance does seem to suggest broadly that variations in the criminal careers of young women and young men, perhaps unsurprisingly, may be related to differences in gendered constructions of identity in adolescence and early adulthood. If this points towards the significance of identity changes in desistance, then research which explores offenders' attitudes, motivation and narratives of desistance makes the case even more clearly.

Attitudes, motivation and narratives of desistance

Returning to Jamieson *et al.*'s (1999) study, it is also important to note that 'persisters' in the youngest age group were more optimistic about their ability to desist, whereas 'for older respondents, who may have become more entrenched in patterns of offending and drug use, desistance was rarely considered to be an immediate or achievable goal' (McIvor *et al.* 2000: 9). The significance of this finding is underlined by Burnett's (1992) study of efforts to desist among 130 adult property offenders released from custody (see also Burnett and Maruna 2004). Burnett noted that while eight out of ten, when interviewed pre-release, wanted to 'go straight'; six out of ten subsequently reported reoffending post-release. For many, the intention to be law-abiding was provisional in the sense that it did not represent a confident prediction; only one in four reported that they would definitely be able to desist.

Importantly, Burnett discovered that those who were most confident and optimistic about desisting had greatest success in doing so. For the others, the 'provisional nature of intentions reflected social difficulties and personal problems that the men faced' (Burnett 2000: 14). More recently Burnett and Maruna (2004) have written persuasively about the role of hope in the process of desistance and equally importantly about how social circumstances can suffocate hope (see also Farrall and Calverley 2006: ch. 5).

On the basis of her interviews, Burnett (2000) delineated three categories of *persisters*, though she notes that these categories are neither fixed nor mutually exclusive. 'Hedonists' were attracted by the feelings of well-being gained through criminal involvement, whether in terms of the 'buzz' at the time, the emotional high afterwards or the place of the financial rewards of crime in funding lifestyles sometimes associated with alcohol and drugs. The 'earners' varied in their enthusiasm for crime, but regarded it as a viable money-making enterprise. The 'survivors' were generally dependent on substances and unhappily committed to persistent property offending to fund their substance misuse.

The *desisters* also fell into three broad categories. The 'non-starters' adamantly denied that they were 'real criminals' and, in fact, had fewer previous convictions than the others. For the 'avoiders', keeping out of prison was the key issue. They appeared to have decided that the costs of crime outweighed the benefits. The 'converts', however, were

> the most resolute and certain among the desisters. They had found new interests that were all-preoccupying and overturned their value system: a partner, a child, a good job, a new vocation. These were attainments that they were not prepared to jeopardize or which over-rode any interest in or need for property crime. (Burnett 2000: 14)

Although Burnett notes that for most of the men involved in her study, processes of desistance were characterised by ambivalence and vacillation, the over turning of value systems and all-preoccupying new interests that characterised the 'converts' seem to imply the kind of identity changes invoked in the notion of secondary desistance.

Maruna's (2001) study offers a particularly important contribution to understanding secondary desistance by exploring the subjective dimensions of change. Maruna compared the narrative 'scripts' of 20 persisters and 30 desisters who shared similar criminogenic traits and backgrounds and who lived in similarly criminogenic environments. In the 'condemnation script' that emerged from the persisters, 'The condemned person is the narrator (although he or she reserves plenty of blame for society as well). Active offenders . . . largely saw their life scripts as having been written for them a long time ago' (Maruna 2001: 75). By contrast, the accounts of the desisters revealed a different narrative:

The redemption script begins by establishing the goodness and conventionality of the narrator – a victim of society who gets involved with crime and drugs to achieve some sort of power over otherwise bleak circumstances. This deviance eventually becomes its own trap, however, as the narrator becomes ensnared in the vicious cycle of crime and imprisonment. Yet, with the help of some outside force, someone who 'believed in' the ex-offender, the narrator is able to accomplish what he or she was 'always meant to do'. Newly empowered, he or she now seeks to 'give something back' to society as a display of gratitude. (Maruna 2001: 87)

The desisters and the persisters shared the same sense of fatalism in their accounts of the development of their criminal careers; however, Maruna reads the minimisation of responsibility implied by this fatalism as evidence of the conventionality of their values and aspirations and of their need to believe in the essential goodness of the 'real me'. Moreover, in their accounts of achieving change there is evidence that desisters have to 'discover' agency (the ability to make choices) in order to resist and overcome the criminogenic structural pressures that play upon them. This discovery of agency seems to relate to the role of significant others in envisioning an alternative identity and an alternative future for the offender even through periods when they cannot see these possibilities for themselves. Typically later in the process of change, involvement in 'generative activities' (which usually make a contribution to the well-being of others) plays a part in testifying to the desister that an alternative 'agentic' identity is being or has been forged. Arguably what Maruna (2001) has revealed is the role of reflexivity in both revealing *and* producing shifts in the dynamic relationships between agency and structure (see also Farrall and Bowling 1999; Vaughan 2006).

Supporting desistance

The implications for practice of this developing evidence base have begun to be explored in a small number of research studies that have focused on the role that probation or social work may play in supporting desistance (for example, Farrall 2002; McCulloch 2005; Rex 1999). In one study of 'assisted desistance', Rex (1999) explored the experiences of 60 probationers. She found that those who attributed changes in their behaviour to probation supervision described it as active and participatory. Probationers' commitments to desist appeared to be generated by the personal and professional commitment shown by their probation officers, whose reasonableness, fairness and encouragement seemed to engender a sense of personal loyalty and accountability. Probationers interpreted advice about their behaviours and underlying problems as evidence of concern for them as people, and 'were motivated by what they saw as a display of interest in their well-being' (Rex 1999: 375). Such evidence resonates with other arguments about the pivotal role that relationships play in effective interventions (Barry 2000; Burnett 2004; Burnett and McNeill 2005; McNeill *et al.* 2005). If secondary desistance (for those involved in persistent offending at least) requires a narrative reconstruction of identity, then it seems obvious why the relational aspects of practice are so significant. Who would risk engaging in such a precarious and threatening venture without the reassurance of sustained and compassionate support from a trusted source?

However, workers and working relationships are neither the only nor the most important resources in promoting desistance. Related studies of young people in trouble suggest that their own resources and social networks are often better at resolving their difficulties than professional staff (Hill 1999). The potential of social networks is highlighted by 'resilience perspectives' which, in contrast with approaches that dwell on risks and/or needs, consider the 'protective factors and processes' involved in positive adaptation in spite of adversity. In terms of practice with young people, such perspectives entail an emphasis on the recognition, exploitation and development of their competences, resources, skills and assets (Schoon and Bynner 2003). In similar vein, but in relation to re-entry of ex-prisoners to society, Maruna and LeBel (2003) have made a convincing case for the development of strengths-based (rather than needs-based or risk-based) narratives and approaches. Drawing on both psychological and criminological evidence, they argue that such approaches would be likely both to enhance compliance with parole conditions and to encourage ex-prisoners to achieve 'earned redemption' (Bazemore 1998, 1999) by focusing on the positive contributions through which they might make good to their communities. Thus promoting desistance also means striving to develop the offender's strengths – at both an individual and a social network level – in order to build and sustain the momentum for change.

In looking towards these personal and social contexts of desistance, the most recent and perhaps most significant study of probation and desistance is particularly pertinent to the development of desistance-based practice. Farrall (2002) explored the progress or lack of progress towards desistance achieved by a group of 199 probationers. Though over half of the sample evidenced progress towards desistance, Farrall found that desistance could be attributed to specific interventions by the probation officer in only a few cases, although help with finding work and mending damaged family relationships appeared particularly important. Desistance seemed to relate more clearly to the probationers' motivations and to the social and personal contexts in which various obstacles to desistance were addressed.

Farrall (2002) goes on to argue that interventions must pay greater heed to the community, social and personal contexts in which they are situated (see also McCulloch 2005). After all, 'social circumstances and relationships with others are *both* the object of the intervention *and* the medium through which

... change can be achieved' (Farrall 2002: 212). Necessarily, this requires that interventions be focused not solely on the individual person and his or her perceived 'deficits'. As Farrall (2002) notes, the problem with such interventions is that while they can build human capital, for example, in terms of enhanced cognitive skills or improved employability, they cannot generate the social capital which resides in the relationships through which we achieve participation and inclusion in society.[1] Vitally, it is social capital that is necessary to encourage desistance. It is not enough to build *capacities* for change where change depends on *opportunities* to exercise capacities:

> ... the process of desistance is one that is produced through an interplay between individual choices, and a range of wider social forces, institutional and societal practices which are beyond the control of the individual. (Farrall and Bowling 1999: 261)

This stress on the interplay between agency and structure is both reminiscent of and consistent with the 'responsibility model' (Paterson and Tombs 1998) discussed in Chapter 1 which, as we have already noted, is 'premised on the view that, through social work intervention which promotes individual responsibility for behaviour together with social responsibility for alleviating adverse circumstance, offending will be discouraged' (Paterson and Tombs 1998: 9). Moreover, the three key findings reported by Robinson and McNeill (2004) concerning the views of Scottish workers – that in order to protect the public it is necessary to assist offenders, that relationships are the main vehicle for change and that social contexts are critical in change efforts – seem to find a good deal of empirical support in the desistance literature. This congruence of Scottish policy and practice perspectives with the desistance research has led McNeill to conclude that:

> the penal professional context in Scotland represents perhaps uniquely fertile ground for the development of more desistance-focused practice, particularly when set alongside the retention of penal reductionism and improving the social inclusion of offenders amongst criminal justice social work's official purposes (Justice Department 2001). Capitalising upon this context may depend in part upon the outcome of the ongoing debate about the most appropriate organisational contexts for interventions with offenders. If this results in the establishment of a new organisation that responds to 'populist punitiveness' (Bottoms 1983) by developing an increasingly correctional ethos, then a significant opportunity will be lost. However, if existing organisations or new organisations can retain, develop and re-focus those aspects of Scottish policy and practice which seem likely to best support desistance, then the possibility of a more constructive way forward may survive the current turbulence. (McNeill 2004a: 433–4)

Conclusions: paradigms for practice

In Part III of this book, where our focus is effective practice, we will develop in more detail our arguments about how both criminal justice social work practice and the work of the new Community Justice Authorities might be best developed in the light of desistance research. However, to conclude both this chapter and, more generally, the scene-setting discussions of Part I of the book, it makes some sense to discuss the paradigm for practice that we would suggest emerges from the research evidence reviewed in this chapter and, drawing on the analysis offered in Chapter 1, to place this paradigm in some historical context.

In a recent paper, McNeill (2006) has drawn on the material presented in this chapter to suggest a desistance paradigm for 'offender management', following the examples offered by Bottoms and McWilliams (1979) and by Raynor and Vanstone (1994) in trying to build both empirical and ethical cases for the development of earlier paradigms for probation practice. The paper also discusses the 'what works?' paradigm that has dominated probation since the mid-1990s. In many respects, as historical artefacts, these previous paradigms lend weight to our analysis (advanced in Chapter 1) of how probation has adapted in order to survive changing penal policies and public sensibilities, while retaining a core focus on seeking to reduce the prison population by developing constructive ways to tackle offending and reoffending. Chapter 2 outlined our analysis of the contemporary problem of reoffending in Scotland, suggesting the scale of the challenge that currently faces criminal justice social work services. Like its predecessors, therefore, the desistance paradigm draws on the best available evidence to seek self-consciously to reinvent social work with offenders in the context of the challenges that it currently faces.

In summary, the argument that McNeill (2006) advances is that desistance is the process that social work with offenders (whether it is called 'offender management' or not) exists to promote and support; that approaches to intervention should be embedded in understandings of desistance; and that it is important to explore the connections between structure, agency, reflexivity and identity in desistance processes. Moreover, desistance-supporting interventions need to respect and foster agency and reflexivity; they need to be based on legitimate and respectful relationships; they need to focus on social capital (networks and opportunities) as well as human capital (motivations and capacities); and they need to exploit strengths as well as address needs and risks. McNeill (2006) also develops normative arguments for a desistance paradigm, noting that desistance research highlights the relevance of certain 'practice virtues'; that it requires a focus on the role of legitimacy in supporting normative mechanisms of compliance; that it is consonant in many respects with communicative approaches to punishment which cast probation officers (or offender managers) as mediators between

Table 3.1 Probation practice in four paradigms

The non-treatment paradigm	The revised paradigm	A what works? paradigm	A desistance paradigm
Treatment becomes help.	Help consistent with a commitment to the reduction of harm.	Intervention required to reduce reoffending and protect the public.	Help in navigating towards desistance to reduce reoffending, to reduce harm and to make good to offenders and victims.[2]
Diagnosis becomes shared assessment.	Explicit dialogue and negotiation offering opportunities for consensual change.	'Professional' assessment of risk and need governed by structured assessment instruments.	Explicit dialogue and negotiation assessing risks, needs, strengths and resources and offering opportunities to make good.
Client's dependent need as the basis for action becomes collaboratively defined task as the basis for action.	Collaboratively defined task relevant to criminogenic need and potentially effective in meeting them.	Compulsory engagement in structured programmes and case management processes as required elements of legal orders imposed irrespective of consent.	Collaboratively defined tasks which tackle risks, needs and obstacles to desistance by using and developing the offender's human and social capital.

(Source: adapted from McNeill 2006)

offenders, victims and communities; and that it suggests a rights-based approach to rehabilitation which entails both that the offender makes good to society and that, where injustice has been suffered by the offender, society makes good to the offender.

Table 3.1 summarises the contrasts between the constructions of practice implied by the non-treatment, revised, what works? and desistance paradigms. Unlike the earlier paradigms, the desistance paradigm forefronts processes of change rather than modes of intervention. Practice under the desistance paradigm would certainly accommodate intervention to meet needs, reduce risks and (especially) to develop and exploit strengths, but whatever these forms might be they would be subordinated to a more broadly conceived role in working out, on an individual basis, how the desistance process might best be prompted and supported. This would require the worker to act as an advocate providing a conduit to social capital as well as a 'treatment' provider building human capital. Moreover, rather than being about the technical management of programmes and the disciplinary management of orders, as the current term 'offender manager' unhelpfully implies, the forms of engagement required by the paradigm would reinstate and place a high premium, wherever possible, on collaboration and involvement in the process of co-designing interventions. Critically, such interventions would not be concerned solely with the prevention of further offending; they would be equally concerned with constructively addressing the harms caused by crime by encouraging offenders to make good through restorative processes and community service (in the broadest sense). But, as a morally and practically necessary corollary, they would be no less preoccupied with making good to offenders by enabling them to achieve inclusion and participation in society (and with it the progressive and positive reframing of their identities required to sustain desistance).

The potential of the paradigm depends not only on its own strengths and weaknesses but on the legal and organisational contexts within which it might be developed and operationalised. Before developing our arguments about effective practice in Part III, therefore, it is necessary to explore these legal and organisational contexts in Scotland. This is the task to which we now turn in Part II.

Notes

1 Significantly, Boeck *et al.*'s (2004) emerging findings suggest that bridging social capital in particular (which facilitates social mobility) seems to be limited among those young people in their study involved in offending, leaving them ill-equipped to successfully navigate risk.

2 It is with some unease that we have merely mentioned but not developed arguments about the importance of making good to (and for) victims. I am therefore grateful to Mike Nellis for highlighting the contingent relationships between offenders' making good and making amends to victims. There is little empirical evidence that desistance requires making amends or making good to *particular* victims, although there are of course independent and compelling reasons why this matters in its own right. As Nellis suggests (personal communication, 18 August 2005), the case for making amends requires separate justification. He further suggests that from the point of view of interventions with offenders, it may be important not so much as an *enabling* factor in desistance as a *signifying* factor. Drawing on this distinction, our own view is that although making amends is neither necessary nor sufficient for desistance to occur, it may be useful nonetheless in consigning the past to the past (for victims and offenders) and thus in entrenching redemption scripts (for offenders).

Part II
The Legal Context

4. Advice and services to court

Preparing social enquiry reports demands a high standard of professional practice. It requires skilled interviewing, the ability to collect and assess information from different sources and the art of writing a report which is dependable, constructive, impartial and brief. (SWSI 1996: i)

Introduction

Practice that best supports reintegration and desistance needs to be grounded within a clear understanding of the legal and policy contexts of the core professional tasks. In Part II, therefore, we aim to provide a more detailed discussion of the legal and policy requirements of the three main criminal justice social work services in Scotland, along with a critical examination of their stated overall goal of reducing reoffending. This chapter examines the technical requirements for providing advice to the courts in Scotland, in preparing reports based on professional assessment of needs and risks and in assisting the court with information on the feasibility of a community disposal or the need for supervision on release from custody. Central to the task is the critical use of evidence within the framework of values, principles and research evidence discussed in Part I.

Each local authority in Scotland is required to make 'arrangements for the attendance of officers of the local authority at court' and for 'co-operation . . . with the courts' (Social Work (Scotland) Act 1968, section 27(3(c))). There are a number of ways in which social workers can assist the criminal court in sentencing on a day-to-day basis by providing information, advice and a range of services. These include assessment to assist disposal or sentencing, and providing bail-related services which offer the court an alternative to remanding an accused person.

National Objectives and Standards (NOS) for social enquiry reports and related services were first developed in 1991 (SWSG 1991a) and were reviewed and reissued in 2000 (Scottish Executive 2000a). They identify a range of tasks associated with the provision of information, advice and services to the courts as well as services for offenders and their families, victims and witnesses while attending court. These include the following.

- Dealing with requests for reports.

- Providing oral, stand down or supplementary reports for the court.

- Interviewing offenders following a request for a report by the court.

- Interviewing offenders/accused following a custodial sentence or remand.

- Interviewing offenders following a decision by the court to make a disposal involving social work.

- Providing support to victims or vulnerable people as witnesses who appear before the courts.

- Representing the local authority in the court setting and liaising with other professional groups.

- Seeking to divert people with mental health problems, who may be a risk to themselves in custodial remand, to appropriate care including bail accommodation (under section 200 of the Criminal Procedure (Scotland) Act 1995).

Social work, sentencing and social enquiry

There are three levels of criminal courts in Scotland – the High Court, the Sheriff Court and the District Court – and two methods of prosecution – solemn (with a jury) and summary (non-jury) procedure – which determine the sentencing powers of the Scottish criminal courts. The High Court hears cases only on solemn procedure, the Sheriff Court can hear cases using both methods, and the District Court hears cases only on summary procedure. The legislative basis for most criminal court activity is included in the Criminal Procedure (Scotland) Act 1995 (hereafter 'the 1995 Act').

Generally crime is prosecuted under common law, the exceptions being statutory offences (that is, breaches of specific legislation). Penalties for common law crimes are not determined by statute relating to the crime, they are determined by the powers of the sentencing court (District, Sheriff or High) and by the procedures (solemn or summary) under which the prosecution takes place. The procurator fiscal determines the court and the procedure and therefore plays a key gate-keeping role. The sentencing powers of the different courts under different procedures are outlined in Table 4.1.

Setting a maximum penalty reflecting the relative gravity of that offence is usually the only part that Parliament plays in determining sentencing policy for a particular offence. Within the sentencing framework and the maximum penalty laid down by Parliament, it is entirely for the courts to decide the appropriate sentence in each case which comes before them. As a general rule, it is not Executive policy to provide different maximum penalties for first and subsequent offences. There are exceptional examples in statute (for

Table 4.1 The maximum sentencing powers of Scottish criminal courts

District Court	
Fine	Level 4 (£2,500)
Imprisonment	60 days
Sheriff summary (and stipendiary magistrates)	
Fine	Level 5 (£5,000)
Imprisonment	3 months (on the first conviction)
	6 months (on second or subsequent conviction)
Sheriff solemn	
Fine	Unlimited
Imprisonment	5 years
High Court of Justiciary	
Fine	Unlimited
Imprisonment	Life

example, section 52 of the 1995 Act dealing with the offence of vandalism) where different maximum penalties are provided. But these should not be treated as the norm and there are offences under the Road Traffic Offences Act 1988 for which disqualification from driving or endorsement of the licence is obligatory.

The limits to the sentencing powers of the Scottish criminal courts apply to all common law offences. Statutory provisions may extend or limit these powers. For example, the sheriff court is empowered by statute to impose up to six months' imprisonment on summary conviction for a range of offences. It also has the power to impose exceptionally high maximum fines (up to £50,000 in certain cases) on summary conviction. The Criminal Proceedings (Scotland) Bill currently before the Parliament includes proposals to increase summary sentencing powers including provision to increase the maximum period of custodial sentence to 12 months in some instances.

Scotland has a wide range of measures available to the criminal courts, many of which are community based and involve social work supervision. The following is a brief summary of the main measures available to the courts through the 1995 Act:

- **Absolute discharge.** No penalty is imposed, even though guilt has been admitted or proved. On solemn procedure an order is made 'instead of sentencing' (section 246(2), and in cases of summary procedure 'without proceeding to conviction' (section 246(3)).

65

- **Admonition.** Represents dismissal with a warning, following conviction (section 246(1)).

- **Deferral of sentence.** Technically not a disposal; follows conviction; no restriction on the length of time the person is required 'to be of good behaviour'; may involve social work supervision and assistance; following the period of deferral a supplementary report is normally requested and a substantive disposal can be imposed. Deferrals are commonly used for purposes such as to test behaviour over a specified period of time; to see how a person responds to a recently ordered period of supervision; to enable a person to perform a specific task or service related directly to the circumstances of an offence; to enable the person to receive help or treatment (section 202).

- **Remittal to children's hearing.** For advice or disposal. This is a requirement on summary courts for young people subject to supervision (section 49(1)) and is at the court's discretion for other young people who are not within six months of attaining the age of 18 (section 49(3 and 6)).

- **Caution** (pronounced 'kay-shun'). Money required as financial security of future good behaviour (section 227).

- **Compensation order.** Requires the offender to make financial amends to a victim (via the court) on summary or solemn procedure (sections 249–253).

- **Fine.** Available to all courts, with upper limits in summary procedure; requires the person's 'means' to be taken into account (section 211).

- **Fine supervision order and fine enforcement.** Involves social work supervision of fines (section 217) on solemn procedure or summary procedure but has largely fallen into disuse. A social work fines enquiry report can be requested by courts.

- **Supervised attendance order.** Requires attendance at a specified place for a specified number of hours as an alternative to imprisonment for fine default; legislation allows for its use at first instance instead of a fine for young offenders; no consent is required (section 235–237).

- **Supervision and treatment orders.** Used for those assessed as unfit to plead in relation to mental health problems (section 57).

- **Probation.** Consent is required (section 228) (see Chapter 5).

- **Community service.** Unpaid service or work in the community. Consent is required (section 238) (see Chapter 5).

- **Community reparation orders.** Unpaid work in the community. No consent is required (section 245K).

- **Restriction of liberty orders.** An order restricting movement for up to a total of 12 hours in any one day, by requiring the person to be in a specified place for set periods of time (section 245); section 245C makes provision for electronic tagging. No consent is required.

- **Drug treatment and testing orders.** Requirement for drug testing and treatment normally imposed by specialised drug courts (Crime and Disorder Act, 1998 (section 72). Consent is required.

- **Criminal anti-social behaviour orders** (CRASBO). Crime and Disorder Act 1998 introduced an anti-social behaviour order made on conviction by a Sheriff or Justice of the Peace.

- **Custodial sentences.** See Table 4.1 and Chapter 6.

- **Supervised release orders, home detention curfews and extended sentences.** See Chapter 6.

The independence of the judiciary is a fundamental principle of the Scottish legal system and great importance is accorded to judicial discretion in sentencing (Hutton 1999). It is for the courts to decide on the most appropriate sentence, within the limits provided by Parliament, in any given case. Each case is unique and only the court hears all the facts and circumstances surrounding the offence and the offender. Local authorities have a statutory duty to provide services to the court, including 'making available to any court such social background reports and other reports relating to persons appearing before the court which the court may require for the disposal of a case' (Social Work (Scotland) Act 1968, s.27(1)(a), hereafter 'the 1968 Act').

The term commonly used for such reports in Scotland is social enquiry report (SER). In England and Wales pre-sentence reports (PSR) are roughly equivalent. While the term SER is contained in NOS, it does not exist in Scots law, but is used to describe reports which local authority social workers prepare and submit to the courts. NOS require that reports are prepared by a qualified social worker, who is an officer of the local authority. This emphasis on professional qualification is also not reflected in Scots law, which simply indicates it must be 'from an officer of a local authority or otherwise' (section 207 of the 1995 Act).

The law provides general powers to the courts to adjourn a case for the purpose of enabling enquiries to be made or of determining the most suitable method of dealing with a case (section 201(1) of the 1995 Act). An adjournment must not exceed three weeks where the offender is remanded in custody (section 201(3)(a) of the 1995 Act). When the offender is remanded on bail or ordained to appear, the maximum period is normally four weeks, although 'on cause shown' the period may be extended to eight weeks.

In law, the report is required to provide 'such information as it can about an offender's circumstances and it shall also take into account any information before it concerning the offender's character and physical and mental condition'. In cases where a custodial sentence is being considered, this is intended to assist the court in determining that 'no other method of dealing with him is appropriate' (section 204(2) of the 1995 Act). In relation to community supervision, it is to ensure 'that suitable arrangements for the supervision of the offender can be made' (section 228(2) of the 1995 Act). Though the courts may request a report in any case, they are obliged to obtain reports under certain specified circumstances to assist them in deciding whether there are ways of dealing with the offender in the community to avoid the use of detention or custody. It could be argued that the court's actions are constrained by law to ensure social work information is available before making key decisions. The court must always obtain a report when dealing with:

- Those subject to supervision or licence following release from prison or any other form of detention; including those under supervised release orders (section 209(2) of the 1995 Act) and extended sentences (section 210(a)(10) of the 1995 Act).

- Those subject to a community disposal, for example, community service order, probation, supervised attendance order, supervision and treatment order, restriction of liberty order (RLO) or drug treatment and testing order (DTTO) (under section 203 of the 1995 Act).

- Those under 21 facing custody and anyone facing custody for the first time or before imposing certain community disposal with the exception of supervised attendance orders (SAO) or community reparation orders (CROs) (under sections 205 and 207 of the 1995 Act).

- Those under the age of 16 or a young person aged 16–18 who is subject to a supervision requirement under the Children's Hearings system (section 42(8) of the 1995 Act).

- A person convicted of incest, intercourse with a step-child or intercourse by a person in a position of trust with a child under 16 (under section 4(6) of the Criminal Law (Consolidation) Act 1995).

The legislation indicates that imprisonment or detention may be imposed only if the court is of the opinion that no other method of dealing with the offender is appropriate (section 204(2) of the 1995 Act). The law can be seen, therefore, to underscore the long-standing (if imperfectly enacted) policy of using prisons sparingly and, at least for some offenders in some situations, as a measure of last resort (as discussed in Chapters 1 and 2). Equally the court is required to consider social work information and assessment for those likely to be made subject to a number of community disposals.

In the past, one source of tension was the notion of defining the social worker's 'client' in the social enquiry process. On this question, Sheriff Aikman Smith noted that:

the term client, ubiquitous in social work, can be misleading in the context of work for the courts. The offender on whom the court directs a social enquiry report to be prepared is in no sense the client of the social worker. The report must be prepared with professional objectivity; if the social worker has a client at all, the client is the judge who has called for the social worker's assistance. (Moore and Wood 1992: xvii)

Though this is perhaps now the generally accepted view, offenders, their families, sentencers, victims, defence agents, social work agencies and policy-makers are each likely to have expectations of the report writer which may be quite different and, at times, conflicting. NOS identify the role and purpose of social work in providing reports for court as follows:

The central task is to provide advice and information about the feasibility of a community disposal or the need for supervision on release from custody by assessing the risk of reoffending, and in more serious cases, the risk of possible harm to others. This requires an investigation of offending behaviour and of the offender's circumstances, attitudes and motivation to change. Reports have a particular role to play in seeking to ensure that offenders are not sentenced to custody for want of information and advice about feasible community-based disposals. (Scottish Executive 2000a: 1.6)

NOS identifies the key focus of social enquiry as addressing issues concerning the offence and offending behaviour and the associated social factors that might impact on the court's decision-making. These include finance, family relationships, education, training, employment, accommodation, lifestyle, physical and mental health, risk of self-harm and substance misuse (Scottish Executive 2000a: 2.8–2.21). The focus on assessing risk of reoffending and risk of harm as a central task of social enquiry is reflected in the emphases in the new national strategy (Scottish Executive 2006d) on reducing repeat offending as an objective for the whole criminal justice system.

As the key entry point to criminal justice social work services, SERs attract a very high level of financial investment, which reflects policy-makers' recognition of the pivotal role they play in pursuit of governmental objectives for social work services to the criminal justice system in Scotland. The Social Work Services Inspectorate (SWSI 1996) reported that some 108,000 reports were completed between 1991 and 1996, at an estimated cost of £23,500,000. This represents an average of over 18,000 reports per year across Scotland. By 2005 the annual figure was 40,265 including supplementary reports. This extraordinary increase in requests for reports from courts has to be set against the backdrop of a broadly static picture in terms of the number of cases proceeded against in court – the figure of 151,000 in 2004/05 is marginally *below* the 1998 figure of 159,000 and approximately 15 per cent below the amount of court business in the mid-1990s (Scottish Executive 2006g).

Around 54 per cent of those on whom an SER is prepared receive a custodial or community-based disposal and, in 2004/05, 20.6 per cent of outcomes were represented by fines or deferred sentence. Almost 90 per cent of reports are requested by lower courts; whether Sheriff Summary or Stipendiary Courts (Scottish Executive 2006g: Table 8).

NOS place criminal justice social work and social enquiry, in some senses, in an invidious position. The policy promotes attempts to assist and influence decision-making within courts – which might suggest some weak form of governance over sentencing – but it gives social work no formal authority or status to bind sentencers' decision-making. In practical terms this tension surfaces in controversies over the issue of social workers making 'recommendations' to the courts; a term that appeared in the first issue of NOS (SWSG 1991a: paras 93–96). While it was never the intention that social workers should make recommendations on sentencing as such – simply that should the court be considering a community disposal or alternative to custody, the most suitable should be recommended – the terminology did imply an assertive approach to engagement with sentencers and sentencing. The reissued standards (Scottish Executive 2000a: 5.6) precluded the term 'recommendation' and clarified that *opinions* should be expressed on the most appropriate community-based disposal or alternative to custody.

Nonetheless, if social enquiry is to play its key part in delivering the stated objectives, the business of making constructive proposals to the court, whether deemed opinions or recommendations, remains vitally important. If criminal justice social workers are to practise in line with the 'twin track' policy of NOS (Rifkind 1989), it is important for them to reach informed conclusions about what kind of view courts are likely to take of individual cases. It is equally important that the report writer does not merely try to assess and respond to the court's view of seriousness or 'second guess' and meet the court's expectations (Raynor 1985).

It may be that SERs at their best provide an aid to sentencing by bringing more of the whole person, in his/her experiential, educational and cultural history, before the sentencer. In this sense, paradoxically, the report may aid fairer sentencing by making the sentencing decision *more* complex (McNeill 2002). Thus, in theory, the report allows the 'system' to individualise the offender, recognising that no two people and no two offences are alike and, somehow, to take account of these differences in sentencing without damaging consistency.

National statistical data show clearly that alongside the very large rise in the use of SERs over the decade between 1995 and 2005, sentencing patterns also changed notably, but not in the intended direction (as we noted in Chapter 2). At the same time that community disposals rose from 7.5 per cent to 12.6 per cent of court decisions, custody rose from 10.5 per cent to 12.3 per cent (Scottish Executive 2006e). These rises were matched by a fall in the use of fines from 70 per cent to 63.4 per cent of court outcomes. There is no national statistical data on the 'match' between social work proposals and 'take up' by the court.

A major Economic and Social Research Council-funded study, 'Social Enquiry and Sentencing in Sheriff Courts', has recently been completed in Scotland.[1] This study used ethnographic methods to explore how social workers went about constructing SERs and how sheriffs subsequently interpreted and used them in the sentencing process. The emerging findings suggest that there are fundamental limitations on the influence of reports on sentencing that arise essentially from criminal justice social work's uncertain status in the legal world (see McNeill and Burns 2005). This marginality led to criminal justice social workers being preoccupied with their credibility in the eyes of the sheriffs but also denied them the means to secure that credibility; the lack of feedback that they received about reports left them perpetually uneasy about their standing and uncertain about their influence. The study reveals that many social workers strive to gain a sense of the sentencing practices of sheriffs in their area to be able to anticipate what would fall within the range of reasonable disposals according to these practices and then adapt their own practice accordingly. Though their reports are therefore indirectly regulated by sheriffs, social workers do strive to exercise influence through the narrative devices that they deploy in telling the story of the offence and the offender. However, their reliance on the offender for the story of the offence (since they do not receive police reports or witness statements) creates a fundamental vulnerability in their narratives at a key point, meaning that their accounts are easily 'trumped' by other narratives deployed by 'insiders' in the legal world (whether procurators fiscal or defence agents). Thus the influence of social enquiry is limited in both structural and cultural ways.

These new research findings may account, in part, for why the very significantly increased use of SERs by courts has not been matched by reduced recourse to custodial penalties (see also Tombs and Jagger 2006). They certainly raise questions about the effectiveness of social enquiry work and suggest that SERs may be used by courts as a kind of insurance policy (against appeals) in showing that all the boxes have been 'ticked' regarding the legal requirements that 'no other method of dealing with [the offender] is appropriate'.

The development of social enquiry

Developments in approaches to social enquiry have reflected broader developments in approaches to probation and social work practice more generally, as discussed in Part I. These developments in practice in turn have paralleled developments in the nature of social work as a profession and, in particular, in the role of criminal justice social work which has faced growing expectations regarding effectiveness in reducing reoffending and assisting individuals in desistance and better social integration.

It is likely that Police Court Missionaries were already undertaking some sort of social enquiry at the time of the Probation of First Offenders Act in 1887 (see McWilliams 1983, 1985, 1986, 1987). The role of the 'enquirer', however, has shifted over time from one of special pleading for those who might be 'saved', clearly a role aligned directly with the offender, to one where the primary responsibility of the report author lies in promoting social welfare under section 12 of the 1968 Act. In this instance it is the community's welfare and safety, as well as that of the offender, that is the priority and focus of assessment and intervention; the role being to examine and make a case, where appropriate, for community disposals or alternatives to custody which will impact on reducing reoffending and, consequently, safeguard the community. The 1968 Act also located the enquirer as part of the local authority – carrying the responsibility of and for the community – rather than part of the formal criminal justice system, symbolising a more detached and objective stance regarding community safety and welfare and emphasising where responsibilities for planning provision to assist the individual desist and community safety lie. Current debates about social enquiry continue to reflect tensions between policy directives and professional ideologies (see Part I).

The Streatfeild Report (1961) provided the first well-developed articulation of the purpose of court reports. The first function was to provide information about the offender and their background, to help the court determine the most suitable method of response. Originally, information was used primarily where the court was considering putting the offender on probation, but information was also helpful where the court was considering whether any other form of sentence or disposal might divert the offender from crime. A number of core elements were identified which should be included in a report, such as 'assessment of personality and character'. Streatfeild took the view that an opinion should be included as to the possibility of the defendant committing further offences, and, as a result, of the possible impact of sentences other than probation; the Morison Report (1962) (see Chapter 1) was less sure. Nonetheless, both committees recognised the SER as a key element contributing to a philosophy of individualised sentencing.

By the late 1970s, the possibility of offering statistical probabilities of reoffending in reports was an intriguing prospect. Davies concluded:

> The use of reports represents one of the most important penal developments of the 20th century, and reflects a crucial change in the balance of sentencing authority. If during the next decade . . . research begins to pay dividends, there seems little doubt that the role of the probation officer as a sentencing adviser will become even more significant than it is now. (Davies 1978: 209)

Such an upbeat conclusion was inevitably vulnerable to concerns that remain nearly 30 years on. As we will see in Part III, the research looked forward to by Davies is still coming to fruition. While structured assessment tools and accredited programmes of supervision may now appear to promise more positive and more predictable effects, the challenges of implementation and the impact of the numbers of intervening variables elsewhere in an offender's life, alongside the low probability of apprehension for most offences, still combine to make 'scientific' prediction highly problematic, if not impossible (Harper and Chitty 2004; see Chapter 2). At best, such tools help to locate the offender's profile within a statistically valid distribution and provide a means of making the evidence for professional decision-making transparent and open to challenge. But the predictive validity of such tools for the purpose of *individual* sentencing remains ethically questionable. Providing government policy and social work practice do not overplay the rhetoric and maintain modest and realistic aspirations, the process of providing critical information about needs and risks will remain important to assisting the court process.

Social work assessment and sentencing

Although the SER is provided for the court, the placement of criminal justice social work services within the local authorities under the 1968 Act ensures that first and foremost the report is a social work document; that is, one that is informed by professional values such as care and respect for persons, and one which uses social work skills in its preparation (Raynor 1985). While tailored to the courts' needs, and conscious of the need to maintain credibility, the report should, nevertheless, be geared towards promoting appropriate community disposals drawing on the basis of available research, professional expertise and a consistent value framework. Any value framework has to deal with the competing and sometimes conflicting demands on the role of social workers, particularly in relation to issues of providing help, intervention and control in varying measures.

Exploring the critical use of evidence within a framework of values and principles equally challenges over-simplistic interpretations of what values entail. For example, a recognition that some offenders in some circumstances may not be able or willing to provide a completely honest account of their circumstances and behaviour (even assuming the successful development of a relationship of trust – see Chapter 7), challenges any simplistic position of 'believing and respecting' the offender's understanding of his/her experience as the only or even the main source of relevant information. Individual narrative is an essential ingredient of social work assessment but has to be set against other available evidence to avoid the well-established risks of operating a 'rule of optimism'.

Similarly the emphasis in social work literature on engagement, motivation, building a purposeful relationship and working alliance has to be matched with appropriate methodologies and the requirements of enforcement, compliance and public protection. Vanstone (2000) noted some of the possible effects of these changes on professional ideologies:

> The increasingly serious criminal profile of the people with whom practitioners engage, and attendant concerns about risk assessment and management have meant that the previously dominant concerns about whether social work intervention with offenders was treatment or help, whether the provision of care was possible within the State apparatus of control and how it could be delivered in anti-discriminatory and anti-oppressive ways have been eclipsed. (Vanstone 2000: 176)

Vanstone may be correct in terms of preoccupations but, in Scotland, the model of practice outlined in the supplement to NOS (SWSG 1991b) stresses the importance of multilevel engagement, intervention and service brokerage to promote compliance and change aimed at better social integration in which positively directed help remains an important element if desistance is to be the long-term objective. The National Standards are much more circumspect about how to achieve this.

These preoccupations, however, reflect the growing recognition that the SER writer needs to understand and respond to crime as a social phenomenon, understanding not only the risks that an offender may pose to others, but also her or his background characteristics, needs and strengths and social context. Until the turn of the twenty-first century, SERs tended to be more offender focused than offence or risk focused, with consequent limitations on the content and impact of the advice on offer to the courts (SWSI 1996). Clearly a difficult balance has to be struck by the report writer.

The wide-ranging review of probation practice in England and Wales reported by the Audit Commission (1990) was influential on both sides of the border in raising the debate about 'value for money' and 'net widening'. The report drew attention to the dangers of over-simplistic evaluations of 'success' and suggested that the increases in the use of community disposals were more related to a reduction of fines than with a reduction in custody. As we discussed above, Scottish statistics belie similar trends. The Audit Commission report also suggested that the effects of probation intervention on reoffending were small and difficult to detect but nonetheless proposed that probation services should take 'centre stage' in the provision of community-based disposals for the key target groups involving medium to serious non-violent offenders, some violent offenders and young offenders. It argued that probation's contribution should be geared to changing behaviour and reducing offending by focusing on underlying causes of offending behaviour and the risks of further offending. This version of offence-focused intervention (as opposed to a narrower focus on risk, deeds and deficits, as discussed in Chapter 3) is now generally uncontroversial when viewed not as a labelling process but as an ethical approach to social work intervention aimed at desistance and better social integration. At the same time it recognises that the only legitimacy for intervening in the life of the individual within the criminal justice process – in most cases an involuntary relationship – is the individual's offending behaviour.

The social worker's role is quite distinct from establishing the 'facts' of the case which remains the responsibility of the court process and is (normally) completed by the time reports are requested. As Stone put it:

> the worker's principal strength is not in tackling factual aspects of a criminal's modus operandi, but in throwing light on the judgements, motives, triggers, associations, anticipation/intent, reactions and mental state of the offender, before, during and after the crime. (Stone 1992: 561)

At the same time he suggests that there may be circumstances in which the skills, values and perceptions of the practitioner in getting alongside the defendant can create a 'misleading atmosphere of the confessional', and could result in disclosure by offenders without awareness of the 'public' nature of the disclosure, creating dilemmas for report writing and for advice offered to the courts in the role of promoting community welfare and safety. The use of information has to be determined by the purpose of the report. In a similar vein, it is a matter of debate to what extent the SER writer can make any judgement or imply an understanding of the nature of the offending without considering it in the light of national/local patterns and trends of crime, set within local knowledge of factors and social circumstances which contribute to or sustain certain criminal behaviour.

Reports for criminal courts

Information for reports needs to be gathered, corroborated, interpreted, compiled, edited and presented within prescribed timescales. Although courts can now continue a case for 28 days for reports (when the offender is at liberty), more commonly they allow 21 days, often less if the offender is remanded in custody. Some authorities have pre-planned interview times which allow speedy arrangements for meeting with the offender. Nonetheless, some time is inevitably lost to administration at the start and at the end of the process, and, typically, the SER author may have about ten days in which to prepare the report. Practice estimates suggest SERs take on average around eight hours to complete and are often based on one office or prison interview with the offender. It has been pointed out by both researchers and inspectors (Whyte *et al.* 1995; SWSI 1996) that many reports contain formulations about dynamic or changeable characteristics of criminal behaviour based on limited information or contact; often as little as 40–60 minutes, direct contact time with the subject of the report (Harris 1992; in the recent ESRC study referred to above similar timescales were noted). As a consequence the nature of the assessment and the basis for any proposal put forward has to be recognised as very limited and, in most instances, as a very 'initial' assessment and action plan.

NOS (Scottish Executive 2000a: 3.12–3.16) outline circumstances in which a second or a further interview will *normally* be required. Arguably, these circumstances pertain in many, if not most, cases. The standards advise that:

> Talking with members of the offender's family and visiting the offender's home provide an extra dimension to the assessment and help build an overall picture. Report writers should as a general rule visit the home. There may however be some circumstances where contact with family members is office based or carried out by phone, for example, where time is limited or where there are concerns about the report writer's safety. (Scottish Executive 2000a: 3.16)

In some cases much more extensive enquiry will be required. However, the practice model reflects more traditional social work literature which recognises that good assessment is ongoing and in-depth assessment is likely only to be achieved in the first phase of a community disposal. Indeed NOS (SWSG 1991a; see Chapter 5) stress that the first phase of a probation order (six weeks) will be needed to develop and confirm any plan of action. Nonetheless, the SER assessment needs to be sufficient to inform and advise the court on disposal.

Content of reports

The first edition of NOS moved Scottish guidance from the exhortatory to the regulatory, prescribing the format and contents of an SER. While the original NOS (SWSG 1991a) specify the role of social work in regard to SERs, the revised NOS (Scottish Executive 2000a) have less to say about professional methodologies of good social work assessment. Arguably, the revised standards are underpinned by a more functional model of the service requirement to the court, placing more emphasis on outcomes and less stress on the professional 'means' and on how these might impact on both the justice system and the offender. The first edition of NOS (SWSG 1991a) identified a format for presenting SERs and, although abandoned in the revised edition, it still has some merits:

- **Introduction.** The basis of the report; offender, court and offence details; brief social history including current domestic and social circumstances.

- **Information relevant to offending behaviour.** Offence history; current offence; offender's view of the offence; personal/social factors contributing, sustaining or supporting offending.

- **Information relevant to sentence/disposal.** Offender's response to previous disposals; financial circumstances; health, physical and mental; substance dependence; family and social networks; education and employment; resources available to the offender.

- **Review and conclusions.** Feasibility of community-based options; consequences of specific disposals; summary of offending needs/risks to be addressed, offender's motivation.

- **Proposals** ('recommendation' in the original version). Community-based options available; author's preferred option; explanation if no preferred option; initial action plan; offender's consent to the plan.

As we have said, the offence is central to the court's concern and is the only legitimate reason for involvement with the subject. The social worker's principal responsibilities are not in tackling the legal facts which belong to the court, but in throwing light on crime-related issues such as judgements about, motivations for and triggers of offending; social associations; expectations and intent, reactions and mental state of the offender, before, during and after the offence. The crime focused nature of the assessment is detailed in NOS (Scottish Executive 2000a: 2.8). The social worker is to explore:

- The offender's attitude to and explanation for his or her offending including his or her perceptions of its seriousness and its consequences for others including any victim.

- Whether there are any discrepancies between the information available about the offence and his or her account of events.

- The extent to which the offender thinks about the behaviour which leads to offending, for example, was the offending pre meditated?

- How the offender feels about the offending – does s/he express any genuine remorse or concern for the victims?

- Whether the offender sees any pattern to his/her offending.

- The extent to which the offender is or could be motivated to try and change his/her behaviour.

There is authority within NOS for report writers to provide *their* professional view on the risk of reoffending and to comment on the subject's 'attitude to and explanation for his or her offending including his or her perceptions of its seriousness and its consequences for others including any victim' (Scottish Executive 2000a: 2.8.1).

Structuralist approaches to social science can overemphasise a deterministic view of human nature – people as products, even passive victims, of their environment, upbringing, peer group, and social circumstances. In the context of sentencing, such explanations can be viewed as providing excuses rather than an understanding of criminal behaviour. This way of thinking contrasts very sharply with the equally unsatisfactory classical view of sole individual responsibility and intentionality which are at the root of much legal and jurisprudential thinking (McNeill 2002). Most contemporary criminology (including much of the desistance literature reviewed in Chapter 3) recognises the interplay between structural factors and personal agency. If report writers are to assist the court's sentencing function, they need to find ways of enabling courts to consider and understand possible explanatory or associated factors in the offender's social circumstances, while at the same time offering interpretations that can be recognised within the ideological terms of reference of the courts.

NOS identify the central task of social enquiry reports as providing 'advice about the feasibility of a community disposal particularly those involving local authority supervision' (Scottish Executive 2000a: 1.5), or 'the need for supervision on release from custody by assessing the risk of reoffending, and in more serious cases the risk of possible harm to others' (Scottish Executive 2000a: 1.6). The NOS requirements include an investigation of the offender's circumstances; the offending behaviour and attitudes and motivation to change. In order to assess the feasibility of a community-based disposal or the need for supervision on release from custody, the report writer is expected to undertake an assessment of the risk of reoffending and possible harm to others offering a view to the extent to which this could be managed in the community and to offer, where appropriate, a proposed plan for supervision (the action plan).

The core responsibility is to offer information and advice which can help the court decide between available sentencing options and to make the court aware of information and circumstances which the court may wish to take into account including family commitments, ill-health, work record/prospects and accommodation (Scottish Executive 2000a: 4.3). To carry out the task of report writing adequately, particularly with the increasing emphasis on assessing the risk the offender may pose to the community, social workers need full information about the person's past criminality, about his/her response to any periods of supervision or to custody, and about his/her physical and mental health, particularly where this is relevant to the possibility of a custodial disposal.

A draft supplement on risk assessment underlines the need to consider factors relating both to the subject's current offence and previous offending history and to his or her personal attributes and social circumstances. It distinguishes between static factors (that is, those factors which cannot be changed) and dynamic factors (that is, those factors which may be amenable to change). It also introduces the idea of criminogenic needs; that is, needs which have been found to have an association with offending.

In assessing the risk of custody, the report writer is challenged to assess the extent to which custody will be considered seriously by the court. As we

Table 4.2 Assessing risk of custody

Custody more likely	Custody less likely
The subject is appearing on indictment.	The subject is appearing on complaint.
The subject is remanded in custody.	The subject has been ordained or bailed.
The subject has previously been sentenced to custody.	The subject has no previous experience of custody.
The court has requested a report on suitability for community service.	

have noted above, NOS stress that reports have a particular role to play in seeking to ensure that offenders are not sentenced to custody for want of information and advice about feasible community-based disposals (Scottish Executive 2000a: 1). They also note that if a report is to help the court decide whether there are ways of dealing with the offender which avoid the use of custody, the report writer has to assess the extent to which custody will be considered seriously by the court (Scottish Executive 2000a: 4.5). This controversial element of the task is hardly a precise science and begs the question how the social worker is to do this without second-guessing the sheriff. Clearly it helps if the sheriff indicates what he or she has in mind; but most will wait for social work advice before deciding. The report writer has to rely on the critical use of evidence within a framework of values and policy principles. The Standards (Scottish Executive 2000a: 4.5) provide some clues to direct the social worker's judgement on whether custody is more or less likely (Table 4.2). Other indicators are likely to include the nature and seriousness of the offence; the seriousness and frequency of any previous offending; and any comments made by the bench. The 'twin track' policy does not focus directly on persistent offending, yet there is some indication that this may be a factor in custody (see Chapter 2).

Because of the increased demand for SERs discussed above, the future is likely to see greater need to provide briefer screening reports as a filter to requests for full assessments reports, if required. The idea is not new and occasionally a court-based social worker may be asked to undertake an interview while a case is adjourned or 'stood down' for that purpose so that they can report to the court orally or in writing later in the day. These interviews are usually associated with the need for specific information and advice to assist decision-making; for example, if there is doubt about the person's plea when they are not legally represented or, more typically, information may be required to assist the court in considering issues of bail or remand. NOS emphasise that oral reports of any sort are not sufficient where the offender is at risk of custody and, unless the subject is currently subject to supervision or licence, they must consent to the information being given. Any disposal or decision which results in a statutory social work activity (an SER request, probation, community service, etc.) will require the person to be seen immediately after the hearing and 'before they leave the court precincts' in order to establish that he or she understands the procedure or the basic requirements of the order to which he/she is now subject. Changes introduced by the Management of Offenders (Scotland) Act 2005 to allow courts to review community disposals may provide a more meaningful mechanism for exploring more comprehensive assessment and its implications for action plans with the court at some subsequent date.

Assessing needs and risks: an initial action plan

Assessing needs and risk is not a new concept for the SER writer, in so far as the social worker's duty to protect the public has been recognised since the Morison Report (1962) and the duty to *promote social welfare* (and not just the offender's welfare) is the foundation of the 1968 Act. The term risk assessment, however, now brings with it an expectation that best practice in report writing should involve the use of standardised tools, incorporated routinely into the exercise of SER writing to assist the development of evidence-based action plans. The limitations of any standardised tool are such that at best they will supplement professional judgement but should never supplant it.

NOS guidance reflects an expectation that more services will be developed on a programmed basis by Community Justice Authorities so that when a community-based option is being considered both the judge and the offender will have as clear an understanding as is practical as to the nature and purpose of the programme of supervision proposed, the time demands and the expected outcomes. This is to ensure that, where consent is required, the offender has made an informed choice (Barber 1991; Raynor *et al*. 1994) and judges understand the undertaking they impose. This can then be accompanied by a resource statement on the availability of services and whether they can be delivered in a timescale acceptable to the court. Reasonable action plans can only be presented where a clear targeting framework has been established by the agency and programmes of intervention developed to address the anticipated crime-related issues for the individuals judged to fall within the target groups. Good liaison with courts and good information are essential if sheriffs are to be familiar with the kinds of programmes on offer to certain offenders, how they operate and to what effect. A judicial website has been commissioned by the Scottish Executive with the expectation that outline service pathways and planned 'packages' or personal change programmes will be identified for the court (see www.scotcourts.gov.uk).

The introduction of a Scottish version of the standarised risk assessment tool Level of Service/Case Management Inventory (LS/CMI) from 2007 should assist in providing more transparent structured assessments and initial action plans. It is important, however, to acknowledge that the application of standardised measures can have major limitations. One unintended consequence is to support a political and bureaucratic ideology based on the assumption that offenders are no longer individuals to be reintegrated, but are risks to be managed (Hannah-Moffat 2006). Standardised assessment has an important contribution to make but is not an end in itself. Organisations comfortable with risk are, in effect, organisations open to change and learning. The Association of Directors of Social Work noted recently that while there are many different styles of organisations in the social services, 'learning organisations are at the opposite end of the continuum from the "blame organisation" or low trust culture' (ADSW 2005: 12). However, the combination of increased emphasis on risk and the existence of a 'blame culture' in public service can focus concern on overt social regulation, placing an emphasis on risk avoidance rather than on social integration as an effective form of community safety. Indeed, such a social context for risk assessment may provide one explanation for the apparent 'dispersal of discipline' discussed in Chapter 2. An issue reported consistently in the consultation as part of Scotland's twenty-first century review of social work is that in all areas of practice, professional autonomy is seen to have given way to agency self-protection, with professional judgement and accountability subordinated to defensible decision-making and procedural accountability (Scottish Executive 2006a).

The purpose of structured assessment in SER writing is to support practitioners who can produce skilled, intuitive, and well-reasoned risk assessments, combining both actuarial knowledge and clinical judgement, based on a sound understanding of individual, situational and environmental risk factors. The dynamic information generated by such assessment allows for some formulation of how these risks might be tackled through a community disposal and provides explicit information for developing the initial action plan required by the national standards for probation (SWSG 1991a: paras 20 and 4.8). Given the limitations on time to complete an SER, it is likely that the outline plan will be brief and indicative only.

Social enquiry reports and rights

Offenders have no right to prevent a court ordering or requiring a report. However they can offer varying degrees of non-cooperation with the preparation of the report. The report is prepared for the court and is the court's property and issue of consent from the subject does not arise in legal terms. Where reports are ordered or required post-conviction, and there is nothing the subject can do to prevent this.[2] The SER writer acts with the authority of the court and non-cooperation can be construed as contempt of court, entailing additional penalties. In practice, persistent non-cooperation in the community may lead to remand in custody for the report to be compiled. Consequently it is of critical importance to establish and evidence the reasons for non-cooperation, whether deliberate or accidental.

The subject of the report is entitled to see the report: 'a copy of every report shall be given by the clerk of the court to the offender or his or her solicitor' (section 203(3) of the Criminal Procedure (Scotland) Act 1995). This is the duty of the clerk of the court, not the social worker. The law is silent on the offender's right to *retain* a copy of the report after the hearing, although it is likely that they have a right to retain it (Moore and Whyte 1998: 90). In any case it is a matter of good practice for the social worker to discuss and explain the content of the report with the offender in advance so as to check the veracity of the information included and to allow the offender to consult his/her solicitor about any disputed areas.

Although Scots law says little directly about offenders' rights in respect of SERs, the law in general has much to say about the rights of accused persons, for example in regard to representation and fair trial. The issue of discrimination remains a practical one, for example for refugees or for the growing number of migrant workers in Scotland in regard to the intelligibility of legal proceedings, particularly for those for whom English is a foreign language, for people with sensory impairments and for people with learning difficulties. NOS draw attention to the need to ensure that the nature, purpose and content of the SER is clearly explained to the offender and the need to investigate and corroborate information provided by the offender is also stressed; it is made clear that permission from the offender to contact third parties, while desirable, is not required (see Scottish Executive 2000a: 3.3).

Conclusion

The evidence for the impact of social work advice to the courts remains equivocal. Nonetheless, both formal and technical requirements present substantial challenges for criminal justice social workers. At the same time the requirements provide an opportunity to assist the court consider the potential consequences of sentencing options against the policy objective of reducing reoffending and to reflect on sentencing within a framework of principles, rights, values and potentially positive outcomes for public safety and well-being. The SER provides a platform for identifying needs and risks and a doorway to meaningful provision should the courts order a community disposal.

Notes

1 'Social Enquiry and Sentencing in the Sheriff Courts', ESRC Award No: R000239939. The research was conducted by Nicky Burns, Simon Halliday, Neil Hutton and Cyrus Tata (of Strathclyde Law School) and Fergus McNeill (of the Glasgow School of Social Work). Some preliminary findings (McNeill and Burns 2005) can be accessed at: http://www.gssw.ac.uk/ppt/redemption_risk.ppt and (in audio form) at: http://www.sieswe.org/node/130
2 Because of the assumption of innocence, the issue of consent does arise in the case of pre-trial reports ordered for the High Court. The NOS provide guidance in this regard.

5. Supervising offenders in the community

... there will need to be a move away from overdependence on assessing risk to finding interactive means of managing that risk with offenders and local communities ... and to develop some of the ideas of how offenders can be actively reintegrated. (Spencer and Deakin 2004: 225)

Introduction

Completing the social enquiry reports (and the initial assessments that are integral to them) forms an essential part of the criminal justice social worker's role. However, it is *implementing* meaningful plans relevant to the individual offender and to the safety of the community that lies at the heart of effective supervision. This chapter examines the technical requirements of supervision in the community and the role of the criminal justice social worker as key to exercising the local authority's responsibility to promote social welfare.

Scotland's Criminal Justice Plan (Scottish Executive 2004a: para. 4) claims that social justice is at the heart of safer, stronger communities. In recognition of the association between crime and social disadvantage, it stresses that criminal justice practices cannot operate apart from the communities they serve and that crime cannot be resolved by the criminal justice system alone. The theme reflects directly the legislative basis for criminal justice social work in promoting social welfare. While promoting effectiveness in reducing offending is the key focus of the agenda, *Smarter Justice, Safer Communities* (Scottish Executive 2005c) stresses that effective engagement with communities is needed to tackle offending effectively and promote public confidence. The Criminal Justice system is, interestingly, presented as a 'public service', which needs to command the confidence and consent of the community at large.

A key theme in this twenty-first century policy is that unacceptably high reoffending rates cut to the heart of communities and the criminal justice system (see Chapter 2). The suggestion is that so long as reconviction rates remain high, the criminal justice system is likely to remain locked into an 'unproductive, volume led, demand driven cycle which clogs up Scottish courts' (Scottish Executive 2004a: para. 13) as the same offenders appear time and again. This, in turn, is seen to drive up custody, in particular the number of short-term prisoners caught in a revolving door and in circumstances in which it is much harder for prisons to offer interventions to reduce the likelihood of further offending upon release (see Chapter 2).

Statistical and empirical data give weight to the policy direction. High rates of reoffending in UK jurisdictions may be disputed (see Chapter 2) but what is certain is that both English and Scottish jurisdictions have among the highest prison populations in Western Europe. International comparisons (Coyle 2003) demonstrate that more needs to be done to reduce the likelihood of reconviction particularly after a prison sentence and as a consequence the revolving door effect. While there is no evidence to suggest that the increasing use of community disposals has resulted in a reduction in the prison population, the fiscal cost of high rates of custody in Scotland – on average £16,342 for six months custody compared to an average of £1,157 for a standard probation order and £1,432 for a community service order (Scottish Executive 2006h) – is a strong political motivator for promoting community supervision.

Community-based supervision is cast within a policy whose priorities are prevention and crime reduction, not as an alternative to custody but as credible mainstream disposal in its own right against which consideration of custody should be a last resort. The thrust of current policy remains consistent with Rifkind's (1989) 'twin track' policy that custody should be 'used sparingly' (SWSG 1991a) and reserved for those offenders who present a serious risk to the public.

Given the different forms of community disposals available in Scotland, this chapter covers a wide range of issues. The first section of the chapter briefly addresses diversion from prosecution which, as we will see, some-times requires social work supervision. The second section provides a much more detailed account of the legal and policy contexts of probation supervision, addressing the related national objectives and standards, the specific requirements around action plans for supervision, the legal require-ments that orders impose, issues of enforcement and compliance and (briefly) issues around effectiveness (to which we turn in more detail in Part III of the book). Third, we explore supervision as a means of making amends in the community, briefly introducing restorative justice principles and practices before going on to discuss reparation and mediation, compensation, the legal and policy requirements around unpaid work in the community (that is, community service) and the new community reparation orders. In the fourth section we briefly review developments in Scotland around supporting victims at least in so far as they relate to the responsibilities of those supervising offenders.

1 Diversion from prosecution

The Criminal Justice Plan (Scottish Executive 2004a: 4.7) reiterates the policy that for minor offenders decisions to prosecute may not be the most appropriate solution, citing the long-standing arrangements that allow the procurator fiscal to offer an alternative, such as a financial penalty (the 'fiscal fine') or diversion to social work services or mental health care, where the public interest would not be served by prosecution. This is partly in recognition that the criminal justice system can further damage individuals who get into trouble, and often does little to remedy the harm that individual offenders have done to others. It is also a practical response to the volume of business in the summary courts which have become 'slow and congested and needed urgent attention' (Scottish Executive 2004a: 4.7).

Diversion from prosecution or from the criminal justice system altogether has remained central to Scottish policy for young people for over 30 years. However, the policy and practice of adult diversion has been somewhat limited, despite decades of documentation on the economic, social or humanitarian value of diversionary measures. Research evidence has highlighted a reluctance on the part of procurators fiscal to operate more 'adventurous' diversion, particularly for people with mental health or psychological problems (Duff and Burman 1994). Diversion projects tend to focus on specific groups, such as drug users, using both waiver and deferred prosecution methods (Scottish Executive 2004d).

Social work supervision in diversion operates in cooperation with procurators fiscal. The Stewart Report (HMSO 1983) set the platform for current diversionary practice. It suggested that 'frequently . . . it will be an offender's personal or social circumstances that cause concern, and the prosecutor may wish to investigate the possibility of making a referral for counselling or practical assistance' (HMSO 1983: 3.29). The report indicated that 'in minor cases, where . . . stresses are identified, we are of the opinion that an early offer of assistance by a social worker or volunteer helper may prove a constructive alternative to prosecution' (HMSO 1983: 3.29). In some instances, procurators fiscal waive prosecution following an undertaking from the accused. However, the deferred method of diversion is more commonly used in association with social work, to await a satisfactory outcome to any arrangement made. Specialist social work provision has developed, for example in relation to drug-related offences, where attendance at drug treatment and counselling can be part of an agreement for diversion.

Following the McInnes review recommendations (Scottish Executive 2004h), *Smarter Justice, Safer Communities* (Scottish Executive 2005c) outlined plans for a considerable expansion of the use of alternatives to prosecution, for example the introduction of formal police warnings, greater use by police of fixed penalty notices and fiscal fines, and the introduction of a new fiscal compensation order designed to ensure that victims of offending behaviour can be directly compensated by the perpetrator in appropriate circumstances. These are aimed at improving the collection and enforcement of fines, which it is argued have little credibility among the general public and offenders alike and will be administered by a single public sector fine enforcement agency with powers to relieve police of these responsibilities.

Research on community attitudes gathered as part of the consultation on the Criminal Justice Plan (MRUK 2004) showed little public knowledge of alternatives to prosecution and many respondents confused them with alternatives to custody. While public attitudes varied enormously, there remained a strong view that diversionary compensation or community work and 'not going to court' or 'not getting a criminal record' would be like 'getting off'. It is difficult to know whether political rhetoric in the last decade has promoted the view that the criminal justice system and courts, in particular, are the most effective way of resolving social and community problems or whether politicians have simply taken their lead from existing community attitudes. Either way, the challenges involved in creating major shifts in attitudes away from formal process and towards informal community problem resolution are clearly considerable.

2 Supervision in the community – probation

The Criminal Procedures (Scotland) Act 1995 provides the legislative framework for probation supervision in Scotland. Scots law retains some continuity with the history of probation practice in the UK (see Chapter 1) and despite the terminology in NOS referring to probation as a 'community sentence', in Scotland probation follows conviction but is imposed 'instead of sentencing' (section 228 of the 1995 Act) with the offender subject to supervision. The effect of probation is that successful completion of the order should mean the probationer receives no sentence *per se* for the original offence. The court retains the right, if the person commits another offence or is brought back to court for not keeping one of the requirements of probation, to impose sentence in respect of the original offence, as if the probation order had never been made. Successful completion of probation is intended to result in the person 'living down' or 'making good' for his or her offence.

The legislative basis for providing probation supervision in Scotland is located in section 27 of the Social Work (Scotland) Act 1968 and the organisational arrangements in section 3 of the Management of Offenders (Scotland) Act 2005. The legislation clearly identifies probation as a social work provision and part of local authorities' duty to promote social welfare, both of the community and of its citizens, where the underlying assumption is that community supervision is an effective means of protecting the public and the victims of crime while protecting the rights and interests of the offender.

NOS stress that the services 'should be fully aligned with systems for the organisation and management of all social work services provided by the local authority, including arrangements for strategic oversight and review of social work services generally' (Scottish Executive 2004d: para. 18); that 'the roles ... must be clearly stated, in terms of service delivery, management, coordination, policy planning, service development, monitoring and evaluation'; and that 'maximum use should be made of those resources available elsewhere in the local authority or in the wider community where needed' (Scottish Executive 2004d: para. 19). However, the NOS remain silent on how this might happen in practice.

Two important factors have been significant to changes implemented in probation practice in Scotland in the last decade. The first is the effectiveness or 'what works?' agenda (see Chapters 1, 3 and 8) which has provided evidence that community supervision can have a positive effect on assisting individuals reduce their offending. The second is the professional, managerial, financial and organisational arrangements for Community Justice Authorities in Scotland, set within the framework of the 2005 Act, to provide criminal justice social work services.

The establishment of Community Justice Authorities (CJAs) is intended to provide leadership and direction for improved strategic development, as well as addressing issues of effectiveness, scale and locally integrated provision intended by the 'one door' strategy of the 1968 Act. Location within Community Justice Authorities should improve the capacity of supervisors to connect offenders to community provision, such as accommodation, education, employment training, drug and mental health provision, social and leisure opportunities, so as to assist offenders maintain positive change over time, reduce the impact of social exclusion, and promote desistance. CJAs will consolidate a community-based framework for delivering effective supervision in the community which includes NOS, 100 per cent central funding of criminal justice social work services, specialist criminal justice social work teams, a National Effective Practice Unit (located in the Community Justice Division of the Scottish Executive Justice Department), a Criminal Justice Social Work Development Centre, a Scottish Accreditation Panel for Offender Programmes (see Chapter 8), and government-funded post-qualifying training in criminal justice social work.

Research on community attitudes and views (MRUK 2004) found expectations that members of the public should be heard, have a say and contribute in some way to community justice processes. For example, 40 per cent of respondents felt that they should have a say in deciding what types of community service work offenders should do locally and 19 per cent felt that they should have a say in supervising offenders in the community. Few had any realistic understanding of what was involved. When explanations about community-based responses were offered, most respondents expressed belief that some forms of community measure would work but may depend upon the age of offender, acts of contrition and the nature of the offence.

Respondents further refined their views to suggest that crimes that involved violence were deserving of a prison sentence. These views have some resonance with the 'twin track' approach to supervision in the community outlined in NOS and present strong messages to which Community Justice Authorities, if they are to harness positive community support and participation, will have to respond in order to assist communities to better understand what is likely to be effective in community supervision, and what is actually done.

Probation and national objectives and standards
A probation order can be made for not less than six months and not more than three years in respect of any offence for which the penalty is not fixed by law if 'it is expedient to do so' (section 228 of the 1995 Act). In practice very few orders are for over two years. This may well indicate that despite the increase in use of probation, its full potential, particularly for offenders who otherwise would receive custody, has been underdeveloped. The 1995 Act requires the court to obtain a report before making any probation order (section 228 (1)(a)). The person must consent to the order and the court is required to explain the undertaking 'in ordinary language' (section 228(5)). The importance of the person fully understanding what he or she is undertaking is self-evident.

NOS identify a three-tiered structure within probation: standard probation; probation with requirements; and intensive probation. Probation's versatility means it has the potential to be used across a wide range of situations and levels of risk – from standard probation for less serious or persistent offenders to 'intensive probation' for more serious or persistent offenders. Distinctions between different types of probation may reflect differences in degrees of help provided but, equally, may involve different levels of control, surveillance and monitoring. The NOS for probation require combinations of control in the form of obligations placed on offenders which include restrictions on their personal freedom (Scottish Executive 2004d: 6.1), with help and assistance over issues associated with offending (Scottish Executive 2004d: 6.2) and with opportunities for 'social integration' (Scottish Executive 2004d: 6.3).

While restriction is not the prime reason for imposing an order, just as punishment *per se* is not the main objective and character of the order, probation imposes significant requirements and should be reserved for medium to high risk offenders where the need to reduce offending is set alongside assistance with better social integration.

Probation action plans
Legislation requires that the court should be 'satisfied that suitable arrangements . . . can be made' (section 228(2) of the 1995 Act) for supervision and NOS stress the importance of building on the initial action plan established by the SER and the legal requirements of the order.

89

> The plan should set out what will be done during the course of the order to address the problems and issues associated with offending behaviour with the aim of reducing the risk of reoffending. (Scottish Executive 2004d: para. 20)

NOS stress in particular the importance of the first three-month initial phase of supervision which provides the opportunity for a fuller assessment, confirming or adapting the initial action plan and incorporating the risk 'domains' from LS/CMI or a similar assessment tool. NOS also stress that the supervision plan should be focused *primarily* on factors related to offending and aimed at assisting the cessation or reduction of that offending. The wider context noted in NOS requires this focus to be allied to meaningful assistance towards reintegration and desistance.

The principles of effective practice emphasise the importance of matching intensity of intervention to the level of risk and the identified risk factors; matching the focus of intervention to the objectives set; and matching supervision style to the learning style of the probationer (see Chapter 8). One important way to convince sentencers about the value of probation is the provision of information and promotional accounts of work carried out within action plans and the kinds of outcomes expected. Local authorities will, increasingly, be required to provide such information on services through the Judicial website (www.scotcourts.gov.uk). At the same time, however, NOS equally recognise the importance of addressing other aspects of social need and integration either directly or through the advocacy and brokerage role of the supervisor (see Chapter 7).

Probation requirements
Section 228(6) of the 1995 Act requires the clerk of the court to provide a copy of the order for the probationer, the supervising officer, and any person in charge of an institution in which a probationer may be required to reside. In practice, the supervising officer 'serves' the order explaining the requirements and expectations. The probationer should sign and date a copy of the order to confirm they understand as well as agree with the undertakings. The signed copy is retained by the supervisor and a copy is kept by the probationer. This is the beginning of the process of confirming the initial action plan.

There are some requirements which are common to all probation orders. These are to be of good behaviour; to conform to the directions of the supervising officer; to inform the supervising officer at once of any change of place of residence or place of employment. The 1995 Act provides the court with a general power to include extra requirements in a probation order and specific powers to include particular kinds of requirements, such as attendance for mental health treatment, as a formal condition of an order. These must be reasonable, legally enforceable and capable of being supervised (section 229 and Scottish Executive 2004d: para. 23). It should not be necessary to have a formal condition to provide supervision on a groupwork or programme basis. This can be agreed with the probationer and the court as the appropriate standard means of supervision in any given case from the outset. Detailed negotiated requirements can also be included as part of a standard order without recourse to formal requirements.

Additional formal requirements, given the additional risks of default that they create, should reflect higher levels of risk, a history of non-compliance or a need for specialist interventions (such as drug treatment) and may have much more emphasis on 'management' and restriction as well as supervision and help. It is important to ensure that positive help is made available to the offender in conjunction with any restrictions to avoid the poor outcomes of restrictive measures without positive help which have been well demonstrated in USA (Petersilia and Turner 1990). Whatever the case, it is important to distinguish between the various working agreements of supervisors and probationers and the legally defined requirements which are enforceable by law. Formal requirements can include unpaid work, compensation or restitution, reparation and mediation, requirements of treatment for a mental condition, residential or day centre requirements, and drug treatment requirements.

Formal probation reviews (within the local authority) involve the probationer, the supervisor and the supervisor's line manager and aim to establish progress in meeting agreed aims and objectives outlined in the original plan and to plan again for the next phase of supervision. The guidance in the NOS specifies that formal reviews of progress should be carried out at three and six months, and where the length of the order permits six-monthly thereafter. Minutes of the review should be countersigned by the probationer and the supervisor's manager (Scottish Executive 2004d: 66.1). McIvor and Barry (1998a: 24) found that 51 per cent of initial reviews were carried out within the time period required but found 'reluctance on the part of social workers to convene formal reviews'. In most cases the supervisor assumed the sole responsibility for providing services. Use of other agencies was most common in relation to employment, alcohol, drug and health issues.

Courts should be informed about confirmed supervision plans and about notable changes to the plan following reviews. NOS requires that a completion report summarising progress is submitted to the appropriate court and sent to the clerk of the court holding the order no later than two weeks from the date the order is terminated. It is important that at the completion of the order the offender is reminded of the legal implications of having been on an order with respect to the Rehabilitation of Offenders Act 1974. Identifying service gaps as well as resource usage is essential if CJA planners are to set priorities for service development, otherwise there is always a risk that the review process could become merely a bureaucratic and procedural exercise to meet the minimum requirements of NOS.

Compliance and enforcement

NOS detail areas in which the supervisor must exercise his/her statutory authority, particularly in regard to non-compliance; for example, requiring evidence such as medical certificates where medical reasons are offered for non-attendance. The legislation for breach of probation (sections 232 and 233 of the 1995 Act) includes two types of breach of probation which are dealt with separately: breach of requirement of probation and breach by further offence. Breach by further conviction (offence) is an automatic breach and has to be brought to the attention of the court (section 233 of the 1995 Act). The court has the power to take no action in respect of the breach or to sentence the person for the original offence, as well as for the breach itself which constitutes a 'new' criminal offence. Breach of requirement, however, entails day-to-day decision-making on the part of the supervisor and the use of professional discretion along a continuum from taking no formal action to taking the probationer back to court. NOS suggest that formal warnings should be issued to probationers for failure to comply with the requirements of their orders and that breach proceedings should be initiated in the event of non-compliance following a maximum of two formal warnings; 'all warnings must be put in writing' (Scottish Executive 2004d: para. 84).

Advice from the procurator fiscal may help in considering the adequacy of the evidence of non-compliance available to the supervisor. In addition to seeking advice from colleagues and managers, in the past some sheriffs may have been prepared to have informal discussions with supervisors, or even to meet with the offender to review progress. This has sometimes occurred in the context of failure to comply and has been used as a means of avoiding formal breach to re-contract the probation order. This had no standing in law and in recent years an appeal decision clarified that the court had no power to call a progress review for any purpose.[1] The Management of Offenders Act 2005 rectified this situation and introduced section 229A to the 1995 Act. This allows the court on making the order, or in regard to failure to comply under section 223(2), to make arrangements for a probation progress review. The supervisor is required to provide a written report on the probationer's progress and both the supervisor and the probationer are required to attend, whether or not the prosecutor elects to attend. Following the review the court may amend the order providing the probationer expresses a willingness to comply. The normal duty to explain to the probationer, in ordinary language, the effect of making the amendment remains.

To bring an allegation of breach of requirement before the court, the supervisor (or the chief social work officer or his or her appointee) needs to present or 'lay' information that a breach has occurred. Where breach proceedings are initiated, verified evidence is required to substantiate the legal grounds for the breach. The onus of proof, as in any criminal case, is that the prosecution must prove the case 'beyond reasonable doubt'. However, the evidence of one witness (usually the supervisor) is sufficient to proceed (section 232(3) of the 1995 Act) and it will be important to give the background to the specific allegation and to give a reasonably comprehensive account of what transpired during the probation period. This reinforces the importance of the probationer having fully understood the original terms of the order to which s/he agreed in court, and that these terms and their consequences have been spelled out in 'ordinary language'. It also underlines the importance of adequate recording systems.

The supervisor's reasoned view of what might be a suitable response to breach will be important to the court outcome. It is assumed that through review and warning mechanisms, every effort has been made to re-engage the probationer. Nonetheless, continuation of the order, with or without additional requirements, formal conditions or increased intensity, remains an option.

Role legitimacy and the use of positive authority by supervisors can generate short-term compliance with an order (Bottoms 2001) contributing to long-term compliance with the law. Ordinary everyday encounters can have crucial implications for the nature of power relations and for the validity of the practitioner's claim to justified authority. Procedural fairness is also associated with perceptions of legitimacy. Bottoms (2001) identified some important practice principles which characterise the qualities of an authoritative supervisor:

- Representation – providing opportunity for offenders to state their point and have their viewpoint taken into account; negotiation and linkage to other services.

- Consistency – treating people the same over time, setting realistic expectation, minimising personal bias.

- Accuracy – demonstrating ability to make high-quality decisions by being open about the nature of issues and using reliable information.

- Correctability – reviewing and being willing to change decisions where necessary.

- Ethicality – treating the person with respect and dignity.

Compliance theories highlight that a person may be compliant to different aspects of supervision for quite different reasons (Bottoms 2001):

- instrumental (self-interested calculation)

- normative (felt moral obligation)

- constraint based

- habit/routine related compliance.

Nellis' typology of compliance (2004: 239–40) similarly recognises different mechanisms, including incentive-based, trust-based (creating working alliance and sense of obligation), threat-based, surveillance-based, and incapacitation-based compliance. These issues are discussed further in Chapter 7.

Effective supervision in the community
While NOS do not carry the force of law, they do have regulatory weight and are subject to external inspection by the Social Work Inspection Agency (SWIA). However, effective practice requires a much more specific and substantive matching of intervention to the objectives set in a given supervision plan (see Chapters 7 and 8). Research supports the view that the outcomes of a programme of intervention are significantly better when the programme is focused and well structured, involves multiple methods and is multidisciplinary (see Chapter 8). The most successful outcomes are associated with programmes which have clearly stated and measurable objectives which are understood both by the practitioner and the participant; where practitioners are sufficiently trained and know what they are doing; where the intervention has a chance of achieving its objectives; and where evaluative information is gathered on an ongoing basis to check that what was agreed is actually done. These are the key elements of programme 'integrity' (Andrews *et al.* 1990).

Structured assessments are aimed at identifying a range of associated dynamic (changeable) factors seen to sustain and support individual criminality. Despite the limitations discussed in Chapters 4 and 7, a structured approach to assessment can provide the basis for more integrated and holistic supervision planning. It is, of course, one thing to assess risk and need factors, it is another to identify how to provide meaningful and effective help for an individual dealing with their difficulties. Intervention programmes make no coherent sense unless they are embedded within locally defined responses to need as well as risk (Petersilia 1990; Rumgay 2000). Any division of the relationship between offence and offender-focused and community-wide provision is unhelpful. Rumgay suggests that the concept of 'minimisation of harm' can help overcome any conflict of choice between community/victim on the one hand, and offender on the other, and to avoid the risk of co-option of community support services as pseudo-penal services or law enforcement agencies. She argues that this is not equitable and is likely to create harm and should be resisted by adopting a broader community enterprise approach. In many ways Scots law, in casting the social work role in terms of promoting social well-being, has endeavoured to achieve this, but with little success to date. It remains to be seen if the establishment of CJAs will promote partnership working aimed at assisting mainstream services respond to offenders as part of their own social welfare responsibilities.

The intensity of supervision needs to be the minimum necessary to achieve the objectives set for the individual probationer – in some instances this will be very intensive. There has been little discussion in Scotland about the meaning of 'intensity', and while NOS refers to 'intensive probation' (Scottish Executive 2004d: 13.2), there is little in the guidance about its meaning or its uses. Intensive probation in many jurisdictions has tended to be developed within a context of probation as a punishment, with the 'intensity' relating to the restriction and the surveillance demands made on the offender. Intensive probation need not, of course, involve punitive delivery and most research indicates that the more punitive the supervision, the less effective it is likely to be in terms of reducing reoffending (Palmer 1992). Most effective programmes of intervention for those presenting greatest risk combine intensive monitoring with constructive help aimed at changing behaviour. Intensive probation should, by definition, be intensive and involve significant time demand and resources. Commentators suggest that intensive programmes should 'occupy 40–70% of the offender's time' over a period of three to nine months (Gendreau *et al.* 1994: 75) if they are to be effective (Petersilia and Turner 1990).

Inspection reports both in England and Wales and in Scotland have been critical of the lack of holistic and integrated approaches to disadvantage as well as criminality. For example, Morgan (2003) was critical of the high level of investment in programmes alone and called for a more holistic approach, employing the traditional skills of probation officers to nurture offenders' motivation to change. However, this is not a recipe somehow for a return to the past of relationship-only based supervision or to argue that sound administration, or less personal approaches, have no place; quite the contrary. Their place is *within*, rather than *instead of*, a predominantly human service approach. The overhaul of the organisational and managerial elements of probation have been long overdue to ensure that supervision is not separated from structured programme work and effective case management.

3 Making amends in the community

The predominance of 'punishment' as a cultural response in the UK to criminal behaviour has meant that often the public framing of measures responding to crime has been dominated by retributive justice principles without consideration of how best to respond effectively to the characteristics and circumstances of those involved. Adversarial criminal justice often attracts the general criticism that it provides limited opportunity for victim, 'user' or 'stakeholder' involvement in decision-making and retributive criminal processes tend to exclude those with the greatest stake, the victim and other interested parties, limiting the opportunity for 'communities of interest' to participate in the resolution of their own social problems.

This emphasis on involving those most affected by crime has resulted in an increased use of restorative practices by justice systems in different jurisdictions. These seek to balance the concerns of the victim and the community with the need to better integrate the offender. Implicitly or explicitly, they suggest that the state has a major role in creating conditions for promoting social well-being and community safety, in which 'communities of interest' can be co-producers in decision-making (Whyte, forthcoming). Responses that are restorative seek more effective and lasting solutions to local crime related problems and produce mutually beneficial outcomes for participants that state processes cannot achieve on their own. Many of the aspirations of restorative practice articulate well with the requirements for desistance and better social integration of offenders.

Scotland has no formal or integrated policy on restorative practices in adult justice, although there is a long tradition in using victim–offender mediation and unpaid work in the community. Below is a brief examination of restorative practice, and a more detailed existing consideration of orders which involve unpaid work or opportunities to make amends. Our intention in locating a discussion of restorative practice alongside other forms of making amends is in recognising that the latter lacks a clear theoretical and operational framework in Scotland. We argue that this might best be addressed within a policy framework of restoration.

What is restorative practice? Some theoretical directions
Restorative practice in justice is a response to crime that considers the needs of victims, of those who offend and of the community (Zehr 2002). It is an attempt to put into practice a set of ethical ideas about how human beings should relate to each other (in particular how we should relate to those who cause harm), seeking to resolve and strengthen relationships where possible. Restorative practices are designed to give victims[2] of crime an opportunity to tell the offender about the impact of their actions on them and their families, and to encourage acceptance of responsibility for the harm that they have caused, if possible to repair it, and where appropriate to make amends. Its general aims are to address the harm done, to restore to varying degrees the relationship between the parties that was disturbed by the offence, to reduce reoffending and to improve their experience of the criminal justice system (Marshall 1999).

There is no universally accepted or concise definition of restorative practice in justice and practices vary greatly in their apparent intention. Marshall's definition appears to encompass the main generally accepted principles:

Restorative justice is a process whereby all the parties with a stake in a particular offence come together to resolve collectively how to deal with the aftermath of the offence and its implications for the future. (Marshall, cited in Braithwaite 1999: 5)

The United Nations *Declaration on Basic Principles on the Use of Restorative Justice Programmes in Criminal Matters* (2000) defines restorative justice as a process in which the victim, offender and/or any other individuals or community members affected by a crime participate actively together in the resolution of matters arising from the crime, often with the help of a fair and impartial third party.

While active participation is a central concept, none of these definitions stresses better social or community cohesion as an essential characteristic of restorative practice, and the UN definition places little emphasis on mutually beneficial outcomes. Nonetheless, for many advocates for justice to be restorative it must evidence the consistent involvement of all parties affected by the crime, and focus on the development, implementation and mainten-ance of mutual healing, reparation and satisfaction, rather than retribution and punishment (Schiff 1998). Bazemore and Umbreit (1994) argue that the involvement of the person who causes harm and the person who experiences it is essential and that both of these two main stakeholders (victims and offenders) need to somehow benefit in any balanced system of restorative justice. Regrettably, these principles are seldom seen in operation in many Scottish practices incorporated into formal criminal legal processes discussed below.

Braithwaite's (1989) theory of 'reintegrative shaming' suggests that people are generally not deterred from committing crime by the threat of official punishment but by the two informal processes of social control: fear of social disapproval and social conscience. Through restorative practice the offender can be made powerfully aware of the disapproval of their actions by significant others in their lives. The potentially alienating and stigmatising effects of shaming are overcome by reacceptance and affirmation of the person's value in the social community. As a consequence agreements reached with family members, friends, or other individuals important to the offender are likely to be more effective and lasting in their impact than those imposed by an impersonal legal institution.

From this point of view, not only do restorative practices provide an opportunity for people to accept their share of responsibility for their actions, they also affords them the opportunity, where possible, to repair the harm they have caused with the support of their families, while involving victims in the process, strengthening the sense of social cohesion, self-efficacy and responsibility. Equally some commentators argue that restorative practices in justice can operate as another kind of punishment and that reparation and making amends should be incorporated into traditional retributive ap-proaches. Daly (2002) argues that restorative practice within state mechan-isms is intended to be a punishment, albeit an alternative punishment, that is not humiliating, harming or degrading and that can combine retribution and rehabilitation.

Restorative practices

The term restorative practice is used for a plethora of activities within adult and youth justice including mediation and reparation, family group conferencing, restorative and community conferencing, restorative cautions, sentencing and healing circles, community panels or courts, and other communitarian associations (Braithwaite 1999). While restorative practices often provide alternatives to formal justice processes, in some jurisdictions they are police-led, for example in the Thames Valley restorative cautioning scheme, and in others they are incorporated within the formal justice process with explicit justice objectives including punishment and retribution as part of formal judicial disposals (Daly and Hayes 2001).

Family group conferences (FGC) are generally modelled on an approach developed in New Zealand and bring together family members of both the offender and the victim, friends, people from the local community, and professional social workers or justice personnel to look at the facts (what happened and why), the consequences (how the victim and others were affected) and the future (how the person can make amends) – in an effort to produce a mutually satisfactory resolution.

Restorative justice conferences (RJC) aim to enable victims, offenders and their respective families or support people to participate actively in the process of addressing the harm caused by the offence: to talk about why an event occurred and how it affected them, to decide on a plan of action, which may specify what needs to be done to put right the harm and to prevent it happening in the future. The agreed plan should, as far as possible, be based on a consensus of views of those at the meeting and will usually outline what is to happen, and who is to oversee or support those taking action to ensure that the plan is carried out. The plan may include compensating the victim, family and/or friends, changing their routines to provide support and encouragement to both victim and offender, the provision of practical and financial assistance or other services by statutory authorities or other agencies and involvement in local programmes. In some jurisdictions the plan is presented to professionals or to a court who will normally accept it as part of the final disposal. These types of restorative practices place a very clear focus on the co-production of mutually benefi-cial outcomes through direct participation of the people most affected by the event, and on personal 'uplift' achieved in taking responsibility for problem resolution while supported and affirmed by families or other positive social supports.

It is not always possible or the intention to involve victims or other supporters *directly* in restorative practices. In the case of damage to community property, for example, a representative such as a teacher from a school or from the retail community may attend and represent the victim(s) or community perspective. Restorative police cautioning has no explicit aim of repairing family or social bonds and victims are seldom involved directly. This approach has been pioneered in a number of areas in the UK, most notably by Thames Valley police (Hoyle and Young 2002), and it is now a common element in youth justice practice in Scotland (Dutton and Whyte 2006). While it could be argued that processes such as unpaid work really do not conform to the requirements of restorative practice as a form of co-production, they nonetheless attempt to promote and support new understanding and change through the dynamic generated and experienced through the process.

Reparation and mediation

Reparation is a form of making amends by an offender, usually through the intervention of a third party (mediation); either *directly* to the victim to compensate for the offence in some way, for example by financial compensation or an apology; or *indirectly*, where reparation is made to some other person or organisation, often determined by the victim, for example by a donation to charity. Reparation schemes have been established in Scotland for many years mainly as forms of diversion from criminal courts. Mediated reparation can be used as part of social enquiry report preparation or as part of a probation order or other order.

Victim–offender mediation (VOM) provides a range of options aimed at including victims in the justice process as central to the approach. At one end of the range, VOM may simply involve the offender writing a letter of apology to the victim. At the other end, it can involve a structured meeting or conference between the victim, offender and other interested parties, in which the impact of the offence is examined more closely by all concerned. In some instances face-to-face meetings between victims and offender without support persons are arranged and supported by trained staff. Shuttle mediation provides another model where the offender does not come face to face with their victim but someone, usually a trained person, 'shuttles' information between the two key participants to achieve a satisfactory outcome. There are a few schemes in Scotland providing community mediation where the mediator is a catalyst for community action, encouraging and helping those involved deal with the problem creatively and constructively themselves (Marshall 1999: 3). The concept of mediation carried out by trained mediators in criminal justice, though well established in some areas and some jurisdictions, is not yet widespread across Scotland (Warner 1992).

Compensation

In Scots law, there is provision for financial reparation to be made, in some circumstances, in the form of compensation paid to victims (via the court) as part of a court order. A compensation order is available to courts both on summary and solemn procedure and to the district courts (sections 249–253 of the 1995 Act). Compensation orders can be made in addition to other penalties, reflecting the concept that most crimes have two victims – society in general and an individual who has been harmed as a result of the offence. Thus an offender may be ordered *both* to undertake unpaid work for the community *and* to make financial amends to a victim as a result of an offence.

Unpaid work in the community

Community service orders (CSOs) and probation with a condition of unpaid work have a long history in Scotland and the 'ingredients' seem to appeal to a variety of sentencing considerations (retribution, reparation and restoration). The power of courts to order offenders to undertake unpaid work or service for the benefit of the community had its origins in the mid-1960s. The idea was developed in the Wootton Report (HMSO 1970) as an alternative to a short prison sentence. The Community Service by Offenders (Scotland) Act 1978, now consolidated in the 1995 Act, was enacted to enable courts to make a community service order (CSO) requiring a person to perform a specific number of hours of unpaid service for the benefit of the community.

Section 238 of the 1995 Act indicates that community service must be used for a person 'of or over 16 years of age convicted of an offence punishable by imprisonment' and 'the court may, instead of imposing on him a sentence of, or including, imprisonment or any other form of detention, make an order'. Research examining the nature of practice and its outcomes (McIvor 1992) suggested that although it was reasonably popular as a disposal, the use of unpaid work was having limited impact on custody rates.

The use of CSOs grew rapidly in the 1980s and the number of orders, though it has stabilised since then, has continued to grow from 5,399 disposals in 1995 to 5,573 in 2005 (the total is 8,330 if the 2,757 probation orders including a condition of unpaid work are added) (Scottish Executive 2006g). During the same period there has been a major rise in the use of probation, from 6,179 to 9,437, a reduction in the use of financial penalties from 110,019 to 85,253 and a rise in custody from 16,206 to 16,531 (Scottish Executive 2006g). This raises questions about the effectiveness of CSOs and other community disposals in providing an alternative to custody (see Chapter 2). The interpretation by a court of what circumstances justify a prison sentence, to which community service might be the alternative, is still an area of considerable discretion, flexibility and variation. Few people are likely to appeal against the imposition of community service, so whether or not a custodial sentence was in prospect can seldom be tested.

The 1995 Act also contains, at section 229(4), provision for unpaid work as a requirement of probation. There is some ambiguity in the status of this order. The legislation indicates that it should be used only for people 'convicted of an offence punishable by imprisonment' but does not specify, as with a CSO, that the alternative for the offender is custody. This, however, would seem to be implied. NOS support this contention (Scottish Executive 2004e), indicating that this provision should only be available for those at serious risk of a custodial sentence, and where the offender can benefit from the probation component. In both cases, section 238 orders and section 229(4) orders, the social work authority is responsible for arranging or providing placements. No formal differentiation is made in the way work is organised between the two orders.

In 2004/05 male offenders accounted for 88 per cent of CSOs and probation orders with a requirement of unpaid work. Females receiving CSOs (excluding probation with unpaid work) tended to be older, with 64 per cent of such orders relating to over-25 year olds. The corresponding proportion for males was 49 per cent. CSOs (including probation orders with a requirement of unpaid work) were relatively more common among young offenders, with 84.2 orders per 10,000 population for 18–20 year olds and 60.3 orders per 10,000 population for 21–25 year olds (Scottish Executive 2006g).

NOS identify the aim of CSOs as providing 'Scottish criminal courts with a credible community-based penalty by requiring those found guilty of imprisonable offences and who would otherwise have received a sentence of imprisonment or detention to undertake unpaid work for a specified number of hours for the community' (Scottish Executive 2004e: 1.1). Restorative purposes (such as any benefits to the victim that may result from the work or any benefits for the offender from the sense of satisfaction from the task) are rather understated in the objectives. They do, however, stress that there should be a range of opportunities 'capable of enhancing his/her social responsibility and self-respect' (para. 1.6.3); that they should 'present a challenge to the offender' (para. 10) and that they should be 'seen by both the community and the offender to be constructive and enable the offender to make reparation to the community for the offence' (para. 11).

An order made under section 238 of the 1995 Act does constitute a conviction. The normal time period before it becomes 'spent' is five years. The order must specify the number of hours the person has to perform which may not be less than 80 and may not exceed 240 in summary courts (300 in cases heard on solemn procedure). The hours must be completed within 12 months. The order remains in force until the hours have been completed, or the order revoked. The Act makes provision for an order to be made by a district or a sheriff court. In practice few district courts have access to a scheme except through the provision of community reparation orders.

Four sets of circumstances in which an assessment of suitability may be provided to the court are indicated (Scottish Executive 2004e: para. 26):

- The social worker preparing the SER initiates an assessment for suitability.

- The court requests both an SER and an assessment for suitability.

- The court requests an assessment for suitability having received an SER.

- The court requests only an assessment for suitability.

Little guidance is provided within NOS as to who is considered 'suitable' for CSO. They stress that the principal consideration in determining the suitability of an offender to undertake a particular placement must be the physical safety of any person residing or working at the placement (Scottish Executive 2004e: 19.1). The previous offending history must inform risk assessment decisions for those who have a previous custodial disposal for violence who should be assessed 'particularly carefully' before being found suitable. The assessment of risk should be 'informed by previous offending history, the nature of the placement and degree of supervision given, and the vulnerability of the recipient' (Scottish Executive 2004e: 19.3).

Unpaid work: requirements and administrative arrangements

A copy of the CSO containing any detailed requirements to be adhered to is given to the offender. The central requirement is to perform the specified number of hours of service at such times as the officer may instruct. Other requirements derive from this, and have to do with the mechanics of making arrangements for the service to be performed (section 239 of the CP Act 1995). These are:

- To report to the local authority officer appointed for community service purposes.

- To notify without delay of any change of address or in the time, if any, at which he usually works.

The 1995 Act sets out details governing the actual performance of the service/unpaid work, and these apply both to section 238 orders and to section 229(4) orders. The court has to concern itself with the following details:

- The person must consent to the making of the order/requirement.

- The number of hours must be specified.

- The person is 'suitable' to undertake the service/work.

- A report as to the person's suitability has been obtained.

- Opportunities for work/service are available.

- A scheme/arrangements exist in the area where the person resides or is to reside that are approved.

A copy of the order for work/service should be given by the clerk of the court to the offender on the day the order is made or alternatively sent by recorded delivery to the last known address and a copy sent to the chief social work officer. The person should be seen by the community service officer within one week of the date of disposal and should sign and date two copies of the order to the effect that they understand what is entailed. It is the responsibility of the officer to explain, in detail, the nature of the order and to check that the offender understands their obligations and rights. Work should normally begin within two weeks and not later than three weeks from the date of disposal.

Legislation says little about the subject of organising placements although a distinctive feature of CSO has been the considerable number of 'placement' opportunities provided for people in trouble by a wide range of agencies in the community. The 1995 Act simply says that the person must 'perform for the number of hours specified in the order such work at such times as the local authority officer may instruct' (section 239(1)). However, one detail is included: that any instruction shall 'so far as practicable, be such as to avoid any conflict with the offender's religious beliefs, and any interference with the time, if any, at which he normally works or attends a school or other educational establishment' (section 239(3)). Similarly the expectation is that the work placement will not interfere with the regulations relating to unemployment benefit, particularly the '21 hour rule'. NOS stress that while 'there is no reason why an offender should not be instructed to work for more than 21 hours in any one week ... regulations governing entitlement to unemployment benefit, national insurance credits and income support must ... be taken into account where an offender is to be so instructed ... community service must not be seen by the offender as an exemption from seeking employment' (Scottish Executive 2004e: para. 48).

In consenting to the making of an order for community service or unpaid work, the individual agrees to complete a set number of hours as instructed by the local authority officer. The offender has minimal rights to determine what particular piece of work or item of service to be undertaken. In practice, discussion and an attempt to match the individual to an appropriate placement has generally been the norm. NOS indicate that the officer should take into account the skills and interests of the offender and involve him or her in the decision-making about the most appropriate placement. This, however, has to be balanced with a judgement on the kinds of risk that the offender may pose to the community or to the organisation providing the placement. The limited research available suggests that where the offender is carrying out work he or she considers to be worthwhile and where there is direct contact with the beneficiaries of the service, the experience is likely to have the greatest impact on the offender (McIvor 1992).

A person subject to a community service order has no responsibilities under the order other than to perform the work satisfactorily within the 12-month period. However, the person who is subject to a probation order with a requirement of unpaid work is subject to all the other obligations and requirements of a probation order, since unpaid work is only one component of a larger order.

Unpaid work: compliance and enforcement

In a section 229(4) order, a further offence constitutes an automatic breach of the probation order. However for a CSO, a breach of requirement of the order is constituted by:

- A failure to perform the work as instructed.

- A failure to complete the number of hours within the 12-month period.

- A failure to report or to perform the work satisfactorily.

- A failure to report any change of address, employment or employment circumstances.

NOS set out a framework of discipline to be applied consistently in the interests of justice. Disciplinary procedures are required when the person fails to comply with the following requirements without reasonable excuse (Scottish Executive 2004e: para. 77):

- Failure to attend.

- Lack of punctuality.

- Failure to report as required by the community service officer.

- Failure to notify a change of address without delay.

- Failure to notify a change in employment circumstances without delay.

- Failure to perform work to a satisfactory standard.

When absence from work is considered unacceptable, the guidance requires the officer to set a series of formal warnings in motion and limits the officer's discretion to two such warnings. On a third unacceptable absence, the guidance requires that breach proceedings are instituted and the order suspended. The same is true for other breaches of requirement, on the third failure. Judgements on satisfactory work performance standards are inevitably subjective. NOS emphasises that the standards must be set at an attainable level and that the context of the placement agency is important. Some guidance is offered to assist in applying consistent criteria (Scottish Executive 2004e: para. 72):

- **Quality of performance.** The work done and the manner in which it is done conforms to the standards laid down by the placement agency.

- **Work effort.** Offenders are expected to apply themselves energetically to the demands of the work required of them by the placement agency.

- **Behaviour and attitudes.** Offenders are expected to conduct themselves in such a way as to demonstrate respect for the rights of others and willingness to cooperate with others in the placement agency.

It is the supervisor's responsibility to decide whether a breach has occurred and whether return to court is the appropriate response to that breach. Any breach which is presented to the court may be challenged and must therefore be supported by sufficient evidence. As with probation, the evidence of one witness can provide sufficient evidence to establish a breach (Scottish

Executive 2004e: para. 103). If the allegation of breach is admitted or proved, the court can do one of four things:

- Impose any penalty in respect of the original offence that it might have done at the time had it not made a community service order.

- Impose a fine not exceeding level 3 and let the order continue.

- Vary the number of hours, except that the overall total ordered must not exceed the maximum allowed, and let the order continue.

- Take no action, and let the order continue.

In view of the legislation's insistence that a community service order should only be made as an alternative to a custodial sentence, logic would suggest that the penalty for breach should be a custodial sentence. However, in practice the law is interpreted more flexibly, and courts do not routinely impose a custodial sentence for a breach of requirement. However, the imposition of, for example, a fine for serious non-compliance only serves to demonstrate the ambiguity of the legislation with regard to the imposition of an order only as an alternative to custody.

With respect to probation orders with a requirement of unpaid work, the court can deal with breach as with any breach of requirement of probation (section 232(2) of the 1995 Act). It can either vary the probation order by including a requirement for unpaid work and thus allowing both for the probation order to continue in force and for a substantial period of work/service to be performed; or make a community service order, as an alternative to custody for the breach, though this would terminate the probation order. The legislation also makes provision for a (separate) community service order as a possible penalty for a breach of requirement of probation (section 232(2)(d) of the 1995 Act) while still leaving the original probation order in force, thus maintaining all the other requirements for that order. Although uncommon, the outcome in theory could be two entirely separate orders, a community service order and a probation order, running in tandem, except that the one (the community service order) has been made in respect of a breach of requirement of the other (the probation order).

Amendments to the 1995 Act introduced sections 233(3) and (4) and 241(1) and (2), where, if the subject of an order commits an offence in any place where the work was performed up to three months after the end of the requirement (which could be beyond the expiry date of the order), this will be treated as an aggravating factor for the purposes of sentencing in respect of that offence. NOS (Scottish Executive 2004e) stress the importance for supervisors of making sure that people subject to orders involving unpaid work are well informed about these provision and their implications.

Community service orders can be amended under section 240 of the 1995 Act on application either by the supervisor or the individual. This may be to deal with changes of circumstance, such as a move of residence to a different court area, or to change the timescale to accommodate changes in work patterns, and so on. Powers to revoke an order are set out in section 240 of the 1995 Act. The possibility of revoking an order applies only to CSOs. Two related criteria must be met, namely that circumstances have arisen since the order was made, and for that reason it would be in the interests of justice for the court to consider amendment or revocation. There are no specified circumstances contained in the legislation. The provision for revocation may cover the following kinds of situation:

- To allow for changes in life circumstances (for example, obtaining a new job or moving to take up work) such that the number of hours originally ordered cannot be performed in the time available; or suitable work cannot be found, and it is not considered in the interests of justice to penalise the person for the changed circumstances.

- Medically certificated ill-health over a lengthy period which prevents the work being carried out.

It is possible for courts in Scotland to make a CSO on people resident in England and Wales. The Scottish court must forward to the equivalent court in England or Wales copies of the orders and three copies of the amending order. The clerk of the court is responsible for sending these documents. The supervising officer is responsible for transferring other relevant documents or information to assist the new supervisor. Where the transfer involves a probation order with a requirement of unpaid work, the maximum number of hours allowed for 'combination orders' in England and Wales is 100 hours. If the order exceeds 100 hours, an application to the Scottish court under Schedule 6 of the 1995 Act is required to consider reducing the hours.

A report must be submitted to the appropriate court, and to the original SER author, on the satisfactory completion of an order. The report should outline the setting and nature of the work undertaken, the standard of work achieved and any information available on the impact of the order on the offender's attitudes or behaviour or its contribution to the development of new skills or interests. It is important that at the completion of the order the offender is reminded of the legal implications of having been on an order with respect to the Rehabilitation of Offenders Act 1974. If Community Justice Authorities are serious about measuring effectiveness, in the absence of a national database, this is also an opportunity to seek the offender's permission to make contact with him or her at 6, 12 and/or 24 months to gather information, in confidence, on his progress. Reconviction rates for a minimum of two years are now a standard measure in most research. It will be essential for authorities to generate follow-up data if future strategic planning is to be based on evidence.

Community reparation orders

With the growing emphasis on victims, restorative practice and making amends, it is perhaps not surprising that the approach has been further extended by the introduction of community reparation orders (CROs) under the Antisocial Behaviour, Etc. (Scotland) Act 2004. The CRO is designed to deal with offences where there is an anti-social behaviour element, particularly harassment (for example, vandalism and breach of the peace). The CRO is a low-tariff disposal available under summary proceedings in the district and sheriff courts to allow for reparation including between 10 and 100 hours of unpaid work in the community. Unlike a CSO, which is clearly a 'fine on time', CROs have the additional objective of producing changes in attitudes – rather a high-level objective for a low-tariff order. That CROs do not require consent is, of course, contrary to restorative practice principles and an SER is not required for such an order to be imposed. Community reparation orders were introduced as pilots and ran in Inverclyde, Inverness and Dundee until March 2007. The types of activities the offender carries out are intended to be predetermined by prior consultation (between the local authority and relevant community stakeholders, for example police, community councils, residents' associations and so on) to help develop general principles for reparative activity.

4 Supporting victims

The European Union's (2001) *Framework on the standing of victims in criminal proceedings*, adopted in 2001, is aimed at ensuring that victims of crime receive equitable treatment throughout the EU. Scotland's response, *Victims in the Scottish Criminal Justice System*, was published by Scottish Executive (2002) and identified existing and proposed developments. Article 1 of the EU framework defines a 'victim' as follows:

> 'victim' shall mean a natural person who has suffered harm, including physical or mental injury, emotional suffering or economic loss, directly caused by acts or omissions that are in violation of the criminal law of a Member State.

The *Scottish Strategy for Victims: Scottish Executive Justice Department Action Plan* (Scottish Executive 2000b: 1.2.1) had already adopted a wider definition than that required by Article 1, including within the special status group families of victims who lose their lives. The framework recognises the rights and legitimate interests of victims, including in relation to them having an appropriate role in the criminal legal system (Article 2). Article 3 deals with safeguarding victims as witnesses during proceedings and Article 4 deals with victims' right to receive information, including compensation and support. A range of developments ongoing within Scotland come within the direction of the framework. These include:

- A Victim Statement scheme to allow victims of crime the opportunity to provide an account of how the crime has affected them.

- Arrangements for victims of certain crimes to make representations to the Parole Board on any concerns which may exist about the offender's release from prison for custodial sentence.

- Re-examination of the definition of 'vulnerable person' in section 271 of the Criminal Procedure (Scotland) Act 1995 and special measures to assist such persons.

- 'Appropriate Adults' schemes relating to a suspect or a witness with a mental disorder.

- Increased protection for victims of sexual crime who have to give evidence in court.

- Specialist support and advice services.

In some criminal cases, victims have a right to receive information about the release of a prisoner and public guidance is available in the *Victim Notification Scheme – Guidance for Victims* (Scottish Executive 2004f). Victims also have a right to be told when the prisoner is being considered for parole and to make written representations about his/her release to the Parole Board for Scotland. The Victim Notification Scheme (VNS), generally speaking, applies where the offender has been sentenced to four years or more for a crime of violence, a sexual or indecent crime, a crime involving firearms, house-breaking, a hate crime or fire-raising. Victims who are eligible for the scheme include direct victims aged 14 years and over; a parent or carer if the victim is a child under 14 years; a near relative if the victim is incapacitated; and up to four near relatives if the victim has died.

There are two parts to the VNS and people can choose whether to be involved in either or both parts of the scheme. Part 1 provides information on:

- The date of release of the offender from prison or detention about a month before the date of release.

- If the offender dies before being released, the date of the death.

- If the offender has been transferred out of Scotland, the date of the transfer.

- If the offender has become eligible for temporary release.

- If the offender has escaped or absconded.

Under Part II, when the Parole Board for Scotland is due to consider the case, the victim will be given the chance to send written comments to the board. The full implementation of the ISCJIS (Integrated Scottish Criminal Justice Information System) should improve the transfer of information between the Scottish criminal justice agencies, such as the police, the courts and the procurator fiscal, and to victims as appropriate.

The EU framework expects members to provide specialist services and victim support services to (Article 13):

- Provide victims with information.

- Assist victims according to their immediate needs.

- Accompany victims, if necessary, and possibly during criminal proceedings.

- Assist victims, at their request, after criminal proceedings have ended.

Legislation provides police powers to pass information regarding victims to an organisation that provides counselling and other forms of support to victims of crime as well as providing specialist services. Specialist services developed within the police service in recent years include:

- **Domestic violence liaison officers** providing a specialised service to victims of domestic abuse, including advice, assistance and personal safety advice.

- **Family protection officers**, who are trained to deal with sensitive crimes, particularly those where children are victims.

- **LGBT (lesbian, gay, bisexual and transgendered) liaison officers**, who are trained in the particular difficulties experienced by members of these communities.

- **Racial awareness officers**, who again are trained in the particular sensitive issues in this area.

- **Family liaison officers**, who are appointed to act as an intermediary for families who have been victimised by serious crime, or who have experienced a bereavement as a result of a road death.

In addition to Victim Support (Scotland), who provide specialist training to volunteers and staff in relation to families of murder victims and victims of rape, sexual assault and other crimes, a wide range of agencies provide specific information, advice and support service to victims, such as Rape Crisis, Women's Aid, PETAL (People Experiencing Trauma And Loss) and FOMC (Families of Murdered Children).

Victims are not prohibited from taking action in the civil courts, even if a compensation order has been made by a criminal court. The Criminal Injuries Compensation Board was set up to make payments to the victims of crime or to the relatives if the victim had died as a result of being the victim of criminal activity. It is not empowered to compensate for loss in respect of property offences. The offender does not require to be apprehended or convicted for a claim to be considered. Awards can only be made where the value of the claim is £1,000 or more. This figure is varied upwards from time to time, although the appropriate figure is always the one applicable when the incident giving rise to the claim took place. Any award made will be reduced by any amount awarded by the courts.

In a number of areas, victim support schemes are well established, using volunteer helpers to visit and assist people who have been the victims of crime. The ADSW policy statement on victims (ADSW 1996) indicates that 'concern for victims of crime should be a major consideration' for social work and that a 'victim perspective should form a core part of the content of supervision of the offender' (ADSW 1996: 1.1–2.1). While most of the work of the supervisor will be on behalf of victims rather than directly with victims, there is scope for social workers to make referrals to such schemes, and indeed to learn from the experience of these schemes about the effects the crimes of their supervisees are likely to have had on their victims.

Article 10 of the EU framework directs member states to promote mediation in criminal cases for offences which it considers appropriate for this sort of measure and that any agreement between the victim and the offender reached in the course of such mediation in criminal cases can be taken into account. This article does not have to be complied with until 2011. It is reasonable to assume, however, that in the light of the growing focus on victims and restorative practices, a major task in Scotland is to create an integrated policy that links the diverse provision discussed in this section.

Conclusions

It should be apparent from the foregoing discussion that supervision in the community exists in a wide variety of forms and serves a wide variety of purposes. Effective, legitimate and appropriate supervision (of whichever form) requires a clear understanding of its legal and policy contexts. However, while such an understanding may be a necessary condition of good practice, it is certainly not sufficient. The technical-legal requirements of supervision, on which we have focused here, should not operate separately from strategic, managerial, professional and administrative dimensions of supervision and case management. Mobilising self-efficacy and intrinsic motivation is crucial to changing the hearts and minds of individuals. To ensure ongoing reinforcement of learning from supervision, good strategic case management is essential with effective arrangements for ensuring active collaboration not just with offenders but also with other community agencies (as we will argue in Chapter 7).

The effectiveness of supervision in the community is obviously related to its quality. The trading standards definition of quality is 'fit for purpose', which implies that there should be clear and stated purposes for intervention. The core purposes of community-based supervision are outlined in NOS (Scottish Executive 2004d, 2004e). However, considerations of quality and effectiveness must also recognise that there can be different purposes for different orders and that, at the individual level, supervisors have to match *individual* characteristics related to risks, needs and strengths (including gender, ethnicity, age and learning style) with the relevant mix of resources and skills to achieve the desired objectives. Quality in the real world cannot always mean a premium service. A reporting service is 'fit for purpose' if the purpose is merely to hold an individual to account, reporting changes in circumstances, and providing an opportunity to make a judgement on the need to review their allocation status. It cannot, however, be described as a *change* service aimed at acquiring knowledge, understanding or skills; nor can it be expected to reduce reoffending except possibly for people well on the way to change or for those who already represent a low risk of reoffending. Not all cases will require in-depth 'supervision' although the evidence of Chapter 2 is that most 'medium to high risk' offenders will.

In sections 3 and 4 of this chapter we have introduced the idea of restorative justice and, more generally, the issue of supporting victims partly because it is important to stress that there is more to community supervision than 'just' reducing reoffending. It is also necessary for both ethical and practical reasons that community supervision itself involves fair and restorative processes that take victims' *and* offenders' needs, rights and concerns seriously. This is a critical issue to which we will return in the book's Conclusion.

Notes

1 The case referred to is *McLaughlin v McQuaid*, 2006 JC 95; 2005 SLT 972; 2005 SCCR 630. The case is 'McQuaid' in the Justiciary Cases and Scots Law Times reports, but it is also known as *McLaughlin v McQuade* (see the SCCR report). A precis of the case is reported in Greens Weekly Digest (2005 GWD 25–476). The case was a Bill of Suspension heard on 12 July 2005 by Lords Macfadyen, Kinclaven and Temporary Judge C. G. B. Nicholson QC. The opinion was delivered on 2 August 2005 by Temporary Judge Nicholson.
2 The terms 'victim' and 'offender' are used hereafter for simplicity; this risks narrowly labelling them when it is their range of qualities and characteristics that are crucial to co-production in restorative practice.

6. Prison throughcare and resettlement

Unless something is done to tackle the causes of offending behaviour, and the social and economic exclusion from which it commonly springs, and to which it contributes, prisons will continue to have revolving doors, and the public will not in the long term be protected. (HMIP 2001: 4)

Introduction

Successful resettlement of an offender within the community is probably the best guarantee against reoffending and represents a good investment, short of preventing custody altogether. This chapter examines provision for prison throughcare and resettlement in a fast-changing landscape. More specifically, it focuses on criminal justice social work's role in assessment, preparation for release and post-release supervision in the community.

Work done through prison-based programmes and services aimed at helping individuals change their attitudes and behaviour and meet their needs has the potential to be complemented, fulfilled and maintained by the work of criminal justice social work services during the sentence and on return to the community. Until recently prison throughcare has been the 'cinderella' element in criminal justice social work provision, despite the increasing demand for the services and challenges presented by post-release supervision of sex offenders and other serious offenders.

This chapter tries to capture some of the complexities of the legal requirements and policy contexts of throughcare and resettlement work. It begins with a brief discussion of proposed changes in release and post-custodial management of offenders in Scotland, before moving on to describe existing law, policy and guidance in relation to early release, parole board decision-making and post-release supervision. It also briefly addresses issues in relation to throughcare and resettlement of 'high-risk offenders'.

Proposed changes in release and post-custodial management of offenders

Following recommendations from Sentencing Commission for Scotland (2006), the Scottish Executive decided, in 2006, to end automatic unconditional early release and replace it with a new regime which will mean that most offenders will be under some form of restriction or licence conditions for their entire sentence. The Commission's report focused primarily on how best to manage prisoners leaving custody and rather avoided the issue of why so many are admitted in the first place. The Executive's response to the Commission's report were outlined in *Release and Post Custodial Management of Offenders* (Scottish Executive 2006i). At the time of writing (March 2007), the Custodial Sentences and Weapons (Scotland) Act 2007 (hereafter the 2007 Act), which contains provisions for introducing changes to the system of throughcare and early release in Scotland, has been recently passed by the Scottish Parliament.

The rationale for the changes proposed by the Executive was that the public, particularly victims, found automatic unconditional early release confusing and that it undermined the credibility of the criminal justice system. In addition, it was argued that the current system of determining release dates largely on length of sentence criteria does not take into account the risk to the public that a prisoner may pose on release. The 2007 Act is intended to bring greater transparency to the sentencing process and to make it easier to understand.

The proposed regime is intended to allow for sentences to be tailored to the risks and needs presented by an individual in a way that will enhance public protection and reduce reoffending while meeting criminal justice requirements for punishment, deterrence and protection of the public. The main provisions within the Act include:

- For sentences of 15 days or more, a combined sentence management structure comprising a period in custody (the custody part) which will be a minimum 50 per cent of the sentence and a period on licence in the community (the community part). The courts will set the custody part when passing sentence.

- The courts will have the power to increase the custody part (up to a maximum of 75 per cent) at the time of sentence for the purposes of retribution and deterrence (punishment).

- The courts will explain the consequences of the combined structure when imposing the sentence.

- An offender's risks and needs will be reviewed during the custody part. If there are indications that the offender still presents a risk of serious harm to the public at the end of the custody part (provided that this is not the maximum 75 per cent), the case will be referred to the Parole Board for Scotland to consider whether or not the offender should continue to be detained in custody on grounds of risk. The Parole Board cannot order an offender to be detained beyond the [overall sentence] period imposed by the court.

- The community part will be a minimum 25 per cent of the sentence. The offender will be on licence throughout the duration of the community part. Conditions will be attached to the licence to allow for a variable and flexible package of measures and obligations that the offender must meet.

- Serious breaches of licence conditions which show that the offender is an unacceptable risk to public safety will result in the offender being recalled to custody.

- For sentences of less than 15 days the offender will spend the full period in custody and will be released unconditionally.

- The statutory provisions that support the Parole Board for Scotland will be amended to reflect its revised role and functions under the new arrangements. (Custodial Sentences and Weapons Bill, Policy Memorandum: para. 11)[1]

The proposals for a 'combined sentence' do not represent new measures as such but a recognition that there should always be two elements to a custodial sentence – the part served in prison, including preparing for resettlement, and the part in the community which can be tailored to the particular needs and risks presented by the individual as they make the transition. They represent a very clear endorsement of the concept of throughcare, inclusive of elements of constructive work in prison, resettlement and aftercare, but integrated more effectively.

Three major practical challenges are presented by the proposals to have all prisoners under some form of restriction for the full sentence. First, the new requirements around risk assessment during the custody part will mean that the integrated case management system (discussed below), which has only recently been introduced, will need to be applied to an estimated 9,241 prisoners rather than to the 3,000 to whom it currently applies (Custodial Sentences and Weapons Bill Explanatory Notes: para. 157). Second, the number of released prisoners subject to some form of post-release supervision is predicted to rise from its current level of about 600 to 4,300 (Custodial Sentences and Weapons Bill Explanatory Notes: para. 164). Third, and most important, the Bill's provisions are predicted to lead to an increase in the prison population of between 700 and 1,100 (Custodial Sentences and Weapons Bill Explanatory Notes: para. 178).[2] The effect of this would be that Scotland's prison population would become the highest in the EU; it might also require the construction of a new prison. Evidently, these three problems are interrelated. Increasing pressures of over crowding (and understaffing) in the prisons will place the risk assessment process and release decision-making processes under pressure, which in turn will affect the quality of pre-release planning and of post-release supervision. While some attention has been paid to the workload issues that the Bill's provisions would create for prison and social work staff, the *workforce* implications of the proposals have not yet been properly identified, far less addressed. Other concerns that have arisen from the evidence submitted to the Justice 2 Committee during its stage 1 scrutiny of the Bill include various practical and principled objections to the proposals around the setting of the custody part by sentencers; lack of clarity about the meaning of and processes for risk assessment pre-release; lack of clarity about the nature of post-release licence conditions, about recall and about re-release; and lack of detail about the type, scope and quality of post-release supervision that is intended.[3]

It is clear that the demand for prison throughcare and resettlement work will rise significantly both because the prison population is rising and because many more prisoners will now be subject to post-release supervision. The changes proposed by the 2007 Act reflect long-standing debate about the importance of throughcare and resettlement work and are the culmination of a number of stages of development. In 2001 the Scottish Executive established a Tripartite Group, representing the Scottish Executive Justice Department, the Scottish Prison Service, local authorities, and the Association of Directors of Social Work, together with representatives of the Scottish Executive Health Department, to address the issue of the 'revolving door syndrome' of prisoners released in Scotland only for many to be returned to prison after committing further offences. The group was established with the remit of looking at ways of promoting a more coordinated approach to return to the community and closer partnership working, especially in relation to the transitional arrangements for prisoners when they return to the community. The Tripartite Group report http://www.scotland.gov.uk/Publications/2003/01/16093/16159, *Developing the Service* (Scottish Executive 2003b), concluded that in order to provide the coordinated service envisaged by policy, there was a need to ensure closer collaboration between agencies, so that policy initiatives could be better integrated and good practice developed in ways understood and accepted by all the relevant partners. *Developing the Service* resulted in new guidance (Circular 12/2002) and a legislative framework for achieving this was introduced by the Management of Offenders (Scotland) Act 2005.

Nature of throughcare and resettlement

National Objectives and Standards (NOS) on Throughcare were revised in 1996/7 and reissued electronically (Scottish Executive 2004g), with a view to re-establishing a clear framework for throughcare practice. NOS use the term throughcare to denote the provision of a range of social work and associated services to prisoners and their families from the point of sentence or remand, during the period of imprisonment and following release into the community. The term aftercare is generally used to mean social work supervision, support and assistance to prisoners on release. Resettlement is increasingly used where prisoners and their families receive assistance and support to help them prepare for life after prison and their return to the community.

Throughcare has two interrelated elements: work in prison and supervision in the community, reflected in the most recent proposals, which have three key objectives (Scottish Executive 2004f):

- To assist prisoners and their families to prepare for release.

- To help prisoners resettle in the community whether required by statute as part of a licence or because the prisoners seek such a service.

- To promote greater public safety.

While NOS stresses the primary concern with the safety of the public, the service objectives and standards promote a reintegrative approach in that 'successful resettlement of an offender within the community is probably the best guarantee against offending' (Scottish Executive 2004f: para. 3). Social work activity in throughcare cannot be undertaken without reference to prison policy and practice on sentence management and integrated case management (ICM, see below) and the growing expectation that prison staff will be required to undertake more risk assessment and intensive intervention, in conjunction with social workers and other specialists. Social work services in prison are funded by the Scottish Prison Service (SPS) and delivered by local authority social work, on the basis of service level agreements, as part of the local authority's statutory throughcare responsibilities.

Social work supervision and integrated case management

NOS and subsequent guidance aims to integrate the responsibilities of social work in prison and social work in the community within a single integrated case management framework. The guidance contains explicit commitments which represent a joint commitment by SPS and the local authorities towards common objectives and service outcomes (Circular No. JD/8/2006). The 2005 Act (section 10) requires that the responsible authorities for each area must jointly establish arrangements for the assessment and management of the risks posed in that area by certain categories of offenders. Responsible authorities are the police, the local authority, health boards, Scottish Prison Service and Scottish Ministers.

Ideally throughcare should be part of a continuum of services, geared on one hand to reduce the numbers in custody by the provision of credible community-based disposals and on the other to provide effective resettlement programmes for those in custody, aimed at protecting the community and preventing reconviction and readmission. The overall aim of the service is to assist prisoners reduce their risk of reoffending and to help them resettle and reintegrate within the community. Specific objectives for social work in prisons outlined in NOS are (Scottish Executive 2004f: para. 37):

- To offer prisoners access to a range and level of social work services similar to those in the community.

- To contribute to public safety by making available a range of individual and group work programmes to address offending behaviour.

- To provide support and assistance to help prisoners resettle and reintegrate into society following release.

Scottish Prison Service Guidance on Sentence Management and Circular 12/2002 processes (Circular No. SEJD 12/2002, revised May 2004) are to be incorporated within and superseded by a system of integrated case management (ICM) for use by social work and SPS staff. The ICM manual is aligned with and includes direct reference to social work national standards. A cross-sectional project board and associated working sub-groups were given the job of (1) considering specific parts of the sentence management and Circular 12 processes; and (2) finding ways by which a new unified ICM process could improve upon the particular task to be completed. ICM is intended to keep the positive features of throughcare and sentence management, while ensuring that there are strong joint operational processes in place between all criminal justice partners, particularly for those prisoners subject to statutory supervision in the community. Key features of integrated case management are that it is intended to:

- Be delivered to all convicted prisoners and not just those sentenced to four years or more.

- Differ in intensity according to risk and not, as previously, sentence length.

- Adopt a *case conference* approach to action planning involving all the relevant service providers who have contact with prisoners subject to post-release supervision.

- Utilise the input of all service providers through an IT-based system.

- Have the same entry and exit procedures for all prisoners regardless of sentence length. All prisoners will undergo a Core Screen assessment on

117

entry to prison and will leave with a Community Integration Plan/Pre-release Plan.[4]

- Provide prisoners with a clear pathway through custody to encourage greater engagement with the action planning process, a more responsible approach to addressing difficulties and ultimately desistance from offending on release.

- Sequence interventions appropriately.

- Ensure all relevant information is shared with appropriate service providers to facilitate a holistic planning process.

- Facilitate fully integrated service provision (e.g. addictions, learning skills and employability and social care) using assessment tools that have been consistently developed.

- Provide a greater recognition of the diversity within the prisoner population. (Circular No. JD/8/2006)

ICM is predicated on a case conference model, which will bring together the prisoner, their family and key staff to examine the prisoner's progress through custody. The case conference will consider the actions/interventions that are necessary to help make the prisoner's stay in custody successful. The case conference will also examine the assessed risks the prisoner poses and help decide on appropriate interventions aimed at reducing those risks. This particular approach should prove useful in (a) keeping the prisoner at the centre of the ICM process; (b) maintaining a focus on issues which are external to the prison as well as internal; (c) the sharing of relevant information across agencies; and (d) assessing and managing risk.

Guidance on enhanced throughcare identifies the key components of the role of the supervising officer. These key components include scheduled visits with the prisoner, the preparation of home background reports, contact, where appropriate, with the offender's family, and participation in the sentence management of the prisoner to ensure that work done following release is built solidly upon work already undertaken with the offender while in custody. The guidance emphasises the importance of effective communication between agencies and disciplines, particularly

- following admission and during the initial stages of the custodial sentence in the context of visits of supervising officers;

- at points of significant change in the prisoner's circumstances, including completion of prison programmes or risk assessments;

- in preparation of reports for referral to the Parole Board or other pre-release planning;

- on recall or other return to custody while on post-release supervision.

The expectation is that, unless there are exceptional reasons to prevent it, the offender will be interviewed following sentence by social work staff at the courts to explain the sentence to establish whether there are any immediate problems to be dealt with, and to inform the offender of the availability of social work services in prison and what contact to expect (Scottish Executive 2000a: 8.5–8.6; Scottish Executive 2004f: paras 29–30). Offenders sentenced to a period of extended sentence, long-term prisoners convicted of sex offences and those subject to supervised release orders are to be afforded highest priority. Court social work staff should be alert to the possibility of self-harm when conducting the post-sentence interview and ensure that this information is passed on to appropriate community and prison social work staff. Detailed procedures relating to the assessment of self-harm are set out in paragraph 2.19 of the NOS (Scottish Executive 2000a).

NOS and supplementary guidance set clear benchmarks and timescales that require the prison to notify the respective local authority ('the designated supervising authority') within seven days of receipt of the relevant information from court, together with a request to assign a supervising officer (Scottish Executive 2004f: para. 32). In practice, the prison governor will generally discharge this responsibility through the social work unit in the prison. All prisoners subject to mandatory supervision on release must be interviewed by prison-based social work staff within seven days of receipt of this information. The allocated supervisor must notify the prison governor, within seven days of appointment, sending a copy to the prison social work unit. Within 14 days, social work staff in the prison unit should provide the supervising officer with copies of the information they have received from the sentencing court and liaise to ensure that any work already undertaken with the prisoner in the community prior to sentence is built into the sentence management for the prisoner. Specific requirements for the serving of SROs are detailed in NOS at paragraphs 376–377 (Scottish Executive 2004f).

An explicit timeline for action is outlined in the introduction of Circular No. JD/8/2006. The required steps, which are discussed briefly below, include core screening (initial contact); a prison-based social worker interview (seven days); notification of the relevant local authority by the prison (14 days); appointment of a community-based social worker as supervising officer (21 days); transfer of all available information to and from the local authority (28 days); family visit by community-based social worker (within six weeks, thereafter annually); initial needs and risk assessment (within three to five months); and initial case conference six months from sentence. These are intended to update community integration plans and allow for implementation of sequenced interventions

Core screening
A standardised core screening process will be undertaken by prison staff as part of initial contact for all prisoners involved in the integrated case

management system regardless of sentence length and post-release supervision status. The aim is to identify any immediate needs as soon as possible in order to have the best possible plan of action in place, and to make referrals to specialists where appropriate and available, particularly for very short-term prisoners' community integration plans. The information is intended to provide a platform for specialist agencies to contribute to the plan for the prisoner and as a starting point for more in-depth risk and needs assessment for those subject to post-release supervision. A strong emphasis is placed in the guidance on the importance of identifying issues that may impact on a person's ability to engage with particular interventions (responsivity issues), including issues of culture and ethnicity, sexual orientation, disability. An electronic screening tool has been designed to gather data on social needs 'domains' which relate to key outcomes for local prisons. These include accommodation; benefits and finance; family contact during imprisonment and on release; learning, skills and employability; substance misuse; offending behaviour and relevant programme requirements (such as general offending programmes or anger management); and resettlement needs and supports, including voluntary throughcare, statutory supervision/monitoring and community supports.

All prisoners subject to statutory supervision on release should be interviewed by prison social work staff shortly after their admission, normally within seven days of receipt of the relevant information from the court. The purpose of this interview is as follows:

- To establish whether there are any immediate problems of a personal or family nature to be dealt with.

- To inform the prisoner of the social work services available in the prison and how to access these, together with an indication of what contact to expect from the unit staff and the community-based supervising officer.

- To explain to the prisoner what the requirements of statutory supervision will mean for them. This should take into account the particular requirements of the licence or order to which the person will be subject.

- To inform the prisoner of the parole process, where applicable. This also includes explaining to the prisoner that they will be subject to statutory supervision post-release even if they are not released early on parole.

- For Schedule 1 offenders (that is, those convicted of offences against children), this interview must also combine the purposes outlined in NOS paragraph 324 (Scottish Executive 2004f) and SEJD Circular 18/2003.

Prison-based social workers may complete a risk assessment to guide their work with the prisoner, and these assessments are likely to be repeated throughout the sentence in order to assess progress in addressing the level of risk. This is particularly the case with prisoners who are long term, have an extended sentence, or are subject to a sex offender licence. Risk Matrix 2000

(Thornton *et al.* 2003), which is used specifically with sexual offenders to assess their risk of sexual reconviction, is used as standard practice across Scotland. The Risk Management Authority in Scotland has responsibility to disseminate best practice in risk assessment and risk management as well as playing an active role in overseeing these procedures with certain high-risk offenders (i.e. those subject to an order for life-long restriction).

The community-based social work supervisor is expected to make an initial visit to the prisoner within the first six weeks of sentence to underline their role during sentence, the nature of obligations following release, and to offer appropriate assistance from community-based throughcare services. If this is considered inappropriate the reasons should be recorded and countersigned by a line manager. The purpose of this initial family visit is for the supervisor to do the following.

- Introduce him/herself, explaining their role.

- Outline the nature and implications of the sentence and supervision.

- Explain the possible nature of future contact, including preparation of home background reports, pre-release planning, etc.

- Assess the impact on the family of, and their reaction to, the prison sentence.

- Extend an offer of appropriate assistance to the family in dealing with the consequences of the prison term (including access to housing or money advice, childcare supports, voluntary organisations and prison visiting assistance, etc.).

At the same time the supervisor should meet with the social worker in the prison, the prisoner's personal officer and any other relevant staff to gain first-hand knowledge of sentence management planning for the prisoner. The supervising authority (in practice the supervisor in consultation with the first line manager) should draw up a schedule of visits, in conjunction with the social work unit in prison. This should comprise at least one visit to the prisoner per year. Decisions on the number of visits will be influenced by various factors including the attitude of the prisoner towards supervision, overall length of sentence, outcomes from prison-based work or programmes, changes in personal or family circumstances, expected difficulties in securing compliance and demands on operational resources. In cases where the prisoner refuses a visit, details should be recorded in the case file and countersigned by a line manager. Each scheduled visit to the prisoner should be preceded by a home visit to the prisoner's family. While ICM relates to the prison-based process, contact for those subject to an extended sentence should be undertaken within the guidelines in SWSG Circular 14/98 which applies post release.

Case conferences

The ICM guidance stresses that case conferences should be held at set intervals during a prisoner's sentence with the following aims:

(a) To examine, utilise and agree the risk assessment in relation to the prisoner.

(b) To affirm the prisoner's level of need across a number of key areas relating to their risk.

(c) To explain (a) and (b) to the prisoner and seek their views on same.

(d) To discuss ways of reducing or managing the assessed risks, particularly by meeting the assessed needs.

(e) To involve the prisoner in developing an action plan for the next reporting period, including referrals to service providers for appropriately sequenced interventions.

The purpose of the case conference approach is to create a mechanism for regular multidisciplinary risk and need assessment reviews in which service providers can contribute to annual action plans with appropriately sequenced interventions and evidence-led milestones, particularly for long-term prisoners. The 'iterative loop' is intended to ensure regular progress reviews updated by all providers, to feed into community integration plans and a 'route' map for pre-release preparation and planning.

An initial case conference should take place within six months of sentence, and prisoners should go no more than 12 calendar months between annual case conferences. They should focus on four key tasks: risk assessment, planning, intervention and evaluation and should involve, at a minimum, the case coordinator, prison-based social worker, community-based social worker and the prisoner. Where possible, attendance should also include the prisoner's personal officer or life liaison officer where applicable, services providers, those involved in risk assessments, and family members, where appropriate. A key task for the case conference is to review, amend (if necessary) and ratify the prisoner's risk assessment and interventions plans, in particular to ensure that all interventions delivered by relevant agencies are carried out in a coherent and planned way. Fundamentally, this process involves all the relevant parties sharing information; being clear about the accuracy, validity and usefulness of that information; making explicit their views on what action is necessary to minimise the risks; and setting timescales for a review of the risk assessment.

Pre-release

In the pre-release phase, it is likely that case conferences will focus on the progress the prisoner has made overall; their plans for release; the support on offer to the prisoner from family/friends; an explanation of the licence conditions; an explanation of what supervision will entail; and the possibility of other services being involved in that supervision action plan. The expectation is that pre-release planning will accelerate in the final three months of confirmation of the prisoner's release date and a pre-release case conference will be scheduled for three months before release, involving the prisoner, the supervisor, the social worker in the prison and any other relevant parties, as discussed above. Where possible, a meeting should take place with the prisoner's family to contribute to the pre-release plan. The plan must provide an overall assessment of (the prisoner's) needs, and must address any outstanding issues surrounding accommodation, finance, relations and personal or behavioural problems (Scottish Executive 2004f). Plans also need management approval and it is not envisaged that the community-based social worker will have another meeting on their own to draw up a plan. SPS will send the confirmed notification to the Multi-Agency Public Protection Arrangements (MAPPA) coordinator for those prisoners captured by the legislation, so that work can begin there.

Early release provisions

The legislative basis for statutory prison throughcare lies in section 27 of the Social Work (Scotland) Act 1968 as amended, which requires every local authority to provide a service for:

> the supervision of, and the provision of advice, guidance, and assistance for ... persons in their area who, following release from prison or any other form of detention, are required to be under supervision by the terms of an order or licence ... or of a condition or requirement imposed in pursuance of any enactment. (section 27(b)(ii))

These duties were extended to those leaving prison without a supervision requirement who are entitled to seek 'voluntary assistance' and request advice, guidance and assistance from local authorities in the 12 months following their release from prison.

The Prisoners and Criminal Proceedings (Scotland) Act 1993 provides for the current system of early release based on the recommendations of the Kincraig Report (HMSO 1989). This replaced an earlier system of aftercare and licence, with a structured system of unconditional early release for most prisoners, supplemented by a more focused and restricted system of conditional early release on licence. Section 71 of the Criminal Justice (Scotland) Act 2003 amended the 1968 Act (section 27) to strengthen the existing throughcare arrangements as recommended by the Tripartite Group. The Management of Offenders (Scotland) Act 2005 introduced additional measures to allow for early release subject to supervision including home detention curfew (HDC) and orders of life-long restriction (OLR). Up-to-date circulars on HDC, ICM and the OLR can be found at: http://www.

scotland.gov.uk/Topics/Justice/jdcirculars/listjdcirculars. As we have seen, the 2006 Bill proposes further changes including the removal of automatic early release and the addition of supervisory conditions for short-term prisoners.

The statutory system of throughcare and early release from prison is complicated and deals with two groups of prisoners. The first group is subject to statutory supervision on release and consists of 'long-term' prisoners – those serving service sentences of four years and over. The second group are 'short-term' prisoners – those serving less than four years, but who are subject to post-release supervision as part of extended sentences or supervised release orders (SRO). Short-term prisoners form the major group of released prisoners – about 23,000 out of a total 25,000 per year – and reoffending and reincarceration rates are highest among this group. In the current system, apart from those on extended sentences or subject to SROs, short-term prisoners are not subject to any form of statutory supervision on release but are eligible for voluntary assistance.

A supervised release order (SRO) (under section 209 of the 1995 Act) can be made by a court at the point of sentencing for those sentenced to 'imprisonment for a term of not less than twelve months and not more than four years', if it considers that supervision is necessary to protect the public from serious harm from the offender on their release from prison. Conditions can be inserted in the order. SROs are available for young offenders as well as adults.

Post-release supervision through 'extended sentences' can be ordered on indictment cases for violent offenders sentenced to four or more years, and for sex offenders receiving a determinate custodial sentence of any length (under section 210 of the 1995 Act). The maximum length of post-release supervision is ten years for both sex offenders and for violent offenders (see the statutory instrument, the Extended Sentences for Violent Offenders (Scotland) Order 2003). The extended period is the aggregate of the 'custodial term' plus the 'extension period' considered necessary to protect the public from serious harm once the offender is released, either unconditionally (in the case of short-term prisoners) or when they would otherwise have ceased to be on licence (in the case of long-term prisoners).

An order for lifelong restriction (OLR) (under section 210F of the Criminal Justice (Scotland) Act 2003) is available from 2006 in the High Court for the most serious sexual, violent or life-endangering offences and is specifically aimed at protecting the public. It provides for lifelong supervision and allows for a greater degree of intensive supervision than has hitherto been the norm in such cases. The period spent in the community will be an integral part of the sentence. A risk assessment order (RAO) allows a case to be adjourned for no more than 90 days for a risk assessment report (RAR) to be carried out by an assessor, accredited by the Risk Management Authority (RMA). The offender must be assessed against statutory risk criteria:

> that the nature of, or the circumstances of the commission of, the offence of which the convicted person has been found guilty either in themselves

or as part of a pattern of behaviour are such as to demonstrate that there is a likelihood that he, if at liberty, will seriously endanger the lives, or physical or psychological well-being, of members of the public at large. (Criminal Justice (Scotland) Act 2003, section 210E)

A risk management plan (RMP) will be prepared for each offender sentenced to an OLR, specifying the measures and detailing the roles of each agency involved.

Section 15 of the 2005 Act amended the Prisoners and Criminal Proceedings (Scotland) Act 1993 (by adding section 3AA) and introduced a scheme of home detention curfew (HDC) for prisoners considered to present low risk on their return to the community. The home detention curfew arrangements will be retained in any new regime as an incentive in appropriate cases; in the first instance for those serving 12 months or less. High-risk offenders and sex offenders will be automatically excluded. Section 3AA of the 1993 Act gives Scottish Ministers the power to release certain prisoners on licences which include a curfew condition (compliance with which will be monitored remotely by means of electronic equipment or devices) and certain prescribed standard conditions. Additional conditions can be added to the HDC licence by Scottish Ministers in accordance with recommendations made by the Parole Board. The power to release on HDC will allow certain prisoners to leave prison between two weeks and four months prior to the date on which they would otherwise be released under the 1993 Act (such prisoners will continue to serve their sentence during the period of the HDC licence and will be required to remain at the place specified in their licence for up to 12 hours per day). The primary aim of the HDC scheme is to ease reintegration of prisoners within the community while restricting their movements. It also provides a practical way of easing the prison population.

HDC is currently available initially for short-term prisoners. Accordingly, this order prescribes the standard conditions for such short-term prisoners. The standard conditions to be prescribed are:

- To be of good behaviour and keep the peace.

- Not to commit any offence.

- Not to tamper with or intentionally damage the electronic monitoring equipment or device(s) or knowingly allow these to be tampered with or intentionally damaged.

- To allow the electronic monitoring service provider access to the specified address to install and check electronic monitoring equipment.

The current arrangements that give courts the power to order an additional period of supervision (extended sentence) under section 210A of the 1995 Act will be retained under any new provisions for throughcare. Extended sentences practice (Circular No. SWSG 14/1998) is considered a model for the standard for good practice in all post-release supervision. These important 'best practice' principles include the following:

- Designation of both the supervising authority and a supervising officer from the point of sentence.

- An enhanced role for the supervising officer throughout the sentence including prison visits, family contact work, an increased emphasis on coordination and case management.

- Greater attention to the importance of information and assessment exchange between the prison and the supervising authority.

NOS were updated based on this model (see Circular No. SEJD 12/2002, revised May 2004) and applied to all prisoners released from prison on any form of statutory supervision except those who are subject to extended sentence, for whom the procedures detailed in Circular No. SWSG 14/1998 continued to apply. The application of the extended sentence model to all statutory throughcare prisoners placed an increased emphasis on continuity of risk and needs assessment, sharing of relevant information between prison and the community and across disciplines and agencies as well as allocation of a supervising officer at the start of the custodial sentence and early identification of the supervising authority on release. Local authority criminal justice social work services were required to produce plans to implement this 'enhanced' throughcare service. This model is likely to be applied to all community supervision introduced by the Custodial Sentences and Weapons (Scotland) Act 2007.

Table 6.1 provides a summary of the current post-release supervision requirements.

Provisions within the Custodial Sentences and Weapons (Scotland) Act 2007 are implemented in their current form, these provisions will change, as indicated in Table 6.2.

Parole Board decision-making and release

The system of parole came into being in Scotland on 1 April 1968 (Criminal Justice Act 1967, sections 60 and 61). The Parole Board currently exists under the provisions of the Prisons (Scotland) Act 1989, the Prisoners and Criminal Proceedings (Scotland) Act 1993 and the Convention Rights (Compliance) (Scotland) Act 2001. The Parole Board consists of Scottish Ministers' appointees, including judges, psychiatrists, social workers, criminologists and business people and at the time of writing is chaired by a former director of social work. The board deals with matters of early conditional release and recall. The Parole Board has the following powers, to:

Table 6.1 Current post-release supervision requirements

Length of sentence	Supervision in the community		
	Sex offence	Violent offence	Other
Under 12 months	None Voluntary Extended sentence	None Voluntary SRO	None Home detention curfew (3–12 months) Voluntary SRO
12 months to 4 years	None SRO Extended sentence	None SRO	None Home detention curfew SRO
4 years or over	Automatic licence Extended sentence OLR	Automatic licence Extended sentence OLR	Automatic licence
Life sentences	Life licence OLR	Life licence OLR	Life licence

Table 6.2 Proposed post-release supervision requirements

Length of sentence	Supervision in the community		
	Sex offence	Violent offence	Other
Under 15 days	None Voluntary	None Voluntary	None Voluntary
15 days to 12 months	Community licence Extended sentence	Community licence SRO	Home detention curfew (3–12 months) Community licence SRO
12 months to 4 years	Community licence SRO Extended sentence	Community licence SRO	Community licence SRO
4 years or over	Community licence Extended sentence OLR	Community licence Extended sentence OLR	Community licence
Life sentences	Life licence OLR	Life licence OLR	Life licence

- Direct the release of determinate sentence prisoners serving four years or more. It may also make directions as to the licence conditions of such prisoners.

- Direct the release on life licence of life prisoners.

- Direct the recall to custody of determinate sentence prisoners serving sentences of four years imprisonment or more, life sentence prisoners who have been released on parole or life licence and extended sentence prisoners in circumstances where such action is considered to be in the public interest.

The Parole Board can direct Scottish Ministers to re-release any prisoner who has been recalled to custody without a recommendation of the board or any prisoner who has been recalled with the board's recommendation and who makes representations against recall to the Scottish Ministers and the board. The cases of life prisoners and extended sentence prisoners who are recalled to custody must be considered by a Tribunal of the board. The board also can direct Scottish Ministers concerning additional conditions to be attached to prisoners' release licences.

Non-standard conditions can be imposed on released prisoners following advice from a home background report (HBR) prepared by a social worker in the community and a report from the social worker in the prison. Prisoners have right of access to reports and other information contained in their dossiers, with suitable safeguards in non-tribunal cases for withholding of information that would be potentially damaging to disclose. Specifically the prisoner has the right to see the report; have its contents explained to them, and have the opportunity to challenge what they think is incorrect.

Life and designated life prisoners
A life prisoner's sentence is one fixed by law. A designated life prisoner is sentenced to life imprisonment for an offence the penalty for which is not fixed by law – in practice a life sentence for a crime other than murder and, for those under 18 years, a life sentence for murder. It should be noted that young people between 18 and 21 convicted of murder, 'shall not be sentenced to imprisonment for life but to be detained in a young offender's institution and shall be liable to be detained for life' (section 205(3) of the 1995 Act). The life prisoner becomes a 'mandatory life prisoner'; the other a 'designated life prisoner'. Both categories of prisoners can be subject to release on 'life licence'.

It is for a court to decide, taking into account the seriousness of the offence, the length of the 'designated part' of the life sentence and, in effect, the point at which parole can be considered. The matter of release can be referred to a Tribunal of the Parole Board by Scottish Ministers or by application of the prisoner. A Life Prisoner Tribunal (LPT) consists of three Parole Board members appointed by the chair of the board and chaired by a serving or former High Court judge or sheriff operating under tribunal procedures.

LPTs have the power to order Scottish Ministers to release the prisoner immediately, if satisfied that the prisoner no longer needs to be kept in custody to protect the public, or it can make recommendations about the prisoner's future location, the timing of the next review, and the steps needed to deal with their offending.

Parole and non-parole licences last until the sentence expiry date, whereas a life licence lasts for the whole of the person's natural life. The standard conditions within a licence (section 12(2) of the 1993 Act) require the person to be subject to the supervision of a relevant officer of the local authority and to comply with such requirements as that officer may specify, for the purposes of supervision. Conditions may be subsequently added, varied or cancelled by Scottish Ministers following consultation with the Parole Board. Similarly, early termination of conditions is possible by the same process.

Legislation allows for licences to be revoked by Scottish Ministers if 'recommended to do so by the Parole Board' or if revocation and recall are considered expedient in the public interest and it is not practicable to await such recommendations' (section 17(1) of the 1993 Act). Where Scottish Ministers act without a Parole Board recommendation or the prisoner has made written representation, the case must be referred to the Parole Board for review. If during the supervised period a further offence 'punishable by imprisonment' is committed, the court may order the person to be returned to prison 'for the whole or any part of the period' calculated from 'the date of the order for his return'. This is in addition to any disposal the court may make for the new offence.

Home background reports

The social work authority in the area in which the prisoner intends to reside on release is required to provide a home background report (HBR) to provide assessment and information on a range of factors likely to influence the resettlement prospects of the prisoner on their release. In particular, the focus is on the risk of harm posed by and to the prisoner. HBRs should also address the suitability of a particular address or area and whether an application for additional licence conditions where public protection considerations require this.

NOS provide a detailed structure for reporting and stress the importance of indicating the source of any information, differentiating throughout between fact and opinion:

- **Basis of report.** Knowledge of family and prisoner and details of visits and contacts.

- **Family circumstances.** Social relationships and functioning; accommodation, finance.

- **Family attitudes.** The impact of the sentence and attitude to the person's return, and to their criminality.

- **Environment.** Employment prospects, peer associations and other significant relationships; their likely influence; anticipated impact of the prisoner's return on the local community.

- **Specialist resources.** Programmes or resources.

- **Overall assessment.** Risk factors for reoffending; social or personal needs; level of support available from family and network.

- **Provisional release plan.** Aims, objectives, level and nature of supervision and services to be provided and by whom.

The issue of 'rights' is important and the writer is required to ensure that those interviewed understand that any information supplied is likely to be made known to the prisoner (under the Parole Board (Scotland) Rules), with the exception of damaging information. The nature and duration of discretionary release and statutory supervision following release should also be explained, with an offer to revisit, if requested, to explain the outcome of the parole review.

The very limited available Scottish research on Parole Board decision-making and social work's contribution to it is now somewhat dated (McAra 1998: 20) but found that reports tended to be descriptive rather than analytic; and while much of the information outlined by NOS was included, only 10 per cent of reports included all the required types of information. Reports were judged to have minimal impact on Parole Board decision-making, partly because of the patchy information relevant to risk of reoffending and the very limited information on specialist resources available on release. Paterson and Tombs (1998) noted that communication between Parole Board members and community-based and prison-based social workers was problematic and needed to improve. SWIA performance inspections (between 2004 and 2006; see www.swia.gov.uk) show variations in the levels of good practice in this area with some authorities performing well but others requiring significant improvement. In some inspections, for example, only half of the reports reached a minimum standard. Too many reports did not contain a provisional release plan. A consistent message from the inspections is that all reports should have a provisional release plan, should pay greater attention to the assessment of possible risk to the community, and provide clearer description of the levels of oversight and support that would be available on release. SWIA also noted the need to ensure that quality assurance procedures are in place.

NOS stress the importance of providing available information on the attitude of victims or the local community, particularly in relation to violent or sexual offenders, though they do not indicate how this is to be assessed. Prisoners and licensees should be made aware of the formal appeals and complaints systems that exist, both within SPS and local authorities.

The benchmarks set by NOS are ambitious, given the volume of work proposed. A major challenge for CJAs will be to establish enhanced throughcare and meet these standards with integrity.

Post-release supervision

The proposed new measures in the 2007 Act are intended to build on the structure introduced in the Management of Offenders (Scotland) Act 2005[5] to secure 'end-to-end' sentence management so that sentences are managed in an integrated way, in custody and in the community. The new proposals for throughcare will place increased demands on criminal justice social work when writing reports for courts and in contributing to assessment of offenders throughout their time in prison to help inform decision-making authorities of the offender's risk of reoffending at each and every stage. The details of these demands and responsibilities are unknown at the time of writing.

Until the provisions in the 2007 Act are introduced, short-term prisoners (those serving less than four years, except sex offenders) will continue to be released 'unconditionally' and without restrictions as soon as they have served half of their sentence, provided they are not subject to statutory post-release supervision (under section 1(1) of the 1993 Act) such as extended sentences or supervised release orders. No consideration of the risk that they might pose to the public on release is required.

Short-term prisoners serving a sentence of three months or more, who have served at least a quarter and not less than four weeks, may also be released on licence subject to standard and curfew conditions (under section 3AA of the 1993 Act). Curfew conditions (under section 12AB of the 1993 Act) include remote monitoring (electronic tagging) and can require the released person to remain at specified places for defined periods of time of not less that nine hours in any one day or can bar him or her from specified places or types of places for certain periods or days. This licence is subject to revocation or prison recall provisions. The same provisions can apply to a long-term prisoner whose release on having served half of the sentence has been recommended by the Parole Board.

The long-term prisoner, those serving four or more years in aggregate, are eligible for parole 'after half sentence' (section 1(3) of the 1993 Act) and can be considered for parole annually thereafter until there is less than 16 months of the sentence to serve. Decisions on this form of discretionary release are made by the Parole Board and prisoners are released subject to social work supervision on a 'parole licence'. Discretionary release applies both to adult offenders and to young offenders detained under section 208 of the 1995 Act. Curfew provisions under sections 3AA and 12AB of the 1993 Act, discussed above, can also apply to a long-term prisoner whose release has been recommended by the Parole Board.

For those not recommended for parole or who did not put themselves forward, section 1(2) of the 1993 Act allows for long-term prisoners to be released on licence automatically on completion of two-thirds of their sentence, subject to any lost remission. The remainder of the sentence is served in the community under social work supervision on a 'non-parole licence'. NOS recognise that such prisoners are 'likely to present a high risk in terms of response to supervision' (paragraph 204) which should inform the approach adopted on their return to the community. Prisoners on licence who commit a new offence resulting in a further custodial sentence of under four years during the period of supervision are released on a 'short sentence' licence which for practical purposes is dealt with as a non-parole licence.

Provisions under the 2007 Act, for all practical purposes, end both parole and non-parole licences as all prisoners will be subject to supervision in the community at some point. If introduced, these provisions will introduce risk assessment as an ongoing part of the sentence management programme. If the assessment indicates that the prisoner will remain an unacceptable risk at the end of the minimum 50 per cent period of the sentence (the custody part), Scottish Ministers will have the power to refer to the Parole Board with a recommendation for continued custody. If, having considered the case fully, the Parole Board agrees with the assessment, the board will direct that the prisoner is kept in custody beyond the minimum 50 per cent point and will specify the further period of custody. The prisoner will be subject to further reviews by the Parole Board to determine whether they should continue to be kept in custody until they have served three-quarters of the sentence, at which point they will be released on licence. This is intended to ensure appropriate sentence management and to ensure that the offender does not simply walk away at the end of the sentence; the offender will always serve a part of the sentence on licence in the community.

Whatever the legislative regime, the role of the supervisor becomes central following the release of the prisoner. The initial period following release is likely to be a testing one and their practical needs will often be particularly acute following lengthy periods in custody or where they return to particularly isolated or vulnerable circumstances. On release, the person will be given a travel warrant, subsistence money, and a letter of introduction to the benefits agency, and should normally be seen on the day of release by the supervisor. If a prisoner on licence fails to attend, this should be investigated by visiting the release address 'within two working days' and if contact is not established, the Scottish Executive Justice Department should be notified. Failure to attend without good cause constitutes a breach and the necessary action to take will be dependent on the factors of each case especially in terms of the risks posed. However, failure to attend on the day of release for those subject to an SRO who are homeless will trigger an automatic breach report.

The purpose of the initial meeting is to offer immediate assistance, clarify the conditions of the licence, confirm address details and to go over the pre-release plan, particularly arrangements for contact in the first three months. The expectation is that the supervisor will see the person weekly for the first month, and at least fortnightly for the remainder of the first three months, and monthly for the subsequent three months. NOS represent minimum standards only. Formal reviews are required at the end of the first three months, at the end of the second three months, and thereafter at six-monthly intervals to examine progress against the release plan. In the case of life licensees, regular progress reports are required for the Scottish Executive Parole and Life Sentence Review Division.

Voluntary assistance

Voluntary assistance is available, in general terms, under section 27 of the 1968 Act. The Law Reform (Miscellaneous Provisions) (Scotland) Act 1990 added a subsection (c) to section 27 of the 1968 Act that 'the provision of advice, guidance, and assistance for persons in their areas who, within 12 months of their release from prison or any other form of detention, request such advice, guidance, or assistance'.

Following proposals included in the 2007 Act most prisoners will again be subject to some form of statutory community supervision. It is unlikely that all short-termers, particularly those serving less than six months, will receive more than signposting to services. It is likely to be important for CJAs to make planning arrangements whereby this vulnerable group can seek additional assistance on a voluntary basis. The objectives of voluntary assistance are ambitiously outlined in NOS:

- To provide and facilitate a range of services for prisoners and ex-prisoners and, where appropriate, their families, to assist them to deal with any problems they may face particularly following release.

- To assist offenders to reduce the risk of their reoffending through the provision of a range of services to meet identified needs.

- To seek to limit and redress the damaging consequences of imprisonment including the dislocation of family and community ties, the loss of personal choice, and the resultant stigma.

- To help prisoners and their families to develop their ability to tackle their own problems.

- To help prisoners and their families, on request, to prepare for release.

- To assist the families of released prisoners to adjust to the changed circumstances arising from the prisoner's return, where such a service is needed and requested.

- To assist ex-prisoners to reintegrate successfully into the community and thus reduce the incidence of crime.

NOS recognise that some prisoners not subject to statutory supervision will seek voluntary assistance, while others may, because of their own vulnerability or the risk they constitute to others, be judged as needing assistance but may be unlikely to seek it. The Tripartite Group report, for example, identified specific groups as priorities for voluntary assistance:

- High-risk offenders not currently subject to statutory supervision.

- Young offenders.

- Those who show a commitment to address their offending behaviour or take up and continue with the offer of assistance under the Scottish Prison Service's Transitional Care Scheme.

Revised voluntary throughcare guidance (Scottish Executive 2005g) identified only two priority groups: high-risk offenders (sex offences and recurrent violence), and those eligible for the Throughcare Addiction Service. In practice almost all high-risk offenders and many young offenders will fulfil the criteria for the Throughcare Addiction Service. The priorities for phase 2 of the throughcare arrangements for voluntary assistance will therefore largely concentrate on the sex offenders and on the Throughcare Addiction Service offenders. It remains to be seen, with the introduction of section 15 of the 2005 Act dealing with high-risk offenders, which high-risk offenders will actually receive a voluntary service and whether any voluntary assistance will be available for other young offenders.

The revised guidance recognises that engaging prisoners on a voluntary basis can be very difficult and stresses the importance of the prisoner being able to see what is on offer and having confidence that what is promised before release will be delivered afterwards. A framework for a Throughcare Service or Going Straight Contract is provided to set out both the content and delivery of voluntary assistance after release and to allow the prisoner to be a full partner in the process. The prisoner and supervisor are expected to sign up to a Going Straight Contract following a full assessment of their needs. The contract assumes the active participation of mainstream agencies, such as Jobcentre Plus, and local authority housing departments. Voluntary and private sector organisations will also play important roles in providing

- education and training
- help with family issues and parenting
- advocacy – benefits and housing
- participation in offending behaviour programmes
- participation in drug and alcohol programmes
- constructive use of leisure time (Annex B).

A national Throughcare Addiction Service (TAS), provided through Community Justice Authorities as the lead agency working alongside SPS, the Drug Action Teams (DATs) and other partners, is intended to be an integral part of the overall throughcare arrangements. The aim of TAS is to provide continuity of care for those leaving custody who wish to go on to receive addiction services in the community in Scotland. TAS is expected to work with the offender in the latter stages of custody in order to form a relationship which can be sustained in the six-week post-release period, a period of major vulnerability to the offender (in terms of resettlement and the lowering of tolerance to the substance of misuse) and a period of significant fall-out of service provision. The guidance (para. 13) provides principles to underpin good practice on tackling social exclusion:

- Augmenting offender self-assessment with professional assessment of social inclusion, risk and social learning needs of the offender.

- Formulating an action plan for service delivery reflecting the holistic nature of the assessment and setting out *the clear practical benefits to the offender*.

- Building on any structured work undertaken during the custodial term.

- Providing a focus on promotion of social inclusion, lifelong learning and stable family relationships and living conditions.

Whether subject to short periods of supervision in the community, following changes in legislation, or simply eligible for voluntary assistance under the current system, criminal justice social work will have to target services and resources at those who have shown willingness to pick up services in prison, for example participants of the SOTP 2000 (sex offending) programme, and who are willing to continue with this work in the community. The continuity of services is crucial since a major problem with short-term prison sentences is the limited time available to initiate or complete programmes while in custody. These could be taken forward in the community following release.

Particular priority is expected be given to Schedule 1 (Sex) Offenders and other high-risk offenders not subject to statutory licence on release, reflecting growing concerns about the supervision and monitoring of this group of offenders within the context of public safety and child protection. As well as providing practical resettlement help for the offender and their families, for example by assisting with benefits/housing needs, services should also extend to advice on specific offence-related issues such as registration requirements. However, unlike those subject to statutory supervision or licence, there is limited 'leverage' with this group and so supervisors have to be very proactive in their approach.

High-risk offenders

Concern about high-risk offenders, particularly sex offenders, has risen greatly in recent years. Many of those convicted of serious violent offences will be sent to prison and on return to the community will be subject to social work supervision and, in the case of sex offenders, to registration requirements. In June 2003 there were 1,931 registered sex offenders in Scotland. This had risen to 2,809 by June 2005. Data on serious and (non-sexual) violent offenders are less readily available and orders of lifelong restriction (OLR) have still to be implemented for serious (non-sexual) violence (see http://www.scotland.gov.uk/Topics/Justice/criminal/17309/8067). These orders and the establishment of a Risk Management Authority,[6] and a Violence Reduction Unit[7] as national centres for practice excellence, are a reflection of government's growing concern about violence in Scotland. No fully coordinated and integrated strategy for dealing with serious and violent offenders yet exists in Scotland. A national strategy on violence is to be published in 2007 and currently strategic developments are most detailed for dealing with sex offenders.

The recommendations of an Expert Panel on Sex Offending, established under the chairmanship of the Lady Cosgrove in 1998, reflected many of those which had been included in *A Commitment to Protect – Supervising Sex Offenders: Proposals for More Effective Practice* (SWSI 1997). More recently the Irving Report (Scottish Executive 2005e) and SWIA/HMIC (2005) report into the management of Colyn Evans recommended review of the arrangements and best practice for dealing with serious and violent offenders. The resulting expectation that the Scottish Prison Service and local authorities should develop national protocols determining the pertinent information to be exchanged on high-risk offenders has now been established in law under the 2005 Act.

The VISOR (Violent and Sex Offender Register) system will be adopted across Scotland and has been piloted in three local authorities since 2005. The system is to be linked to and will become an integral part of the Scottish Information Database (SID) and Police National Computer (PNC). A longer-term objective is to coordinate and integrate local authority criminal justice social work and Scottish Prison Service data and information with the police-controlled VISOR system. This should facilitate information exchange and more effective monitoring and tracking of sex offenders. VISOR is expected to facilitate cross-checking with other established databases, for example the Department of Work and Pensions, DVLA, Passport Office, Automatic Number Plate Recognition system (ANPR).

While the VISOR system is police led, it is likely, over time, to operate as more than just a register (particularly in regard to serious (non-sexual) violent offenders and for OLRs) and has the potential to be adapted to become a case management tool, a workload planning system, a contact record, a monitoring device and a work diary; all of which are likely to have a direct impact on the role of supervisors with serious and violent offenders. Research on how best to assist positive personal change with serious offenders, particularly sex offenders, remains contentious, and as a result there is a strong emphasis on offender management and administrative approaches to monitoring and supervision within the VISOR system. The term offender management captures the authority and surveillance elements of social work supervision with such cases and presents challenges for criminal justice social workers in their role of promoting the social well-being of the community outlined by *A Commitment to Protect*.

Notification and registration periods under the Sex Offenders Act 1997 and the Sexual Offences Act 2003 relate to the sentence or order imposed by a court and can vary depending on sentence or disposal:

- Life imprisonment or imprisonment of 30 months of more (indefinite).

- Admission to hospital subject to a restriction order (indefinite).

- Imprisonment for less than 30 months but more than six months (ten years).

- Imprisonment for six months or less (seven years).

- Admission to hospital but not subject to a restriction order (seven years).

- Others e.g. probation order (five years).

The notification periods involving ten, seven and five years are halved for those 'under the relevant age' (section 82 of the 2003 Act), which in Scotland is 16. Most children who fall into this category in Scotland are dealt with by children's hearings and are not subject to registration. However, those prosecuted and convicted in the courts will be subject to these arrangements. Special measures are required to safeguard such young people and other children in an authority's care, whether they are subject to registration or not. The adoption of Risk Matrix 2000 (Thornton *et al.* 2003) by police, criminal justice social work and the Scottish Prison Service has brought a consistency and standardisation to the risk assessment process in establishing low, medium, high or very high-risk adult offenders. The Association of Chief Police Officers in Scotland (ACPOS) has produced a Memorandum of Understanding to facilitate the sharing of information with other appropriate agencies, including Scottish Prison Service and social work. A national Information Sharing Steering Group (ISSG) chaired by the Solicitor General for Scotland subsequently agreed a National Concordat in 2005:

- To work together to manage the risk to the public posed by sex offenders.

- To share any relevant information about sex offenders necessary to ensure that this objective is achieved, while ensuring that the rights of individuals are protected.

- To presume that all relevant information will be shared where it is legal to do so.

- To ensure that information is gathered and managed in a way that facilitates sharing.

Sexual offences prevention orders (SOPO), aimed at protecting the public or any particular members of the public from serious sexual harm, were introduced by the Sexual Offences Act 2003 and are intended to place specific restrictions on the activities or circumstances of offenders, for example in relation to employment, and in not frequenting public parks or certain leisure activities. The Protection of Children and Prevention of Sexual Offences (Scotland) Act 2005 amended the Sexual Offences Act 2003 to allow courts to impose a SOPO at the time of sentence. This is in addition to provisions for applications by a chief constable on a convicted sex offender who is currently continuing to exhibit sexually risky behaviour of significant concern. In either case an enhanced social enquiry report will normally be required from criminal justice social work following a joint multi-agency risk assessment. A SOPO is applicable for a minimum of five years. Risk of sexual harm orders (RSHOs), introduced by the 2005 Act, can be applied for by a chief constable in respect of an adult of 18 or more who has displayed sexual behaviour in relation to a child of under 16, who has no previous conviction. The sexual behaviour would need to have taken place on at least two occasions and would need to fall within certain categories. It is expected that specialist VISOR teams will be established to monitor serious and violent offenders in the community, irrespective of formal throughcare requirements.

In addition to the establishment of the Risk Management Authority (RMA) and of related measures discussed above, Multi-Agency Public Protection Arrangements (MAPPA) to coordinate local accommodation, risk assessment and management arrangements through joint working protocols in each local authority area are being established in each Community Justice Authority. These have the potential to provide a corporate multi-agency framework for public protection practice and facilitate effective and consistent information sharing arrangements, through a partnership of criminal justice agencies and with social care agencies such as health, social work services and housing.

Conclusions

After many years of neglect, throughcare and resettlement again form a major part of government policy for promoting community safety. New organisational structures and requirements introduced by the 2005 Act place a greater corporate responsibility for the management of serious and violent offenders returning to the community on local authorities and the Scottish Prison Service as part of a wider community safety strategy. Such a corporate responsibility could provide a more meaningful expression to local authorities' duty to promote social welfare under section 12 of the 1968 Act. These structures set a new landscape for newly established dedicated social work throughcare teams and a challenge to provide meaningful and effective practices aimed both at offender management and positive integrative supervision. However, the measures contained in the Custodial Sentences and Weapons (Scotland) Act 2007, currently before the Scottish Parliament, by very significantly increasing the prison population, the numbers of prisoners subject to risk assessment procedures in custody and the numbers of ex-prisoners under supervision, represent major challenges for all parties involved. Unless the new measures are adequately resourced, particularly through the expansion and development of both the prison and social work workforces, there is a serious risk that the objectives of the Act relating to public protection will not be achieved in practice.

Notes

1 This and other documents relating to the 2006 Bill can be located at: http://www.scottish.parliament.uk/business/bills/80-custsentwea/index.htm, accessed 15 December 2006.

2 The average daily population in Scottish prisons in 2004/05 was 6,779, the highest annual level ever recorded. The average daily female prison population was 332 in 2004/05, also the highest annual level ever recorded. Prison population projections prepared in October 2005 show that the average daily prison population is projected to increase to 7,900 by 2014/15. Long-term prisoners (including life sentences) account for a small proportion (6 per cent) of total receptions, but a very substantial proportion (nearly half) of the total daily prisoner population (Scottish Executive 2005f).

3 Details of the stage 1 scrutiny of the Bill can be found at: http://www.scottish.parliament.uk/business/committees/justice2/index.htm

4 The term 'community integration plan' has been adopted for those prisoners who are not subject to statutory supervision and the term 'pre-release plan' is used for those who are subject to statutory supervision.

5 The 2005 Act (section 15) introduced further amendments to the 1993 Act in relation to short-term prisoners. Sex offenders sentenced to six months or more who are subject to the notification requirements of Part 2 of the Sexual Offences Act 2003 will be released on licence until the expiry sentence, unless otherwise revoked (section 1AA of the 1993 Act).

6 For details of the Risk Management Authority see: http://www.rmascotland.org/home.aspx

7 For details of the Violence Reduction Unit see: www.actiononviolence.com

Part III
Towards Effective Practice

7. Offender management or change management?

. . . offenders are not best served by a system in which they are conceived as 'portable entities', and in which staff are obliged to engage in a 'pass-the-parcel' style of supervision. (Robinson 2005: 312)

Introduction

Chapters 4 to 6 explored the main features of the legal context of criminal justice social work in Scotland. Although that context is critically important in framing the duties, rights and powers of criminal justice social workers, in many respects it leaves open the question of precisely *how* social work practice should be structured and delivered so as to achieve its intended purposes. In this third part of the book therefore, we aim to address that question, returning to the challenge outlined in Chapter 3 concerning the development of practices that can effectively support desistance.

We begin the discussion in this chapter by looking more broadly at the task of the case manager (or 'offender manager') in supporting the process of change as a whole. The title of the chapter is intended to signal our unease about the term offender management. Though the term is useful in encompassing work with offenders serving community penalties, those in prison and those who have been released, for us it sends several unhelpful signals. First, it suggests that the offender is a problem to be managed rather than a person in need of advice, guidance and assistance and also a key resource in the change process. Second, it suggests that the practitioner's task is essentially technical, rather than possessing a moral element. Third, it has a pessimistic tone, suggesting that offenders can be managed or controlled so as to mitigate risks, but perhaps not engaged in change processes that actively reduce risks, meet needs and exploit strengths. The complexity of responding effectively to the needs and deeds of reoffenders does inevitably create a management *task* for workers who must weave together the several threads of an intervention in any given case. However, the point of that weaving together is to provide a coherent intervention that delivers a strong and reliable 'pull' towards desistance, some of the features of which are inescapably about the *moral* legitimacy of the worker's influence over the offender. For this reason, we prefer to describe the focus of this chapter as *change management* rather than offender management or case management.

Drawing on the evidence reviewed in Chapter 3 and on a recent review of the skills required to reduce reoffending (McNeill *et al.* 2005), the chapter is structured around the key stages of the process of intervention. It begins by briefly discussing engagement, assessment and planning, before moving on to a fuller discussion of case management itself.

Engagement: building relationships that support change

It is clear from the psychotherapy and counselling literatures (reviewed in McNeill *et al.* 2005) that the relationship between the 'therapist' and the 'client' is a critical factor in effective interventions in relation to psychosocial problems in general. It is the basis for learning about and gaining the cooperation of the client, and for matching and modifying interventions to suit the individual person. Building effective relationships is, in turn, underpinned by the practitioner's ability to develop and use strong communication, counselling and interpersonal skills. Indeed, these skills are critical to each part of the process of intervention discussed below.

The 'core conditions' of effective psychosocial interventions relate to the ability of practitioners to convey accurate empathy, respect, warmth and 'therapeutic genuineness'; to establish a working alliance based on mutual understanding and agreement about the nature and purpose of the treatment; and to develop an approach that is person-centred or collaborative (Hubble *et al.* 1999; Lambert and Ogles 2004). The literature on the working alliance in particular stresses agreement on goals, agreement that the tasks involved will lead to the achievement of these goals, and the existence of a bond of mutual respect and trust (Bordin 1979). More recently, the core correctional practices (or CCPs) identified in the 'what works?' literature (Dowden and Andrews 2004) suggest that key features of effective practice with offenders include the quality of the interpersonal relationship, the effective use of authority, anti-criminal (or pro-social) modelling and reinforcement, problem-solving, and use of community resources.

The desistance literature more generally recognises that desistance from crime is characterised by ambivalence and vacillation and that, therefore, the ability to foster and sustain motivation is critical to effective work with offenders (Burnett 1992; Burnett and Maruna 2004). This underlines the significance of the skills associated with motivational interviewing in particular, an approach to which we return in the next chapter. Desistance is also an active process and one in which agency (that is, the ability to exercise choice and manage one's own life) is 'discovered' (McNeill 2006; Maruna 2001). This necessitates approaches to supervision that are active and participative and that seek to maximise involvement and collaboration.

The desistance literature also highlights the need to establish relationships within which attempts to positively influence the offender carry *moral legitimacy* (from the offender's perspective). This again underlines the need for the worker's authority to be exercised in a manner that is clear, explicit and fair. It also points to the importance of offering practical help to offenders since this is a vital expression of concern for them *as people*, as well as demonstrating an awareness of their social reality (Burnett and McNeill 2005). Such concern lends credibility to attempts to influence behaviour. A wider body of research attests to the fact that people tend to internalise and thus sustain changes in their behaviour when their compliance with attempts to influence them is based on normative as well as calculative grounds (reviewed in Bottoms 2001). It is for this reason that change-based approaches to reducing reoffending are a necessary adjunct to and corrective for more control-based approaches. While change-based strategies are somewhat uncertain in their effects and inevitably insecure in the short-term public protection that they offer, control-based strategies are only as effective as the technology on which they rely (for example, the security of a prison or the reliable monitoring of an electronic tag's signal) and last only as long as the control is sustained (see McCulloch and McNeill 2007, forthcoming). In other words, the slower process of winning people over by example, by persistence and by persuasion, is in the longer term more effective than mere rewards or threats.

It is clear, therefore, that paying adequate attention to the relational aspects of practice with offenders, and to the skills through which effective relationships are developed, is a necessary (but not a sufficient) condition of effective practice. Little can be achieved within any method of intervention unless practitioners can establish the right kinds of relationships with offenders, despite the challenges that the legal context provides in this regard, for example in relation to compulsory post-release supervision (see Chapter 6). Working to establish consent (albeit constrained consent) to the process of rehabilitative intervention is, of course, also a requirement of ethical practice.

Assessing risks, needs and strengths

The extensive literature about the development, use and limitations of risk and needs assessment is beyond the scope of this chapter. Robinson (2003) provides a recent and succinct summary of approaches to risk assessment in working with offenders. Given the focus on delivering 'defensible' risk assessments (that is, those that can stand up to scrutiny when things go wrong), issues of quality, consistency, reliability and accuracy have come to the fore in risk assessment practice and, in consequence, one of the key debates has been about the relative merits of 'clinical' and 'actuarial' methods. Whereas clinical approaches (or 'first generation' risk assessment) rely on the professional knowledge, skills and experience of individual practitioners, actuarial approaches (or 'second generation' risk assessment) derive from statistical calculations of probability correlating specific risk factors with reconviction data. As a result of the serious limitations of both approaches, 'third generation' approaches to risk assessment have been developed which include attention to 'dynamic' (or changeable) risk factors. Though no better at predicting what specific offenders will actually do, third generation risk/needs assessment tools have the advantage of highlighting specific criminogenic needs, thus (to an extent) individualising risk assessment in order to guide practice without compromising the (already limited) predictive validity of such tools. However, as Robinson (2003) suggests, such third generation instruments generate their own set of issues and problems. These include the demands which their increased complexity make on workers' time, sometimes leading to 'completion fatigue'; related dilemmas in balancing comprehensiveness and predictive accuracy with usefulness and brevity; the reintroduction of elements of professional judgement and related issues of consistency and bias; and concerns about the ability of such tools (derived largely from research involving white males) to accommodate and respect diversity and difference *vis-à-vis* gender and ethnicity in assessing risk.

A further issue, at present, is that it appears that current risk assessment instruments have limited usefulness with respect to arguably the most difficult area of risk assessment: assessing the *risk of serious harm* (Raynor *et al.* 2000). This is concerned not only with the probability of an event occurring, but with the anticipated severity of its impact. With this in mind, and recognising the risks of discriminatory biases in all forms of risk assessment, Tuddenham (2000) argues for and outlines a model of 'reflexive risk assessment' within which practitioners recognise that their knowledge is emergent, tenuous and open to revision; that definitions and discussions about risk are contestable and culturally relative; and that risk assessment functions within certain policy contexts and within a society increasingly preoccupied with risk and its prediction. Reflexive risk assessors need to retain awareness of their own potential for denial of risk; they need to retain the ability to 'ask the unaskable, think the unthinkable, imagine the unimaginable' (Prins 1999: 137). They must encourage and enable offenders 'to say difficult things by asking the right questions; and then hear what the offender wants to tells them, giving the latter confidence that the worker can tolerate the answers' (Tuddenham 2000: 180). With Tuddenham's insights in mind, it is obvious that the quality of the relationship between the worker and the offender will be a critical factor in determining the effectiveness of the assessment; in the absence of sufficient trust between worker and offender, it is highly unlikely that the information on which accurate risk assessment depends can be gathered. In this context, the serious hindrance that high workloads (particularly in relation to social enquiry reports, as seen in Chapter 4) present to the establishment of such relationships should not be underestimated.

This relational aspect of risk assessment and the complexities of and necessity for reflexivity in the process imply the need for a very high degree of professional skill (and specialist training). They also suggest a need to look beyond the qualities of the assessment tools being deployed and to look at the ways in which they are used. One recent study in Manitoba in Canada has explored how probation officers use risk-needs assessments to formulate their case plans and how they manage their cases (Bonta *et al.* 2004). The results showed that the development of intervention plans was based more on what the court mandated than what the offender assessment indicated. As a result, addressing the offender's criminogenic needs in supervision was not as common as expected. Probation officers did engage in behaviours that have been associated with positive behavioural change (for example, pro-social modelling) but more effective practice could have been expected.

More generally, though well-designed instruments are useful in assessment work, the desistance literature also underlines the important part that the qualities and skills of the worker play in developing the relationships within which information is gathered and analysed. Certainly, one of the recurring messages from the desistance research reviewed in Chapter 3 is that practice must be thoroughly individualised. The age and gender-related differences in both persistence and desistance and the significance of the subjective meanings of events and changes for those involved attest to the need for practice that sensitively and thoughtfully individualises the management of the change process. This need is unsurprising since, although there are certain commonalities, for example among young people involved in persistent offending, the categorisation of their characteristics, needs and deeds in large-scale studies tends to conceal their differences (McNeill and Batchelor 2002) and, as we noted in Chapter 2, developmental criminologists now stress the highly differentiated way that risk factors play out in the unique personal social contexts of each individual's life course (Laub and Sampson 2003). It follows that employing styles of assessment, case management and direct practice that value and exploit that diversity seems necessary. Where risk and needs assessment instruments can properly underpin change management by informing thorough and properly argued professional analyses, and where they include resources for engaging people in the process, they can assist in enhancing the quality, credibility and consistency of individualised assessments.

McNeill has argued elsewhere (2003) in relation to the implications of desistance research for assessment practice, that being desistance focused requires an exploration, in partnership with the offender, of each of three

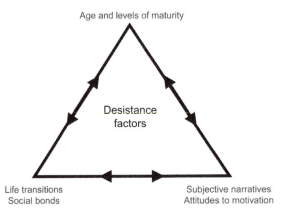

Figure 7.1 Constructing desistance

discrete areas: their levels of maturity; their personal history and current social circumstances; and their narratives around change, motivation, views and attitudes. In each of the three areas, the worker and the probationer would work to make explicit how, in what ways and to what extents the three factors would serve to support or hinder desistance.

Taking the narrative, subjective aspects of desistance as an example, both Burnett's (1992, 2000) findings about attitudes, motivation and desistance and Prochaska's familiar model of change (1982) suggest the need to assess and understand at which stage of the change process workers encounter individuals. The appropriate practical strategies (and the measures of effectiveness employed) would differ depending on whether the work is with 'pre-contemplative' or 'contemplative' individuals as opposed to those who are ready for action in securing change or requiring assistance to prevent or address relapse (McNeill 2000).

Once the three points of the triangle had been explored, the more complex and important task, in the second stage of the assessment, would be elaborating the interrelationships between the three areas (represented by the arrows in Figure 7.1). If there were consonance between the three areas such that all are 'pulling together' in the direction of desistance, then a reinforcing support plan might be relatively straightforward to construct. If all aspects were consonant in the direction of continued offending, by contrast, this would suggest both implications for risk assessment and, if community supervision were appropriate, the need for an intensive and multifaceted intervention. If, as is perhaps likely in most cases, there were some dissonance within and between the three areas, then the task becomes one of reinforcing the 'positives' and challenging the 'negatives'.

Hence, for example, an offender might have secured work and shown some signs of seeking to reconstruct his or her identity through that work, but may seem to lack the personal maturity required to sustain the employment in the meantime. In such a case, the focus of support might be on strategies aimed at accelerating the maturing process (perhaps via motivational work, pro-social modelling, cognitive techniques or problem-solving). Similarly, an offender might have formed a positive relationship with a supportive partner who discourages offending, but remain wedded to aspects of his or her identity as an offender (perhaps within a peer group). In such a case, the worker might work with both partners to build on the strengths of the relationship (reinforcing its pull towards desistance), while working with the offender on issues of motivation, identity and dissociating from the peer group.

Research-based planning and delivery of interventions

The planning of effective interventions should follow from effective assessment practice. Essentially planning (or design) involves the development and continuous review of strategies for change. If assessment requires the development of clear understandings both of the reasons for the offending behaviour (criminogenic needs) and of the available resources within and around the offender to address it (desistance factors), then planning should rest on the development of credible and testable theories of change. In other words, the question becomes: on the basis of the best available research evidence, what do we (the practitioner and the offender) think might best promote the reduction of reoffending in this situation? The planning process thus articulates the core rationale of the intervention: why do we think that doing what we propose to do will bring about the results that we want to achieve? Arguably, this is the logical step that is most commonly neglected in practice (Bonta *et al.* 2004). One reason for this neglect may be that the centralising aspects of 'what works?' have, via processes of accreditation, imposed a generalised and homogenous theory of change at the strategic level, rather than encouraging the development of heterogeneous theories of change, allowing for more subtle and nuanced applications, at the level of individual cases. The evidence reviewed above suggests that, though well intentioned, this method of developing effectiveness is incapable of adequately responding to the individual complexities that practitioners face (McNeill 2001).

The development of individualised theories of or strategies for change, properly conceived and conducted, represents a considerable challenge for practitioners. The skills required include not just the ability to seek, secure and evaluate information from a wide variety of people and sources but also the ability to bring a wide range of theory and research to bear on the information gleaned. Furthermore, it is necessary, as far as is possible, to engage in this kind of theory/practice integration in partnership with the offender. This partnership is critical because however good the 'theory of change' may be, its implementation in practice will fall flat unless the offender recognises its relevance, appropriateness and viability.

Given the range of risk and needs factors that characterise reoffenders, it is clear that strategies for reducing reoffending are likely to involve multisystemic, multimodal interventions; that is, interventions that work in a variety of ways to address a variety of issues (see Chapters 8 and 9). Thus a truly multi systemic intervention might involve, for example, individual work (whether in a group setting or one to one) to develop problem-solving and cognitive skills and to address other personal problems; family work to develop positive relationships capable of supporting desistance; work to encourage either changes within an 'anti-social' peer group or to facilitate withdrawal from the group; advocacy work to access resources to address disadvantages located within the local environment; and work to challenge social structures and attitudes that impede the inclusion of ex-offenders. Evidently, the degree to which practitioners focus on working in and through each system should depend on individualised (and criminologically informed) assessments of risks, needs and strengths and on practical judgements concerning where the most effective degree of positive change can be achieved (see McNeill 2000). However, as we will see in Chapter 9, the emphasis on the significance of social capital in the process of desistance makes clear that intervention plans are likely to include strategies for developing social opportunities as well as individual motivation and capacities.

Whatever the type and level of the intervention, at a practical level change planning also requires the ability, in partnership with the offender, to set specific targets for the work. These targets should be such as to allow the practitioner and the offender to know whether or not the enactment of the plan is delivering the intended outcomes. The review process can then be based on clear evidence that informs thoughtful analysis concerning whether the theory of change is holding good and, where it is not, it should allow the practitioner and the offender to explore whether this is because the theory is flawed or because of other factors. This iterative process then permits the continuous revision of assessment, theories of change and action plans in pursuit of the desired outcomes.

Case management: managing change

Case management cannot easily be made into a simple process. If interventions are likely to be multimodal and multisystemic, and may involve several personnel within the agency and outside it, then the practical difficulties of maintaining sufficient integrity across the different aspects of the supervision process are likely to be considerable. Moreover, implementing complex plans with people who are usually reluctant, often damaged and sometimes dangerous in order to achieve multiple objectives (some of which are in tension with one another) will always be a challenge.

The term case management does not describe a single way of working, but rather a family of related approaches in which resources somehow follow assessments of risks and needs. Nonetheless, the concept is generally of one lead person who is responsible for deciding how the organisation will go about meeting its objectives in relation to a single service user. That person is responsible for ensuring that arrangements are in place to deliver a plan, but other people, often from different organisations, are required to deliver specific inputs to achieve some of the identified and measurable objectives.

Partridge's (2004) recent review of case management practices in England and Wales provides a useful reference point in this regard. Three main models of case management were identified as operating in practice: 'generic', 'specialist' and 'hybrid'. Each model had different benefits for different stakeholders – including senior management, practitioners and offenders. Partridge's (2004) study highlights the choices that have to be made about balancing different priorities.

Generic models

For senior management generic models (that is, those models in which staff retained a mixed caseload) offered greatest flexibility, particularly where staff resources were limited or spread across a rural or geographically dispersed area. For operational staff, working with a mixed caseload of offenders seemed to enhance staff motivation by supporting continuity of contact with the same offenders which enabled them to see the impact of their work; by avoiding fears about deskilling associated with carrying out only one set of tasks; by ensuring staff retained a knowledge and overview of the various supervision stages and processes of working with offenders; and by minimising the stress associated with the intensive demands of working solely with offenders at high risk of harm.

Specialist models

Separating out different case management functions across different teams provided advantages for senior management in coordinating service delivery and targeting resources at specific offender groups. It also allowed specialist resources to be focused on key supervision stages, particularly with high risk of harm offenders. Benefits included monitoring the delivery of service priorities and national standards, due to enhanced accountability resulting from smaller teams with specific aims; creating efficiency gains by allowing staff to concentrate on specific case management functions; and developing skills and expertise in particular subjects and types of offenders.

Specialist models equally showed drawbacks. By separating tasks and responsibilities into discrete functions, resource-intensive boundary management issues were sometimes created, requiring negotiation about when responsibility should be transferred between teams. Some staff became territorial about their specific functions, reducing the flexible sharing of resources across teams and the focus on the overall aims of the probation area. Boundaries also created communication barriers; the greater the level of task separation and fragmentation in a model, the more offenders seemed confused by the range of different staff they saw at different stages of their supervision and about who was overseeing their order and who to contact if they experienced a crisis. This fragmentation was most apparent in the specialist models where poor attendance and poor completion of orders seemed to be associated with higher staff turnover.

Offenders were more likely to build trust with their case manager, address their problems and ask for help if they saw the same person over a period of time, particularly during the initial stages. The local context in which a model operated also seemed to have a large impact on what type of model was feasible and how successfully it was implemented. Important local factors include geography, availability of staff resources at different grades, availability of voluntary and statutory agency provision, staff turnover and caseload size.

Hybrid models
While it is an ideal for one supervisor to oversee an offender throughout their entire community supervision, this is often impractical due to resource issues and staff turnover. Hybrid models varied in their balance between generic and specialist elements. They attempted to maximise continuity of contact by adopting a more integrated team approach, where at least one team member knew what was happening to an offender at each stage and was able to update other team members. The expectation was that hybrid approaches would help alleviate some of the effects of staff turnover, shortages and sickness absences by allowing offenders to have regular contact with a small team of people aware of their circumstances and creating a consistent, familiar and support-ive environment for them to learn, be motivated and complete their order. In a team setting, the named case managers were typically identified as having 'ultimate' responsibility for assessment, progress, enforcement action and overall integration of the order. However, other team members, including probation service officers and administrators, were fully utilised.

Whichever model is adopted, several core case management principles emerged from Partridge's (2004) research as enhancing engagement:

• Models need to acknowledge offenders' experiences and needs.

• Continuity of contact with the same case manager and other staff was essential to building confidence and rapport with the offender, particularly during the initial stages of supervision.

• The greater the level of task separation, the more offenders were confused by why they were undertaking different elements of their supervision, particularly where contact with the case manager had been limited.

- Face-to-face contact with a small case management team was beneficial for both staff and offenders.

- Openness, flexibility and support were key motivating factors for offenders – exemplified by three-way meetings between case managers, practitioners and offenders and where case managers attended initial meetings as offenders moved.

This evidence (which seems consistent with emerging messages from desistance studies) suggests that any service is likely to ensure a better focus on effective practices if it is able to put individual case management at the centre of a holistic service. Some clear, although not necessarily very new, messages emerge about managing effective change with people who offend through a 'human service' approach: developing a single concept of implementation where key stages are mapped on an end-to-end process where case management binds them together into a coherent whole; fostering differentiated approaches, enabling different resources and styles to be matched to different cases; enabling one case manager to implement one plan; and developing variable forms of teamwork and organisational support for the core process of case management.

Though specific models of case management or offender management have yet to be developed for and in Scotland, in England and Wales the National Offender Management Model (NOMM) splits case management into three main elements: offender 'management', offender 'supervision' and offender 'administration' (NOMS 2005). Management at the level of individual cases is the process in which the legal authority of the order or sentence is vested (cf. '... management being management with a view to reducing reoffending', Management of Offenders (Scotland) Act 2005: s.3(d)). It gives the sentence its direction, order, pace and shape, and implies a collaborative, not authoritarian, form of responsibility. Supervision can be described as the sequence of day-to-day, face-to-face tasks and activities which will be required in most cases to secure compliance, generate motivation and achieve cohesion of the plan. Administration is the implementation of service standards and procedures and will be required to meet objectives. Though the NOMM suggests a clear separation between offender management and offender supervision, it may be that if the key elements of the process become too disaggregated, the risks of it going wrong are increased (cf. Maguire and Raynor 2006).

Indeed, contemporary commentators in England and Wales have noted that the shift from generic practice (where the caseworker manages and delivers all aspects of the intervention) towards more specialist practice (where case management and programme delivery functions are typically split) has been one of the most significant changes in probation work in the last decade. Robinson and Dignan (2004), for example, review the shift from generic casework to case management to a fragmented style of offender management in which staff increasingly occupy specialist roles and offenders encounter a variety of staff in the process of supervision. Reflecting on existing research, they argue that offenders are not best served by a system in which they are conceived as 'portable entities', and in which staff are obliged to engage in a 'pass-the-parcel' style of supervision (see also Robinson 2005).

The research evidence that we reviewed above (particularly in Chapter 3), specifically its consistent and compelling message about the importance of the relational aspects of effective practice, would tend to support Robinson and Dignan's (2004) conclusion that the task of managing interventions so as to promote and sustain desistance is not an administrative one; it makes better sense to conceive of the case manager's role as being 'therapeutic', at least in the sense of being an active part of the change process rather than merely a coordinator of services. In reviewing the implications of research on models of case management for effective probation practice, Holt (2000) identifies four overlapping features of case management:

- **Consistency** is a vital ingredient of seamless service delivery. It allows the worker to promote and reinforce effective learning (perhaps from structured programmes) by providing opportunities to exercise new skills; to put theory into practice. Consistency also provides an essential element of the positive working relationships that, as we have seen above, are critical in order to support and enhance motivation to change.

- **Continuity** across all aspects of the intervention and over time is necessary if the intervention is to be meaningful and productive for the offender. The case manager needs to ensure that the offender experiences supervision as an integrated holistic process; a key part of achieving this integration is likely to be the provision of one stable and supportive relationship throughout the duration of the supervision experience.

- **Consolidation** of the learning is achieved when the case manager allows the offender to reflect upon the learning achieved in the different aspects of supervision. This involves enabling the offender to make connections across all aspects of the process; to join up the learning. However, consolidating the learning also requires accessing opportunities for community reintegration, where the offender's strengths can be employed and confirmed.

- **Commitment** of the case manager to the offender and to the supervision process is essential in promoting desistance. This commitment creates stability in the delivery of the intervention and provides a 'holding context for change'.

A fifth feature, to which we have alluded occasionally above, needs to be added to this model of case management given the criminal justice context;

that is, the management of **compliance**. In recent years, a stronger focus on the enforcement of community penalties has emerged, particularly (but not exclusively) where community penalties have been recast as 'punishment in the community'. This recasting of purpose has increased the existing need for effective enforcement in order that courts regard community penalties as credible disposals. Though the language of 'enforcement' implies an emphasis on ensuring the meaningfulness and inevitability of sanctions in the event of non-compliance, Bottoms (2001) has argued convincingly that attempts to encourage or require compliance in the criminal justice system must creatively mix constraint-based mechanisms (those that somehow restrict the offender), instrumental mechanisms (related to incentives and disincentives) and normative mechanisms (related to beliefs, attachments and perceptions of legitimacy). What should be clear from Chapter 3 and from this brief discussion is that, through the establishment of effective relationships, the case manager's role in supporting compliance is likely to be particularly crucial to the development of these normative mechanisms. It is only within relationships of the kind discussed above that the formal authority conferred on the worker by the court is likely to be regarded as *legitimate* by the offender. This legitimacy is likely to be a crucial factor in preventing breach by persuading offenders to comply.

However, the success of case management at the individual level depends on the existence of the local strategic partnerships and pathways that allow the case manager to access and coordinate the required services and resources. Even the best designed, best implemented and most research-based individual case plan will fail if the case manager cannot access the services and resources required to implement it (Robinson and Dignan 2004). Similarly, the best developed approach to securing compliance will fail unless organisational arrangements exist that underpin the worker's legitimate authority by delivering swift and proportionate responses that reward compliance and deal effectively with non-compliance.

Conclusions: what works and who works

Though much more could be said about the case manager's roles, tasks and skills in assessment, planning, delivery, monitoring and evaluation of change processes, this is perhaps a suitable place to end this chapter. Summarising our discussion Figure 7.2 indicates how effective relationships lie at the crux of effective supervision processes (though it signally fails to capture the wide range of related supervision tasks and challenges to which we turn in the next two chapters). The supervision process begins with the establishment of relationships and the effectiveness of every subsequent part of the process will depend in part on the quality of relationships, though good relationships alone will not be enough to bring about change. In other words, although we

155

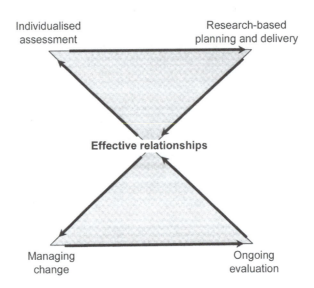

Individualised assessment

Research-based planning and delivery

Effective relationships

Managing change

Ongoing evaluation

Figure 7.2 The supervision process (McNeill *et al.* 2005)

can conceive of the ability to build and utilise relationships as a discrete aspect of intervention in its own right, in fact it underpins each of the other aspects of the supervision process. Whether we look to the latest versions of the 'what works?' research, to the psychotherapy literature or to the desistance research, similar messages emerge. The accumulated weight of evidence, coming from studies that start with quite different assumptions and using very different methodological approaches, drives us towards recognition that relationships are at least as critical in reducing reoffending as programme content.

Clearly, if the individualised and relational interventions required to support desistance need to be multidimensional, then the skills required to deliver them will be similarly broad-ranging. Crucially, the business of reducing reoffending by *supporting change* involves a range of skills that goes far beyond those involved in reducing reoffending by *imposing control*, monitoring or enforcement, important though these measures are. What is required is a complex mix of skills which require significant personal qualities as well as a high degree of training across a range of therapeutic, academic and management disciplines in order that one worker is able to draw together approaches that address various areas of an offender's life so as to coherently and consistently support the change process. It seems to us that, within the criminal justice context at least, social work almost exclusively encapsulates this broad skill base with its holistic attention to the full spectrum of an individual's needs in his or her social context. The development of effective services to reduce reoffending in Scotland therefore requires political and professional investment in equipping the relevant front-line staff with the key skills required for effective practice and in creating the contexts for practice that provide them with realistic opportunities to exercise these skills.

Of course, it is not just practitioners who need motivation, capacities (or skills) and opportunities (or resources) to be effective. Casework theories have long suggested that in order for change processes (like desistance) to occur, the same three conditions need to be present for those who are doing the changing (see, for example, Ripple *et al*. 1964). In other words, offenders need *motivation* to change, *capacity* to be and to act differently and *opportunities* to do so. With this trio of requirements in mind, the next chapter focuses primarily on the role of change programmes in developing offenders' 'human capital' (that is, their *motivation, capacities*, knowledge, skills and personal resources) and Chapter 9 examines the issue of developing social capital (that is, the social networks and relationships within families and wider communities that can create and support *opportunities* for change).

8. Developing human capital

. . . physical capital is created by changes in materials to form tools that facilitate
'production'; human capital is created by changes in people that create the skills
and capabilities that make them able to act in new ways and to do new things.
(Coleman 1990: 302)

Introduction

This chapter seeks to explore how supervision can develop 'human capital';
that is, how it might develop the motivation, skills, resources and qualities *of*
the individual that he or she might need to develop and deploy in the process
of desistance. Though the language of desistance and human capital might
be unfamiliar to some readers, few criminal justice social workers or
probation officers will be unfamiliar with the discourses of and literatures
about 'evidence-based practice' and 'what works?' in reducing reoffending
(for example, Chapman and Hough 1998; McGuire 1995). In many respects,
as we argue below, much of the 'what works?' literature is (implicitly at least)
about the development of human capital. Indeed, some of the literature has
been criticised for being overly preoccupied with human capital and
negligent with regard to the role of *social* capital in desistance (Farrall 2002)
and as a consequence for presenting a naive model of social integration (Mair
2004). Though, as we discussed in Chapter 3, we tend to agree with these
criticisms, in fact it is far from simple (and probably unwise) to separate
human and social capital. Rather, as we will see in the course of the next two
chapters, both in theory and in practice there are complex interrelationships
and interdependencies between the two.

The challenge facing practitioners and managers is to find ways, creatively
but cogently, to combine evidence from research with the art of building a
meaningful working alliance with offenders in order to maximise the
potential of well-directed supervision. Achieving high-quality ('fit for purpose') delivery of such supervision continues to challenge all jurisdictions
(Underdown 1998). Despite the widespread dissemination and discussion of
the 'what works?' literature in recent years, some commentators stress the

lack of strong research evidence in the UK in general about what constitutes effective community supervision (Mair 2004; Kendall 2004). Critics argue that recent emphases on structured programme approaches, particularly those using cognitive and cognitive-behavioural techniques, focus too much on deficits rather than on an individual's strengths, capacities and readiness to change and that effective community provision should be more holistic and socially situated, involving a wide range of focused activities and provision intended to assist individuals to direct their lives in ways that lead to better social integration and desistance. While recognising that there is indeed much more to reducing reoffending than working with individuals to change their attitudes and behaviours, the focus of this chapter is on the development of individuals' motivation, skills and resources; that is, on developing their 'human capital'. The chapter begins by discussing the concept of human capital itself, before considering motivation and 'readiness to change' and then the role of structured programmes in developing offenders' skills. Nonetheless, the discussion leads us inevitably back to the question of social capital, to which we turn in the following chapter.

Human capital

The concept of human capital broadly relates to the personal skills, capacities and knowledge that individuals possess and which, in ordinary circumstances, facilitate access to education, employment and other valued social goods and resources. It is argued that just as physical capital is created by changes in materials to form the tools that facilitate 'production', human capital is created by changes in people that create the skills and capabilities that make them able to act in new ways and to do new things (Coleman 1990). Thus human capital facilitates productive activity and as a result can promote the sense of self-efficacy which is generally recognised as a key quality in successful personal change. If physical capital is wholly tangible, human capital is much less so, being embodied in the skills and knowledge acquired by an individual. As we will see in the next chapter, when allied to social capital it manifests itself in the social relationships, opportunities and networks that exist among and between people. Both social capital in the family and social capital in the community play roles in the creation of human capital.

Coleman defines capital as a 'productive' investment making possible the achievement of certain ends that would not be attainable in its absence. The concept captures the ambition of many social work practitioners in trying to ensure that supervision is both productive and invests meaningfully in the individual for their benefit and for the benefit of the community at large. The concept also stresses the importance of the *mutuality* of the 'investment', which modern management theory refers to as 'co-production'. Co-production takes place when some of the investment used to produce a service is contributed by individuals who are the 'clients' or 'recipients' of the service (Ostrom 1997: 86). The key to a human capital approach then is that the distinction between service provider and user is not rigid and the success of any 'investment' is likely to rely on the provision of services through a sustained relationship between agent/worker and recipient/user, where both make substantial contributions. Applied to human service, power and authority are, consequently, shared between the supervisor and the individual (though not necessarily equally) as an effective means of achieving a dynamic process and mutually beneficial outcomes for participants.

Motivation and readiness to change

One of the most consistent findings related to ending a criminal career is that those who do so have to somehow develop the ability and resolve to overcome problems and obstacles to change. Those trying to make the transition from a criminal to a non-criminal lifestyle often comment on the impact of the stigma of the past on future possibilities. Maruna (2001) and Farrall (2002, 2004a) have commented on impediments and obstacles to desistance experienced by individuals; such obstacles include problems with alcohol and drugs, financial difficulties, problems getting work, other social problems and personal issues including changing associations and relationships with families and friends.

In facing these obstacles or problems, having motivation to avoid further offending is an important factor in enabling change and desistance. Factors that might influence positive motivation and orientation include, for example, the desire to avoid negative consequences; realising that legitimate financial gains outweigh criminal gains; wanting to lead a quieter life; and embarking on a committed personal relationship. As we saw in Chapter 3, Burnett (1992, 1996) found that people who wanted to stop offending, and believed that they could, were more likely to achieve this outcome than those who were unsure. More recently Farrall (2002, 2004a) has described similar outcomes and distinguished between those who see themselves as confident, optimistic or pessimistic about their prospects, with the 'confidents' in his study having the shortest criminal careers (around five years), whereas 'optimists' and 'pessimists' have longer criminal careers (six and over years). Notably, fewer of the 'confidents' faced obstacles in their lives, while half of the 'optimists' and most of the 'pessimists' did. The ability to overcome these obstacles requires personal abilities and human skills, and even for pessimists with many obstacles, attempting to overcome them remained important to successful outcomes. Social and personal circumstances linked to positive life chances were strongly associated with better outcomes, emphasising the interplay between motivation, overcoming obstacles and social circumstances.

These and other research findings suggest that a key role for practitioners is to help individuals identify obstacles to change and to develop the confidence and capacity to take the necessary steps to overcome them, where they can. Farrall (2002, 2004a) found clear evidence that where obstacles to desistance were overcome by probationers, this appeared to be more closely associated with the offender's own motivation and the supportiveness of their social context rather than with direct interventions by probation officers (for example, to challenge attitudes and improve thinking skills). He recognises, however, that 'indirect work' by probation staff (typically work to support offenders in improving their family relationships and their access to employment) did assist some probationers in overcoming obstacles to desistance. If having a strong sense of self-direction, self-control and self-efficacy is essential for successful outcomes then maximising the opportunities for people to take decisions and make the changes they can *for themselves* is clearly important. However, for those with long-standing difficulties, it is hard to imagine that they would feel able to effect significant change in their lives without some sort of influence, leverage, direction, new learning and new opportunity supported by a meaningful working alliance with their supervisor. Effective practice seems likely therefore to involve effective co-production of change, intended to give users a sense of their own success.

In practice, supervision will almost always be about more than building relationships and encouraging motivation, but without motivation and supportive social and personal circumstances, change is less likely to occur. It is this configuration of elements that characterises the concept of 'readiness to change'; a concept which implies more than simply willingness or ambition. Poor motivation before the start of a programme and post-programme is often associated with poor outcomes (as we will see below). People are rarely totally motivated to do something. In general, part of them wants change and part of them feels that change is too difficult, that it will take too long or that it will not be worth the effort. They may feel very motivated one day and less motivated on the next. In seeking to develop motivation, Miller (1983) observed that if a worker advises someone what to do they are likely to find reasons why the advice is not relevant or will not work, and as they hear themselves do so, they will come to believe that the advice is wrong. People therefore have to be helped to find *their own reasons* for change. In this regard, the insights to be gleaned from the literature concerning motivational interviewing, non-directive person-centred counselling, responsivity and pro-social modelling are of particular value.[1]

Motivational interviewing

The approach of motivational interviewing (MI) is now so much a part of work with offenders in the UK that it might not always be appreciated that this is an import from the mental health/substance use field. Because work with people who have problems with substance use is characterised by poor attendance rates and high 'dropout' rates, practitioners have come to see eliciting client motivation as part of their job' (Harper and Hardy 2000). The work of Mary McMurran and colleagues in particular has been helpful in developing similar motivational approaches for work with offenders (McMurran 2004).

The concept of motivational interviewing was introduced by William Miller and Stephen Rollnick, who remain the leading authorities on the subject (Miller and Rollnick 2002). They define MI as a directive, client-centered counselling style for eliciting behavior change by helping clients to explore and resolve ambivalence (Rollnick and Miller 1995). The adjective 'directive' here refers to the approach being focused on the problem and goal-directed; it does not denote that the practitioner should direct the 'client' in an authoritarian or expert manner. On the contrary, a 'quiet and eliciting' counselling style is essential to MI, and the *spirit* of the approach is distinguished from the *techniques*. The rationale for the approach is that ambivalence about the problem behaviour, and a lack of motivation to change it, is commonly at the root of intervention failure. It is this ambivalence or lack of resolve that is the principal obstacle to be overcome.

MI makes use of reflective listening (similar to accurate empathy as operationalised by Carl Rogers) in helping clients to focus on their problems and think about possible solutions. The approach actively *discourages* direct persuasion and advice; arguing that the person needs to change; diagnostic labelling; a punitive or coercive manner; a didactic, expert stance which leaves the client in a passive role; or behaving in a punitive or coercive manner. All of these would be seen as contrary to motivational interviewing and violating its spirit. Instead, MI emphasises the personal responsibility of the client to decide whether they have a problem that needs to be addressed. It is also person-centred (see below) in that a premium is placed on the agency and perspective of the client, with the practitioner's role being that of facilitating the client's articulation of both sides of the ambivalence impasse (Rollnick and Miller 1995). In other words, counsellors are encouraged to use a negotiation method where the clients themselves identify and analyse the pros and cons of their behaviour. By enabling this articulation of what is at stake, the practitioner aims to 'tip the balance' between the perceived positive and negative consequences of the targeted behaviour. Other techniques of MI include eliciting self-motivational statements; providing choice with a variety of alternative change strategies; goal-setting; role-playing; and modelling.

When motivational interviewing works, it involves a sudden shift in how the person perceives the pros and cons of the behaviour and is as though one or more cons have suddenly become dramatically more salient (Miller 1998). MI complements another import from the mental health field that has been adopted in work with offenders: Prochaska *et al.*'s (1984) model of change. MI aims to move the client from the earlier stages of 'pre-contemplation' and 'contemplation' in this model of change to the more advanced stages of 'preparation', 'action' and 'maintenance'.

Person-centred approaches

An important review of outcome research in psychotherapy and counselling concluded that a major operational variable in successful outcomes is the intentional utilisation of the client's frame of reference. The investigators produced a guide for working with 'impossible cases', otherwise referred to as 'heartsink' cases and 'therapy veterans' (Duncan *et al.* 1997). These are long-term clients who do not respond to intervention and whose problems continue or get worse. The main message of this guide is that the key to making progress is for the practitioner to identify and use the client's frame of reference and worldview, and to bring into play the client's own informal 'theory of change'. An underlying premise is that clients themselves know what needs to be done to address their problems, and that practitioners should draw out these insights. In achieving this, clients are to be treated as 'co-therapists', rather than as cases to be managed with a pre-formulated plan. The client's motivation should be honoured, and the client needs to feel that the practitioner sees them as someone with potential and worth. Such an approach taps into what is broadly referred to as a 'person-centred approach'.

The person-centred approach, first introduced by Carl Rogers in 1940, is by no means new to probation services but, in England and Wales at least, became discredited as part of the move away from social work and towards more punitive and directed programme-based approaches (see Burnett and McNeill 2005). Person-centred approaches by definition are focused on clients' own perspectives and concerns, enabling relational engagement as the basis of assisting them and influencing change (Mearns 2003). Clients are related to as individuals rather than as representatives of a type or a label – as people rather than offenders. Person-centred planning (PCP) is again finding its way into criminal justice practice from mental health and disability practice as a more generally applicable method of understanding how knowledge and skill are created and shared that puts learning in the context of social engagement and social inclusion (Wenger 1998). A common misunderstanding is that practitioners of PCP have to like their clients and do not question them, challenge them or hold them to account for their behaviour or, in a criminal justice context, for the requirements of their order. However, in criminal justice practice a clear distinction is made between what a person experiences and how they behave: the former is 'unconditionally valued' but not the latter, and a practitioner, without being critical, will often convey to a client their own feelings in response to how a client has behaved and its consequences for them and others.

Person-centred approaches can be either directive or non-directive, although purists would argue that person-centred planning and counselling is essentially non-directive because it involves engaging with the experiences of the client and becoming a 'fellow traveller' (Cooper 2004) or being 'beside' the client (Mearns 2003). This is in contrast to motivational interviewing which is explicitly 'directive', in the sense of being focused and goal oriented, albeit still person centred. There is some evidence that a non-directive approach may be more effective with reluctant, involuntary clients. This is particularly relevant to work with offenders who, as noted by Marshall and Serran (2004: 315), are typically a 'difficult population to work with at least partly because they are often defensive and oppositional'. Offenders are also likely to have ambivalent feelings about whether they should change or whether they are able to achieve change (Burnett 2004). As such, they are likely to be less cooperative, and less responsive to directive approaches. Person-centred work emphasises that practitioners should find ways of challenging clients that do not involve criticising them or undermining their sense of self-worth. Again, a distinction is made between being 'beside' the client and being 'on the side of the client' (Mearns 2003). As in the criminal justice field, person-centred counsellors have experience of working with some particularly difficult or fragile clients, including those who 'dissociate' or separate themselves from others, perhaps following abuse in childhood or traumatic adult experiences (Prouty *et al.* 2002).

Structured programme approaches

It seems therefore that motivation and readiness to change are multifaceted concepts; moreover they can be developed in different ways with different people. In making decisions about suitability for intervention programmes, an apparent lack of motivation is not in itself a reason for screening people out of community intervention but is, rather, a reason for good programme preparation. Burnett (2004) reported that those most motivated were often less entrenched in criminal careers and criminal associations; this may, of course, reflect lower risks. Those presenting medium to high risks, in contrast, were likely to be more entrenched in their behaviour and attitudes and less motivated to change. Maturity and 'timing' are much harder issues to tackle. As we saw in Chapters 3 and 7, an important factor for consideration by practitioners is whether people are at a point in their lives when they are willing to consider change. Effective supervision involves using interpersonal processes to assist individuals to change, reshape or modify what they think, feel and do, by showing interest and concern, and by using techniques of reflective listening, interpreting, summarising, modelling and coaching.

Encouraging self-efficacy and mobilising intrinsic motivation is crucial to changing the hearts and minds of individuals. The analysis of motivation can be applied to hope, self-efficacy, perceptions, attitudes and other 'within person' variables, all of which are dynamic (changeable) and can be influenced in the course of interpersonal exchanges. However, while the development of motivation or readiness to change represents the generation of an essential form of human capital in any change process, being motivated to change will not be sufficient in itself. The repertoire of skills and personal resources required to enable desistance is likely to extend further and to include new ways of thinking, behaving and problem-solving. It is in this connection that structured programme work has experienced its recent revival and it is to this form of intervention that we now turn.

The Scottish Accreditation Panel for Offender Programmes (which covers both prisons and criminal justice social work) has set demanding standards for the accreditation of structured programmes, in particular for the professional rigour and the substantial resources required to work systematically with those considered to present medium to high risk of reoffending. Structured programmes are, of course, very difficult to deliver in groupwork form in many of Scotland's rural and semi-rural settings and resources are not always evenly available across a wide geographical spread. Even those who strongly support structured programme approaches point out that while the principles on which they have been designed have strong empirical foundations, the provisions of programmes in themselves do not automatically produce successful, widespread and long-lasting outcomes (Hollin *et al.* 2004). Most commentators recognise that practice remains at an early stage in terms of the development of identifiable service pathways to success in supporting desistance.

Reviews of research during the 1960s and 1970s, such as Lipton, Martinson and Wilks (1975), proved inconclusive as to effects on reoffending and fed the view that 'nothing works' in terms of changing criminal behaviour (Martinson 1974). Many commentators challenged this conclusion arguing that it was not that social intervention programmes had no potential to reduce reoffending, simply that it was impossible to draw firm conclusions from the research because the methodologies were so often inadequate that few studies warranted unequivocal interpretations about their effectiveness. Equally the programmes studied were often so poorly implemented and delivered that they could not reasonably be expected to have a positive impact – a warning for practitioners today. Martinson (1979: 245) himself from the 1980s onwards subsequently rejected the 'nothing works' conclusion. Statistical techniques in meta-analysis – a technique for encoding, analysing and summarising quantitative findings from aggregated study findings – have brought optimism back into the debate and have provided practitioners and policy-makers with promising leads and direction in the challenging work of helping young people and adults reduce their offending.

Much of the evidence influencing the structured programme agenda comes from meta-analyses undertaken mainly in North America (for example,

Andrews *et al.* 1990; Sherman *et al.* 1997) alongside a growing number of studies in the UK (Hollin *et al.* 2002; McMahon *et al.* 2004) and Europe (Bergman 2002). While there remains some debate about the effectiveness of social interventions (see Lab and Whitehead 1990), literature reviews have routinely found since the 1950s that between 47 per cent and 86 per cent of better controlled evaluation studies report positive effects on reoffending (Andrews *et al.* 1990). Garrett (1985) surveyed 111 experimental studies carried out between 1960 and 1983, incorporating a total of more than 13,000 offenders, and found a significant overall effect of intervention on a variety of outcomes including reoffending. She concluded that 'the change was modest in some cases, substantial in others, but overwhelmingly in a positive direction' (Garrett 1985: 293). The most powerful practice approaches were cognitive-behavioural, life skills, and family work.

Gendreau and Ross similarly carried out a series of detailed literature reviews (1979, 1981) on studies between 1971 and 1981 and further reviewed over 300 studies published between 1981 and 1987 (Gendreau and Ross 1987). These provided evidence that 'reduction in recidivism, sometimes as substantial as 80 per cent, had been achieved in a considerable number of well controlled studies' (Gendreau and Ross 1987: 350) and they concluded that 'the principles underlying effective rehabilitation generalise across far too many intervention strategies and offender samples to be dismissed as trivial' (Gendreau and Ross 1987: 395).

In a meta-analysis examining predictors of adult reoffending, Gendreau, Little and Goggen (1996) found that factors such as anti-social cognitions, values and behaviours, along with factors such as criminal history, age, gender and race were the strongest predictors of reoffending. Andrews and Bonta (1998: 42–3) argued that these sets of risk/need factors were very robust across various types of subjects (differentiated by sex, gender, age and ethnicity) and across methodological variables (such as self-report vs. recorded crime; longitudinal vs. cross-sectional designs). They concluded that the 'Big Four' risk predictors were anti-social attitudes (including values, beliefs, rationalisations, cognitive states); anti-social associates (including parents, siblings, peers and others); a history of anti-social behaviour (early involvement, habits, perceptions of criminal ability), and anti-social personality.

Lipsey's review (1992), based on 397 experimental outcome studies published between 1970 and 1988, involving 40,000 young offenders, found that 65 per cent of the experiments examined showed positive effects in reducing reoffending. The evidence indicated that type of intervention was important to successful outcomes. Behavioural, skills-oriented approaches, and especially combinations of approaches ('multi-modal'), had the most impact. Deterrence or 'shock' approaches were associated with negative outcomes compared with control groups. When all types of programmes and outcomes were combined, reoffending averaged 9 per cent to 12 per cent lower than for control groups. For 'multi-modal', behavioural and skill-oriented approaches, the reoffending rate was 20 per cent to 32 per cent lower than for control groups. While this may not appear large, given the volume of research carried out, it is scarcely compatible with the proposition that 'nothing works'.

Beyond the average effect size, detailed findings of meta-analytic reviews are complex and beyond the scope of this discussion. However, the mean effect size conceals wide variations and many studies have suggested much larger reductions in reoffending rates. More generally, some clear trends emerge from the research concerning the *content* of intervention programmes with higher and lower levels of effectiveness in reducing offending, in changing attitudes, boosting self-esteem, in developing skills for making better decision-making, for resisting pressures to commit offences and for self-management (Gendreau and Ross 1987; Andrews *et al.* 1990; Lipsey 1992). Andrews and colleagues concluded that 'this pattern of results strongly supports exploration of the idea that some service programs are working with at least some offenders under some circumstances' (Andrews *et al.* 1990a: 374).

Some types of intervention seem less suitable for *general* use; for example, *unstructured* 'counselling', often the mainstay of service provision in the past, may provide some support and fulfil certain monitoring requirements, but it is unlikely to assist a person to change his or her behaviour. Similarly programmes that were long term in nature and frequently employed psychotherapy or group therapy approaches were typically ineffective (McGuire 1995). However, there is evidence to suggest that well-structured person-centred counselling may be effective with more serious offenders (Lipsey 1995).

There is no single way of helping an individual offender change his or her behaviour, and precise knowledge about which methods seem to work best with specific kinds of offending remains limited. Nonetheless, common findings provide direction for addressing the question of 'what works?'. In effect they provide a 'curriculum' for educational activity that can be used with many types of offenders and should play a major part in providing effective services in the criminal justice system. Effective programme intervention is likely to combine work with individuals, with families and significant others and with groups; the most successful approaches offer scope for the involvement of significant family members in the decision-making and supervision process.

Programme-based intervention – that is, structured and planned socio-educational programmes, particularly those which focus on behaviour change and skill development – has been found to be more effective than less structured approaches. According to Andrews *et al.* (1990), effectiveness appears greatest where there is:

- A focus on the nature and consequences of the offending behaviour.

- An emphasis on problem solving and behaviour change, cognitive development, personal or social skills.

- Diversity of methods of intervention.

- Use of positive authority.

- An emphasis on community integration.

Andrews *et al.* (1990) first suggested that the most effective forms of intervention conform to a series of broad principles later summarised by McGuire (1995). First, the level of service provided should match the level of 'risk' assessed; where the risk of reoffending is high, more intensive programmes are likely to be required (*the risk principle*). Second, only some factors contribute to, or are supportive of, offending; the focus of intervention should be on addressing offending by alleviating those factors that sustain and support criminality (*criminogenic need principle*). Third, the learning styles of people involved in offending vary but in general they require active rather than didactic 'programmes' (*responsivity principle*). Meta-analysis on studies of interventions with women offenders suggest that general responsivity factors seem to apply but there may be specific responsivity factors that need to be recognised and addressed (Dowden and Andrews 1999). Fourth, programmes in the community fare better than those in institutions (*community-based principle*). Fifth, effective interventions recognise the variety of problems experienced by people who offend, and therefore employ a skills-oriented approach, using methods drawn from behavioural, cognitive, or cognitive-behavioural (multimodal) sources (*modality principle*). Sixth, effective interventions connect the methods used to the aims stated, are carried out by appropriately trained and supported staff, are adequately resourced, and plan monitoring and evaluation from the outset (*programme integrity principle*).

Implementing structured programmes: lessons from England and Wales

In some respects, these effectiveness principles now seem uncontroversial. More often than not the principal contention/conclusion might be summarised thus: to say that 'nothing works' is erroneous given that the evidence suggests that some things 'work' with some people some of the time. Much more research is required with regard to the specific details before the question mark can be removed from the 'what works?' title and to the direction provided. However, such a cautious and considered approach seems to have been less evident in the drive to engineer 'what works?' principles into probation and youth justice practice in England and Wales (see Bateman and Pitts 2005; McNeill 2004a, 2004b; Mair 2004). Critical commentators have argued that the resultant preoccupation with standardised risk/needs assessments and programmes in delivering effective practice has led to a bureaucratic rather than human service approach to practice.

In many respects the desistance research reviewed in Chapter 3 has provided an important counterpoint to the dominant discourse of 'what works?', though it is possible to overstate the differences between the two bodies of work and to miss the synergies (see Maruna 2001; McCulloch 2005). Perhaps the most important and telling reason why desistance studies based on narrative methodologies (like Maruna's study) offer such a challenge to contemporary policy and practice is that they are based on *listening to* offenders and *respecting* them as people with important stories to tell. It seems significant in this regard that the favoured methodology of effectiveness research is the randomised control trial, in which those undergoing intervention 'often described as 'treatment') are too easily cast as mere *objects* on whom programmes work (in some kind of vacuum) rather than as complex human *subjects* (situated in similarly complex social contexts) that emerge from the Maruna's (2001) rich and robust narrative methodology.

The objectification of programme participants in some treatment research creates practical problems for those seeking to develop effective services. Pre-eminent among these problems in the National Probation Service for England and Wales is what has come to be termed 'scalability' (Carter 2004); that is, the difficulty of turning the small-scale successes of pioneering programmes into effective standardised practices in large-scale public bureaucracies. Neglect of the qualitative evidence offered in offenders' narratives about their change processes (and thus of the diversity of their experiences) might be among the reasons for this. Arguably, underlying the problem of scalability is a misconception about the relative importance of programmes and processes in developing effective practice. Though broad generalisations about effective programmes were undeniably historically necessary in challenging the pessimism that 'nothing works', they too readily lent themselves to a managerialised and homogenising approach to intervention that has predictably struggled to cope with the heterogeneity of offenders to which practitioners must respond on a case-by-case basis. Even at their best, 'what works?' studies tend only to address questions about which types of rehabilitative programme seem to work better than others in which contexts and with which particular target groups. While these are important questions, they can conceal a flawed underlying assumption: that it is only the qualities of the *programme* that are at the core of the pursuit of effectiveness. That said, even within the 'what works?' literature, it is now possible to find strong evidence that challenges this assumption. One authoritative recent review, for example, highlights the increasing attention that is being paid to the need for professional staff to use interpersonal skills, to exercise some discretion in their interventions, to take diversity among participants into account, and to look at how the broader service context can best support effective practice (Raynor 2004a: 201).

169

Despite these more nuanced appreciations of the findings of so-called 'treatment' research, the most influential single finding from existing research on effective intervention remains the reported efficacy of cognitive-behavioural methods, which address the connection between thinking, feeling and doing as a means of preparing people for change. Intervention approaches showing greatest promise and consistency of positive effects and outcomes tend to draw on social learning theory and to adopt cognitive-behavioural methods *alongside others*, to improve problem identification and problem resolution skills, which are then applied to the identification and establishment of alternative positive solutions.

Accredited general offending programmes such as Constructs (developed and accredited in Scotland), Reason and Rehabilitation (developed in Canada but used widely in the UK) and Think First (developed and accredited in England and Wales) tend to be skills based. The underlying assumption is that these approaches may accelerate the maturing process and assist the abandonment of criminal activities; an assumption that fits, in some respects, with findings from criminal career research about impulsivity and poor abstract reasoning among persistent offenders (Farrington 1997). However, perhaps for some of the reasons discussed above, recently published outcomes drawn from rigorously conducted reconviction studies in England and Wales have proven disappointing in their early findings and suggest that we are unlikely to see the major impact on reoffending rates suggested by the 'what works?' literature; at least until and unless accredited programmes run alongside better integrated and more holistic service provision (Hollin *et al.* 2004; Raynor 2004b).

Although these evaluations are recent and (in some cases) ongoing, the published data highlight a number of important issues for practice. The Think First cognitive-behavioural programme in England and Wales (Roberts 2004) identified three groups of respondents readily recognisable to practitioners: 'non-starters', who were assessed as being suitable for the programme but did not attend any of the sessions; 'non-completers', who attended one or more group work sessions but did not complete the programme; and 'completers', who attended sufficiently for the programme to have an impact of some sort. The first very practical lesson for practitioners and managers which emerged as researchers struggled to distinguish non-completers from non-starters was that despite the statutory requirements for attendance, the recording of compliance and completion was poor. Completion rates were very low at only 29 per cent; 42 per cent of the offenders were non-starters; and around half of the non-completers had withdrawn by session four (of 22 sessions). This has major implications for the offenders themselves, notwithstanding the waste of professional resources lined up on the assumption of attendance.

Reconviction rates for completers were significantly better than for non-completers. At 12 months, reconviction rates showed completers were less likely than non-completers to be reconvicted (44 per cent versus 77 per cent), while 74 per cent of non-starters were reconvicted within the same period. Though these findings may be partly the result of selection effects (whereby the completers would have done better irrespective of the programme because they were apparently more motivated to change), they also reinforce long-standing non-intervention principles which suggest that inadequate amounts or poor-quality intervention may be more harmful than none. While design and delivery issues have a part to play in these difficulties, the findings stress the importance of helping people participate in and complete supervision programmes. This in turn emphasises the importance of engaging effectively with offenders (as discussed above) and supporting 'readiness to change' through developing motivation and preparing people for programme work. Not surprisingly, research also highlights structural and systemic issues beyond the control of individual supervisors, in particular the difficulty of losing people to custody.

In addition to the problems referred to above, there are a range of possible reasons for the disappointing impact of programmes in the UK to date. In the first evaluation of the Basic Skills Pathfinder in England and Wales, the number of starters and completers was so small that little useful outcome data could be collected. The Community Service Pathfinder produced significant gains in addressing criminal attitudes and self-reported skills development, but few differences in outcome measures against comparison areas (Rex 2004). The Resettlement Pathfinders for short-term prisoners (Lewis et al. 2003a) also showed a number of implementation problems – getting off to a slow start and failing to meet target numbers – but with some success in the take-up of post-release assistance and significant positive change in criminal attitudes and self-reported problems. What worked best appeared to be a combination of facilitating access to resources relevant to prisoners' needs and taking some steps to address their thinking and motivation (Maguire and Raynor 2006).

Not withstanding the various methodological and implementation issues at play, none of the pathfinders showed a dramatic reduction in offending among those who participated (Hollin et al. 2004). Merrington and Stanley (2004: 17–18) suggest that from the published data 'it is still too early to say what works, what doesn't and what is promising'. Nonetheless, some characteristics are emerging from studies which can assist practitioners identify those individuals more likely to fail to engage or complete programmes of supervision and to identify those areas that are likely to require specific attention in the preparation phase of supervision.

Completers were more likely to be older, to be able to cope in groups, to have better communication and problem-solving skills, to have experienced fewer practical obstacles, to have had more supportive influences, to be more likely to be in employment and to be well motivated (Burnett and Roberts 2004). This presents something of a conundrum and a very real challenge for practitioners. The evidence suggests that those with less entrenched criminal attitudes, fewer criminal associates, limited experience of custody or breach and greater willingness to consider desistance are most likely to complete programmes successfully. People with these existing human 'qualities' are likely to be assessed or considered as at low risk of reoffending in any case and may well be low priority for expensive structured programmes. It is those who do not possess these characteristics (or this 'human capital') who are more likely to be assessed as presenting greatest risk and who need the programmes most. The challenge is obvious. Those *most likely* to be assessed as suitable for and requiring programmed interventions may be, at the same time, those *least likely* to comply and complete – at least without very careful preparation and sustained effort from their supervisors throughout the programme. A key factor in achieving better outcomes is getting people through the whole programme of supervision (Burnett and Roberts 2004).

These findings, therefore, underline the message of the preceding chapters: that good engagement and the development of effective working relationships is a necessary prerequisite to programme work. Structured programmes have to operate alongside the establishment of a meaningful working alliance to support the probationer in committing to and sustaining structured work throughout a programme. Practical steps often need to be taken to assist people to attend. The message from research, as well as from national standards, is that non-attendance needs to be responded to swiftly and every possible step taken to engage and re-engage people. If the wider safety needs of the community are to be met, good assessment and planning work is required to address a wide range of issues that might undermine programme attendance and completion, particularly in the early phases of community supervision as identified by national standards.

Responsivity and learning styles

Workers need different skills for working with different client groups and settings and many writers recommend a flexibility of approach that is tailored to the individual's problems and characteristics. This point resonates with the 'principle of responsivity' (Andrews *et al.* 1990; Andrews and Bonta 2003) which stresses the importance of providing a type of service that is matched not only to criminogenic need but also to the learning capacity, attributes and the circumstances of the person; that is, a service that will assist individuals to acquire essential human capital. In social educational terms, 'learning styles' have been described as qualitative differences between individuals – their habits, preferences and orientation towards learning (Klein 2003: 46).

Effective practitioners need to respond flexibly to offenders and need different skills for different people in different settings (Norcross 2002). While many aspects of the principles of effective practice (see McGuire 1995, and above) have been explored in further research, the notion of responsivity and the importance of learning styles have not been subjected to a similar level of critical and empirical analysis. Some studies have highlighted the importance of action learning, role-playing and skills-based work (including outdoor work) as effective approaches to learning (Lipsey 1992; Home Office 2000).

The literature provides support for the constructive role that learning style models (for example Kolb 1984; Honey and Mumford 2000) can offer in shaping criminal justice interventions to assist individual development and foster a sense of engagement within sessions between practitioners and offenders (Annison 2006). This may offer some scope to addressing the problems of compliance and attrition (discussed above). However, the notion of 'matching' intervention to learning styles (as advocated by Gendreau 1996) is not straightforward. Educational studies have found little evidence that matching an individual to a specific category of learning style in itself improves academic performance (Klein 2003; Coffield et al. 2004).

Learning style frameworks can be seen to offer the potential to open up a genuine sense of dialogue in work with offenders about how they can learn best and how their own learning can be enhanced. In this respect Coffield et al. (2004) suggest that all the advantages claimed for meta-cognition (that is, being aware of one's own thought and learning processes) can be gained by encouraging learners to become knowledgeable about their own learning as well as that of others.

While the concepts of responsivity and learning style allow for a degree of generalisation about the matching of risk and need to key resources, services and approaches, issues of diversity (particularly in terms of gender, ethnicity and age) remain important (Shaw and Hannah-Moffat 2004). There are inevitably challenges and tensions as practice adopts more structured approaches to intervention with a wide range of offenders but nonetheless struggles to respond to differences in learning needs, learning styles, levels of engagement and motivation (Hopkinson and Rex 2003).

Generally, research indicates that 'highly resistant' clients respond better if there is minimal directiveness, whereas directness and explicit guidance is appropriate for those with 'low resistance'. For example, Patterson and Forgatch (1985) found that non-compliance increased when practitioners used directive behaviours such as attempts to teach and confront. Miller and Rollnick (2002) advocate a respectful and supportive stance for use in motivational interviewing. When clients are hostile or resistant, a way through is more likely to be achieved by listening and reflecting on what they say rather than being assertive or pushing expertise or focusing on difficult issues too early. In contrast, Marshall and Serran (2004) found that in work with sex offenders, empathy, warmth, rewardingness and directiveness significantly influenced behaviour changes among the offenders, though they emphasise that directiveness involved suggesting rather than telling the offender what to do.

Pro-social modelling

Pro-social modelling has gained currency in recent years as part of accreditation criteria for effective delivery of intervention programmes. While there are many commentaries, there is, as yet, limited UK research on what constitutes effective pro-social modelling. Perhaps the best-known model of intervention focused on the supervisory relationship, rather than on the features of a given intervention programme, is that developed in Australia by Chris Trotter (1999, 2006). The central principles of Trotter's *pro-social modelling* approach include:

- **Role clarification:** Involves frequent and open discussions about roles, purposes, expectations, the use of authority, negotiable and non-negotiable aspects of intervention and confidentiality.

- **Pro-social modelling and reinforcement:** Involves the identification, reward and modelling of behaviours to be promoted and the identification, discouragement and confrontation of behaviours to be changed.

- **Problem-solving:** Involves the survey, ranking and exploration of problems, goal-setting and contracting, the development of strategies and ongoing monitoring.

- **Relationship:** Involves the worker being open and honest, empathic, able to challenge and not minimise rationalisations, non-blaming, optimistic, able to articulate the client's and family members' feelings and problems, using appropriate self-disclosure and humour.

Trotter's (1996) empirical research tested the hypotheses (formed on the basis of earlier research for example, Andrews and Kiessling 1980) that clients of probation officers who made use of these core practices would be more likely to experience reductions in their problems and would be less likely to offend. Trotter trained 12 probation officers in the approach and followed up 104 of their clients. He compared the outcomes for this experimental group with outcomes for a control group of 157 probation clients. Clients in the experimental group were subsequently significantly more likely to report that their problems were reduced and their reoffence rates were also significantly lower than those in the control group. The use of pro-social modelling was most consistently, strongly and significantly correlated with lower offence and imprisonment rates. The model was *most* effective with young, high-risk, violent and drug-using offenders.

Despite the familiarity of the core practices described above, Trotter's work is important for three reasons. First, although it would be possible to conceive of pro-social modelling as a form of individualised programme, it is perhaps better described as a style of or approach to practice, focused on certain key skills and core practices. He demonstrates therefore that we can conceive of styles and approaches and not merely specific programmes as being evidence-based and effective. Second, Trotter's research directs attention to workers' qualities as well as being about the characteristics of specific programmes. In this regard, Trotter (2000) has also produced evidence to suggest that among staff working in community corrections in Australia, those with a social work background were more likely than those with other occupational backgrounds and qualifications to learn and make use of pro-social modelling and, in turn, to produce lower rates of reconviction. In line with Rex's (1999) findings (discussed in Chapter 3), Trotter suggests that this might be about possession of the social work skills and qualities required to achieve genuinely collaborative problem-solving. The third reason for the importance of Trotter's model is that, perhaps by accident, through its focus on effective relationships and processes, it represents work at the interface of the rehabilitation and desistance literatures and attests to the value of exploring this interface.

Conclusion: a human capital approach

There are clearly risks in focusing exclusively on human capital when working with people who have experienced multiple social disadvantage and exclusion (Farrall 2002) or who have perpetrated serious and violent offences. However, social capital can be most effectively utilised only when the individual also has positive individual resources, particularly social attitudes and skills that can support or resist criminality. Traditional social casework has always been concerned about the interplay between human and social capital, more often cast as the interplay between the person and his or her environment (see Biestek 1961).

More generally, programmes for offenders make little coherent sense unless they are embedded within locally defined responses to individual need (Petersilia 1990; Rumgay 2000). The division between offence-focused, person-focused and community-focused priorities is often artificial and not necessarily helpful to practitioners. Rumgay (2000) suggests that adopting a concept of 'minimisation of harm' can help overcome any conflict that may seem to exist between the needs of the community or victim and those of the offender. The expectation of a more dynamic and holistic approach to intervention is outlined in the Scottish standards (SWSG, 1991b). Offence-focused programmes should be located alongside other activities aimed at building the human capital necessary to participate effectively in programmes themselves, and located within a more integrated intervention plan which covers all the bases associated with non-completion and failure to desist. To ensure ongoing reinforcement of learning from programmes and more integrated objectives for supervision, strategic case management is essential with effective arrangements for ensuring active collaboration with other community agencies and protocols for liaison. Rumgay (2000) cautions, however, that it is important to avoid the risk of utilising community-based services as a form of pseudo 'penal' services or law enforcement agencies rather than as agencies that can help individuals, in their own right, acquire both human and social capital and to move towards a better sense of community and social integration. It is almost impossible for individual supervisors to achieve such a comprehensive approach to supervision without the existence of good strategic planning and of suitable service pathways to respond to the range of needs and risks presented by this client group. This requires a broad community enterprise and strategic approach to service planning, just as is envisaged by the location of Community Justice Authorities as part of mainstream local authority provision in Scotland.

Adopting social learning methods that help individuals acquire human capital or skills while providing assistance in applying them to real social situations looks the most promising approach to developing a strong sense of self efficacy and supporting human agency and personal responsibility. Normative processes play an important part in people's movement away from crime and a common theme is of getting out of crime because they acquire 'something to lose' whether through the investment they have made, for example, a partner, self-respect or personal achievements (see Devlin and Turney 1999). Evidently, if the (pro-social) world apparently has little to offer a person with a criminal record or, for example, with a long history of drug misuse, then its appeal will seem highly limited. It is for this reason that working to develop human capital must be connected to working to develop social capital. It is to this challenge that we now turn.

Note

1 The brief summaries of these three literatures which follow are drawn from McNeill *et al.* (2005) but the material was prepared by Ros Burnett. We are grateful to her for her permission to use it here.

9. Developing social capital

To the extent that felons belong to a distinct class or status group, the problems of desistance from crime and reintegration into civil society can be interpreted as problems of mobility – moving felons from a stigmatized status as outsiders to full democratic participation as stakeholders. (Uggen et al. 2006: 283)

Introduction

This chapter is about the role that criminal justice social work services might play in developing the social capital of those with whom they work and of the communities in which they work. As we have said, by social capital we mean essentially the social networks and relationships within families and wider communities that can create and support opportunities for change. The emphasis in Scottish legislation on the primary duty of social work services to 'promote social welfare' (Social Work (Scotland) Act 1968, section 12) is to a large extent in keeping with emerging thinking on social capital, social integration and desistance. The supplement to the national standards (SWSG 1991b) explicitly identifies better social integration as an objective of criminal justice social work services. This is expressed diagrammatically in the 'triangle' which sets offence-focused and offence-directed work within a context of access to wider social provision and opportunity. While better integration has been an ambition of Scots policy and law for some time (see Chapter 1), data from recent national inspections[1] and from recent Scottish research (McCulloch 2005) would suggest that the reality of practice is some distance away from this ambition. It remains to be seen if the establishment of Community Justice Authorities will promote better partnership working aimed at assisting mainstream services in providing accessible services to offenders as part of their social welfare responsibilities. In terms of the policy at least, we have seen in Chapter 2 that 'bridging the opportunity gap' is certainly a key component of the strategic direction under the new national plan (Scottish Executive 2006d).

We argued (in Chapter 3) – following Farrall (2002, 2004b) – that developing social capital is central to the process of desistance. However, social capital is a somewhat elastic concept and it is necessary to examine it briefly in order to begin to address more precisely *why and how* interventions might facilitate its development. To this end, this chapter begins with a short discussion of the concept of social capital before moving on to examine some of the evidence about the links between social capital, offending and desistance. We then examine some recent research on probation, social problems and social capital, before discussing four related areas in which services might need to work in order to support desistance.

Definitions of social capital

Field (2003) suggests that there are three key theorists of social capital, each of whose definitions of the concept varies in subtle ways. The French sociologist Pierre Bourdieu has famously developed and deployed the concepts of field, habitus and capital to explain how social practices are constructed in and through the relations within particular areas of social life. The three concepts are complex and interconnected but essentially a field is a 'site of struggle' in which various social actors compete over, contest and construct influence and power. Different social fields (for example, the related fields of sentencing and probation/social work) interact at their margins and these margins are also themselves 'sites of struggle' over territorial boundaries and authority. Habitus refers to the 'durable dispositions' that actors in a given field form as a result of their histories within the field; in other words, the habitus is constructed through the influence on the actor over time of the wider conditions in the field. Though the notion of habitus implies the taken for granted unreflective assumptions that shape and structure our practices, Bourdieu suggests that we are not always passive in this process and can be creative and inventive in developing tactics, games and strategies which enable us, within certain structural limits, to recognise and to resist the ways in which the field shapes us. Capital refers to the resources and assets within the field which actors struggle to acquire and on which they trade in pursuit of power and influence. Bourdieu distinguishes between economic capital, cultural capital, social capital and symbolic capital, although he stresses the interactions between them. Whereas economic capital refers to money and other material resources, cultural capital refers to resources acquired through education and socialisation (primarily particular forms of knowledge) and symbolic capital refers to resources linked to prestige, honour and distinction. Most important for present purposes, Bourdieu defines social capital as:

> ... the sum of resources, actual or virtual, that accrue to an individual or a group by virtue of possessing a durable network of more or less institutionalised relationships of mutual acquaintance or recognition. (Bourdieu and Wacquant 1992: 119)

As is perhaps already apparent, Bourdieu does not assume that social capital is benign; in fact, his numerous empirical studies (reviewed in Jenkins 1992) expose how the uneven distribution of social capital in various fields and in various societies is implicated in the maintenance of hierarchies and inequalities.

Though Bourdieu's social theory is widely respected, discussed and deployed, his ideas about social capital have been (regrettably perhaps) less influential than those of two American scholars – James Coleman and Robert Putnam. As we mentioned briefly in the last chapter, Coleman's work relates primarily to education; his studies of educational attainment have shown that, far from being limited to the powerful, social capital can provide a vital and productive resource for marginalised people (see Field 2003: 20–9). Reflecting his concern with education, Coleman defines social capital as:

> the set of resources that inhere in family relations and in community social organisation and that are useful for the cognitive or social development of a child or young person. These resources differ for different persons and can constitute an important advantage for children and adolescents in their development of human capital. (Coleman 1994: 300)

For Coleman, social capital is a public good that we nonetheless pursue self-interestedly; thus social capital provides a bridge between the interests of the individual and our collective interests. Moreover, the development of social capital is facilitated by 'closure' (meaning 'mutually reinforcing relations' between people); by stability and by shared ideologies. Our social relationships constitute resources for us in and through the established obligations, expectations, trustworthiness, communication channels, shared norms and so on that they provide. Essentially, social capital allows us to rely on one another. As the above quote suggests, Coleman's research led him to conclude that social capital was critical in enabling the development of human capital (the subject of our previous chapter); in sum, his studies suggested that, even when social class, ethnicity and other factors were taken into account, educational outcomes were better for children whose families had access to greater social capital (for a brief discussion, see Field 2003: 20–9). Thus while Bourdieu recognises the role that social capital plays in helping to maintain the position of the privileged (and, by implication, the role that lack of social capital plays in constraining the possibilities of the underprivileged), Coleman suggests that it has potential benefits for all social actors.

However, perhaps the most influential social capital theorist to date has been Robert Putnam – a political scientist. Putnam's (1993) initial interest was in the role of civic engagement in supporting both political stability and economic prosperity; an interest that he explored and developed by studying differences in regional administrations in north and south Italy (for a brief account see Field 2003: 29–40). This study led him to the following definition of social capital:

> Social capital here refers to features of social organisation, such as trust, norms and networks, that can improve the efficacy of society by facilitating coordinated actions. (Putnam 1993: 167)

However, both his articulation of the concept and the popularity of his work developed significantly when he turned his attention to an analysis of apparently declining social capital in the USA in his book *Bowling Alone* (Putnam 2000). In this more recent work he suggests that:

> the core idea in social capital theory is that social networks have value
> ... social contacts affect the productivity of individuals and groups ...
> [social capital refers] to connections amongst individuals – social networks and the norms of reciprocity and trustworthiness that arise from them. (Putnam 2000: 18–19)

For Putnam, then, social capital contributes to collective action; it makes it harder to defect or opt out of social responsibilities; it fosters norms of reciprocity; it enables information exchange (including information about reputations); and, most significantly, it enables efficacy and productivity. Its apparent decline (responsibility for which he attributes mainly to the rise of television, although he also stresses the busyness of modern life, the amount of time spent commuting and generational change) is therefore a matter of grave concern. Declining social capital both reflects and exacerbates declining civic engagement and trust. Fundamentally, it threatens social well-being and weakens democracy.

Recent contributions by Putnam (2000) and others (Lin 2001; Woolcock 2001) have further refined the concept by drawing important distinctions between bonding, bridging and linking social capital. 'Bonding social capital' denotes ties between people in similar circumstances (for example, families, close friends, neighbours). These ties are typically strong and often serve expressive purposes, though they also have instrumental uses and benefits. 'Bridging social capital' includes more distant ties (for example, acquaintances, loose friendships, relations with workmates). Though these ties are weaker, because they allow access to a wider range of people and resources they are particularly significant in serving certain instrumental purposes (such as, for example, job-seeking). 'Linking social capital' allows us to connect to people *unlike* ourselves in some senses; people perhaps in dissimilar social situations. Even more so than bridging social capital, this potentially enables access to a much wider range of resources, external to our own immediate community. Whereas bridging and bonding social capital can be thought of as 'horizontal' connections *within* social strata, linking social capital can include vertical linkages with others differently placed in social hierarchies.

Social capital, offending and desistance

In the context of his useful introductory text on social capital, Field (2003) provides a very brief account of the links between social capital, crime and deviancy. This account focuses mainly on North American studies (including Putnam 2000) that suggest an inverse relationship; where social capital is lower, crime tends to be higher. More specifically, he cites a Chicago-based study by Sampson and Raudenbush (1999) which links cohesion and shared expectations in the wider community with lower rates of crime and disorder. The wider literature (including UK and European sources) linking crime to theories of 'social disorganisation' and declining 'collective efficacy' has been reviewed extensively by Bottoms and Wiles (2002). Strong networks seem both to empower people in exercising informal social control over young people (Halpern 2001) and to assist young people in their integration into their wider communities (Kawachi et al. 1997).

But beyond recognising that social capital, community cohesion, shared values and collective efficacy in expressing those values might be correlated with lower crime rates, what might be some of the relationships between social capital and desistance from offending *at the individual level*? We argued in Chapter 3 that desistance resides somewhere in the interfaces between age and maturation, developing social bonds associated with certain life transitions and the subjective meanings that individuals attach to these bonds and transitions. This suggests at least three important questions about the links between social capital and desistance. First, is our access to social capital age-sensitive in some sense and, if so, might this be implicated in explaining offending and desistance? Second, what precisely are the relationships – at the individual level – between our social bonds, our social capital and our offending or non-offending? Third, how do our subjective perceptions about the relative value of our various social relationships and networks reflect and affect the types of social capital that we possess? These questions have only begun to be addressed (directly and indirectly) in criminological research in recent years, but some very recent studies have already provided some important insights.

In relation to the first question, Bottoms et al. (2004), in an important paper which sets out the theoretical underpinnings for an ongoing study of desistance, suggest that:

> it is well to remember that individuals' transition to adulthood is not simply biological, but takes place within structured social contexts, and in an earlier era was much more sudden than now ... Even by comparison with half a century ago, the transition to adulthood in Britain is now very different, given, for example, the rise in the school leaving age, many more people undertaking post-school education, radical changes in the job market for young adults, and altered assumptions about marriage. (Bottoms et al. 2004: 379)

Though we must await the findings of their study in this regard, Monica Barry's (2006) recent book, based on in-depth interviews undertaken with 20 young men and 20 young women in Scotland about their criminal careers, makes a strong case that offending and desistance are best understood as an age-related process of transition. She notes, for example, that for her sample the onset of offending typically occurred in childhood, was maintained throughout youth, and desistance arrived with adulthood. In her analysis (which draws extensively on Bourdieu's work) this pattern is explained in terms of the age and stage-related differences in her subjects' ability to accumulate and expend capital (economic, social, cultural and symbolic). She argues that the status of young people as 'liminal entities' (suspended between childhood and adulthood) is structurally constructed so that they (at least in particular social contexts) are denied the means to accumulate legitimate capital. They are therefore particularly vulnerable in this period to being drawn into offending in order to acquire some sort of status and respect within their peer groups. If Barry is correct, then the much reported elongation of the transition to adulthood (Newburn and Shiner 2005) might itself frustrate desistance – particularly for young people whose access to social capital is particularly limited.

Webster et al.'s (2006) recent longitudinal, qualitative study of youth transitions, criminal careers and desistance provides further evidence in this regard. They interviewed 185 young people aged 16–25 living in very deprived neighbourhoods in Teesside in 1999 and 2000.[2] Thirty-four of the original sample were reinterviewed in 2003. Webster et al. (2006) focus specifically on the changes in the social networks and social capital of the participants between the first and second interviews. The researchers noted that bonding social capital played a very significant role in helping people cope with life in poor communities but that they found very few examples of the participants acquiring new bridging social capital and with it access to new networks and new opportunities. Indeed, for those that were re-interviewed:

> ... coping with the problems thrown up by their various careers and transitions meant that their social networks had become smaller in scope, more focused on immediate family and friends and even more embedded in their immediate neighbourhoods. The geographic and social horizons of our interviewees, therefore, tended to be restricted to the places that they were from ... Our informants' lack of access to wider networks makes individual or collective social mobility unlikely. Seldom did their networks of family and friends provide the sort of social capital that might assist in transcending the limiting socio-economic conditions in which they lived. (Webster et al. 2006: 13)

The situation for the 12 recurrent offenders and/or dependent drug-users who were reinterviewed was worse still. For them, 'the earlier benefits that accrued from social networks became liabilities' (Webster *et al.* 2006: 13) in that their problematic behaviours were often associated with their marginalisation within their own communities (and sometimes within their own families). This damaged bonding social capital, allied to the lack of bridging capital, effectively forced them back into restrictive and destructive networks forged around their offending and/or drug use, frustrating any fledgling attempts to desist. In turn this produced an 'embedding' of the deeper disadvantage rooted in the area's long-term socio-economic decline (Hagan 1993).

These findings perhaps only begin to address our second and third questions about the relationships between desistance and social capital, social bonds and subjective perceptions of their significance. Nonetheless, the major implication is clear – at the individual level, without access to social capital, it may be very difficult indeed to embark upon and sustain a pathway towards desistance. In the Scottish context, this provisional conclusion resonates strongly with Houchin's (2005) study concerning the links between social deprivation and the geographic distribution of imprisonment in Scotland. It seems highly likely that the very population whose desistance criminal justice social work aims to sponsor will lack bridging and linking social capital and will be located primarily in communities in which disadvantage is deeply embedded. As we suggested in Chapter 2, this underlines the scale and complexity of the challenge that services face in attempting to reduce reoffending.

Probation, social problems and social capital

If social capital is largely a product of community organisation and community cohesion it might be suggested that it is beyond the reach of criminal justice social work services; indeed, it could be said that it is more a matter for those concerned with economic and social regeneration and with community development. While we would accept that the development of social capital is largely a matter for social rather than penal policy, this should not imply that criminal justice social work services (and Community Justice Authorities) should neglect its impact and its potential.

Indeed, Stephen Farrall's (2002, 2004b) recent work on probation and desistance (briefly discussed in Chapters 3 and 8) suggests quite the opposite. As we have seen, his findings attest to the importance – at the individual level – of 'indirect probation work' focused on relationships and employment (Farrall 2002) and – at the organisational level – of probation services actively investing in probationers' social capital (Farrall 2004b). More specifically, Farrall conceives of probation officers themselves as being potential links to or activators of social capital. He suggests that there is much that probation officers could achieve through working with probationers' *families of origin* (that is, their parents and siblings) in recognition of the fact that families may provide a key resource in desistance. While Webster *et al.*'s (2006) findings show how the family relationships (and the bonding social capital) of reoffenders are often disrupted and damaged, Farrall's point is that by seeking to repair and rebuild such relationships and with them access to the family's wider resources of practical and emotional support, desistance might be enabled. Moreover, following Laub *et al.* (1995), he also suggests that probation officers should work with probationers in relation to their *families of formation* (that is, their spouses or partners and children) and their attachments to the labour force. Enabling probationers to be better partners or spouses and parents is potentially important in that these ties may provide reasons to desist and resources for desistance. In relation to employment, Farrall (2004b) suggests that probation services should seek to actively develop the work prospects of probationers – not only through employability training (which aims to develop human capital) but also through job creation schemes and 'sheltered employment' opportunities (cf. Caddick 1994, Sarno *et al.* 2000).

Further theoretical and empirical support for these suggestions is provided in desistance studies which have focused more closely on the phenomenological aspects of the process (that is, how the process is experienced and interpreted by those involved). In this regard we discussed (in Chapters 3 and 8) Maruna's (2001) important analysis of the 'life scripts' of persisters and desisters. The most important point in this context is that the desisters' 'redemption scripts' are care-oriented, other-centred and focused on promoting the next generation. They are concerned with having something to show for one's life: rewards, respectability and recognition – all of which are linked to generative pursuits. McAdams and de St Aubin (1998: xx) define generativity as:

The concern for and commitment to promoting the next generation, manifested through parenting, teaching, mentoring, and generating products and outcomes that aim to benefit youth and foster the development and well-being of individuals and social systems that will outlive the self.

In terms of human development over the life course, Maruna (2001) argues that generativity develops at the time that delinquency dissipates; indeed, generative commitments fill a void, making criminality pointless or too risky. As we have already seen, this a theme that has also been taken up by Barry (2006). Although families of formation and employment represent the most obvious means by which we might achieve generativity, there are other possibilities. Uggen and Janikula (1999), for example, have explored the links between civic volunteering, pro-social socialisation and desistance. It may be that other less obvious forms of generativity can produce similar effects; consider, for example, the role of sculpture and writing in the Scottish desistance stories of Jimmy Boyle (1983, 1985) and Hugh Collins (1998, 2000).

For others, political activism and resistance to oppression might become a substitute for criminal activities. Analysing the links between generativity and desistance leads McNeill and Maruna (2007, forthcoming) to suggest that:

> If ... the justice system were to become an environment in which generative commitments were modelled and nurtured, and opportunities for generative activities were promoted and rewarded, it would be more effective at reducing reoffending. Put another way, if we want to encourage offenders to 'give up' crime, we would do well to create opportunities for them to engage in 'giving back.'

They go on to explore existing opportunities within probation and social work services. Evidently, community service has significant generative potential – though unlocking that potential depends very much on the way that it is conceived and constructed. Similarly, they argue that probation work itself should develop its generative potential by drawing on strengths-based approaches to social work (Saleebey 1997; Maruna and LeBel 2003) and moving beyond its current preoccupation with risks and needs. Indeed, McNeill and Maruna (2007, forthcoming) suggest:

> Whereas the former [strengths-based] approach recognises and requires the possibility of the reconstruction of a new generative identity, the latter [risk or needs-based] approach, by identifying the offender with his or her needs/risks/offending, runs the risk of unwittingly reinforcing the passivity and fatalism of the old identity.

However, McNeill and Maruna (2007, forthcoming) take the argument still further by arguing that generativity – like reintegration or reciprocity – is a two-way process. Not only must the ex-offender be willing to contribute, communities must be willing to accept and recognise those contributions and consequently reaccept the ex-offender. As they put it:

> 'Giving up' and 'giving back' will only make sense to offenders in social contexts within which they are offered the realistic prospect of 'getting back' (or perhaps enacting for the first time) their status as fully included citizens. Thus the challenges posed by taking the issue of generativity seriously direct interventions not only towards supporting the development of the individual but also towards developing the communities from which offenders come, to which they belong and for whom *ex*-offenders represent critical but neglected resources. (McNeill and Maruna 2007, forthcoming)

The related prescriptions of Laub *et al.* (1995), Farrall (2002, 2004b) and McNeill and Maruna (2007, forthcoming) are both interesting and challenging in that they in fact echo some of the well-established features of 'traditional' probation work (cf. Drakeford and Vanstone 1996): features that, perhaps because they have hitherto lacked strong empirical support, have been somewhat neglected of late in the pursuit of the 'what works?' programmes that were discussed in the previous chapter. In this regard, McCulloch's (2005) recent study of Scottish criminal justice social workers' and their probationers' views about tackling social problems in supervision provides some encouragement. Like the Scottish workers in Robinson and McNeill's (2004) study, the workers tended to feel that working to address social needs and social problems was a prerequisite of reducing reoffending. Whether through onward referral to other agencies, through direct work typically using task-centred, problem-solving approaches or through family work and home visits, they aimed to impact positively on such difficulties. For probationers, what was most helpful about their workers' support was the provision of an opportunity to talk about their problems, to receive advice and guidance and to be listened to. Rather than social workers directly resolving probationers' social difficulties, however, McCulloch (2005) suggests that their role should be to open up pathways for change linked to wider processes in offenders' lives.

Conclusion: implications for practice

Thus far, we have argued that social capital represents an important set of resources on which people draw in addressing all sorts of issues and problems – from educational attainment to job-seeking to desistance from offending and beyond. By contrast, a lack of social capital – or declining social capital – has been implicated not only in problems of community cohesion, collective efficacy, civic participation and the healthiness of democracy, but more specifically in terms of crime and disorder. In focusing on the individual-level social capital of reoffenders in particular, we have noted that their bonding social capital (associated mainly with their families of origin and local networks) may have become diminished in the course of their criminal careers and that, consequently, their closest social bonds may stand in need of repair. The 'old friends' to whom they may be strongly tied, partly as a consequence of their diminishing social capital, will sometimes represent strong negative ties that frustrate desistance. Moreover, where they have established new families of formation (with partners and children), the resources that these families offer may be merely nascent and fragile, but critical to the process of identity reformation. These new families, as well as providing new bonding social capital, may, in some circumstances, also offer new bridging capital connecting them to wider social networks. However, for many offenders under supervision, their access to the bridging social capital that seems to be so critical in accessing new opportunities, new identities and social mobility will be highly limited. Moreover, their access to linking social capital, and with it any prospect of hierarchical mobility across social strata and access to power and status is likely to be even more constrained.

All of this suggests four main areas that criminal justice social work (and the new Community Justice Authorities) might productively strive to address. First, services need to find ways to engage effectively with families of origin so as to enlist them, wherever possible, in supporting desistance. Clearly the suitability of this strategy will depend on the offender's age and stage of development, on the nature of the family and its dynamics and on an assessment of its potential to support (or hinder) desistance. However, at the very least, the significance of repairing damaged bonding social capital implies that social workers should be routinely engaged in family work and home visits.

Second, the literature around generativity in particular suggests a productive focus for work around new and developing relationships and around parenting (and preparation for it). Moreover, it implies the need for individual workers and for local services to think creatively about other potentially generative activities, including paid employment, civic volunteering and other constructive, creative activities. Work focused around generativity may help ex-offenders to build new bonding social capital *and* to develop new bridging social capital, via wider associations related to generative activities.

While these two suggestions relate primarily to individual-level interventions, the third implication of the evidence reviewed above points to wider strategic priorities for the new Community Justice Authorities linked to community engagement and community development. Probation needs to engage communities because, in terms of desistance, while it may be necessary to prepare ex-offenders for and assist them in accessing wider social networks, including through employment, such work is not sufficient. It is equally important to prepare communities (including employers and other agencies) for ex-offenders and to support them in working with ex-offenders. This kind of mediation and advocacy work – at the community level as well as the individual level – is necessary in order to facilitate the development of ex-offenders' bridging social capital within communities and the development of linking capital across social groups and social hierarchies.

This, in turn, leads to the fourth, and most challenging, implication of our discussion. Developing the social capital of a vilified group is not easy in the context of insecure, late-modern societies like our own – societies that are more preoccupied with punishment of and protection from offenders than their reintegration (Bauman 1997; Garland 2001; Young 1999). Clearly, this wider social context has profound implications for the work of the new Community Justice Authorities. Discussing the impact of 'insecurity' on 'offender management' services more generally (and returning us neatly to the discussion of public protection that closed Chapter 1), McCulloch and McNeill (2007, forthcoming) have argued that contemporary services have little choice but to stand for the promise of public protection, but the question remains open as to what kind of protection and which mechanisms of protection they can or should promise to deliver. They argue that because most of the academic, policy and practice literature about probation and public protection focuses on the technicalities of delivering on this objective more effectively, much of the debate rests on an implicit (and highly optimistic) assumption that the public will *feel* better protected by a more effective service. However, as recent research on high-crime communities and public punitiveness suggests, there is no straightforward relationship between experiences of crime and attitudes to punishment (Bottoms and Wilson 2004). Recognition of the need to *directly* address insecurity and anxiety about crime at the local level underpins the use of high visibility patrols, the targeting of 'signal crimes' and the development of informal controls through communities that characterise 'reassurance policing' (Innes 2004). If, as Bottoms and Wilson (2004) suggest, probation were to target these same insecurities and anxieties, in part by responding to signal crimes with 'control signals', then perhaps the measure of its success would not necessarily be that communities were 'objectively' better protected from crime, but rather communities that were subjectively less anxious about crime and, more specifically, less anxious about the management of offenders within the community. This leads McCulloch and McNeill (2007, forthcoming) to argue:

> Put simply, it might be that probation's intended product should not be communities that are objectively better protected, but rather communities that *feel* safer. At the practical level, the implication that probation would need to engage more visibly and more effectively with local communities raises interesting possibilities, as well as significant problems . . .

In the Scottish context, the implication of this argument might be that the primary aim of Community Justice Authorities should not be merely public protection through reduced reoffending (as emphasised by recent policy developments) but rather a more integrated and holistic concept of 'community justice' (Nellis 2001) as intended by the Social Work (Scotland) Act 1968; meaning an enhanced sense that offending and reoffending were being dealt with not merely *effectively*, but that they were being dealt with in ways that were procedurally and substantively *fair*, *proportionate*, *appropriate* and *proper* and that contribute meaningfully to the wider social well-being of the community. This might imply thinking not merely about 'control signals' or protection signals (important though these would be) but also about visible signals of restitution, reparation and reform and with them better social integration as part of enhanced social well-being. While it may well be possible and desirable to construct a theoretical and normative case for such a model of communicative community justice (Duff 2001; Rex 2005), the evidence reviewed in this chapter suggests that, ironically perhaps, it might also be 'what works' – because the success or failure to send such signals may have major consequences for the capacity of social work and the CJAs to generate wider opportunities for the development of the social capital that seems to be required in order to enable desistance. If desistance requires social capital, then services to support desistance need community support – and that means engaging much more directly and meaningfully with communities than has hitherto been the case.

Notes

1　SWIA inspections are available at: www.swia.gov.uk
2　At the first interview, 21 of the young people in the sample reported one-off offending and 47 reported recurrent offending. Twelve of these reinterviewed had developed long-term criminal careers and/or dependent drug use.

Conclusion: reducing reoffending and community justice

Essentially, societies that do not believe that offenders can change will get offenders who do not believe that they can change. (Maruna 2001: 166)

Much depends on whether or not we want a just and decent society, and whether we have the will and capacity to resist those who do not. There is more at stake here than how we punish and prevent crime, and if we fail to create community justice the rather harsh penal landscape that will be the likely result will, in fact, be the least of our worries. (Nellis 2000: 84)

Reprising the main arguments

In the introduction to this book, we explained that social work and community justice in Scotland are in the midst of critical and potentially far-reaching reforms. Against this backdrop, we described the book's purposes as being twofold. First, to make a timely contribution to these developments by providing an up-to-date (but historically grounded) analysis of the challenges faced by those supervising offenders in the community in Scotland; an authoritative account of the legal contexts for such supervision; and some critical commentary on how the new Community Justice Authorities might best travel towards effective practice. Second, we hoped to provide an accessible but critical introduction for those from further afield (whether scholars, students or practitioners) who share our interest with questions of community justice and with Scottish answers to those questions.

In Chapter 1, our historical analysis revealed significant shifts in emphases in policy and practice from punishment to supervision to treatment to welfare to responsibility to public protection and now to offender management. These various reformations of purposes, discourses and practices can be characterised essentially as the service's adaptations to changing social and political contexts and shifting public sensibilities about crime and punishment. That said, drawing on some recent research evidence (McCulloch 2005; Robinson and McNeill 2004), we argued that these shifts in emphasis and approach have been gradual and that through each of these transitions much of the 'old' survived alongside the 'new'. Arguably, the continuous thread throughout the history of social work with adult offenders in Scotland has been the enduring desire to find constructive and effective ways of *doing* justice by promoting the welfare of both offenders and communities.

Turning, in Chapter 2, to the contemporary challenge of reducing reoffending, we explored and challenged the emerging preoccupation with reoffending in Scotland. We demonstrated both that the last decade has witnessed a significant increase in the 'carceral reach' of the state and that this 'dispersal of discipline' is not evenly spread across the Scottish population; rather, the emerging evidence suggests that it is highly concentrated in the most deprived areas. We also outlined some of the significant limitations of using reconviction as a measure for the impact of penal sanctions and, in exploring the available Scottish data in international context, we suggested that Scottish reconviction rates are neither surprising nor alarming and that they cannot be read simply as being indicative of an under-performing justice system. Rather, we argued that reconviction is strongly associated with the chronic and serious problems of disadvantage, marginalisation and exclusion that commonly characterise the lives of both prisoners and those subject to community penalties and disposals. In seeking to understand those associations, we briefly reviewed some important insights from developmental criminology – in particular concerning why (only) some offenders develop lasting criminal careers. In exploring the scale, complexity and intensity of the needs that provoke reoffending, especially for those persistent property offenders who form the core group with which criminal justice social workers must engage, we cautioned that the potential difficulties that services face in seeking to reduce reoffending should season our expectations about what these services can deliver.

Nonetheless, despite all of these difficulties, people do desist from offending, and in Chapter 3, we turned our attention to understanding how, why and when this happens and, more specifically, what community supervision can do to support desistance. This evidence led us to suggest a paradigm for practice based on the recognition that desistance is the process that social work with offenders (whether it is called 'offender management' or not) exists to promote and support and that therefore approaches to intervention should be embedded in understandings of desistance and better social integration. Moreover, the accumulating evidence about desistance suggests that desistance-supporting interventions need to respect and foster offenders' personal agency and reflexivity; they need to be based on legitimate and respectful relationships; they need to focus on social capital (networks and opportunities) as well as human capital (motivations and capacities); and they need to exploit strengths as well as addressing needs and risks. This paradigm would require practitioners to work out *with* offenders, on an individual basis, how each individual desistance process might best be prompted and supported and to act as an advocate providing a conduit to social capital as well as a 'treatment' provider building human capital. Critically, such interventions would not be concerned solely with the prevention of further offending; they would be equally concerned with constructively addressing the harms caused by crime by encouraging offenders to make good through restorative processes and community service (in the broadest sense). But, as a morally and practically necessary corollary, they would be no less preoccupied with making good to offenders by enabling them to achieve inclusion and participation in society (and with it the progressive and positive reframing of their identities required to sustain desistance).

Recognising that the potential of this paradigm depends not only on its own strengths and weaknesses but on the contexts within which it might be developed and operationalised, we moved on in Part II (Chapters 4–6) to explore the legal contexts of criminal justice social work in Scotland. We suggested in Chapter 4 that the evidence about the impact of social work advice to the courts remains equivocal and that both the formal and the technical requirements around reports present substantial challenges for criminal justice social workers. At the same time these requirements provide an opportunity to assist the court to review the potential consequences of different sentencing options in the light of the policy objective of reducing reoffending, and to reflect on sentencing within a framework of principles, rights, values and potentially positive outcomes for public safety and well-being. The social enquiry report therefore provides a platform for identifying needs, risks and strengths and for positively promoting community-based pathways to desistance whenever this is possible and appropriate.

In Chapter 5 we showed that supervision in the community in Scotland exists in a wide variety of forms and serves a wide variety of purposes and argued that effective, legitimate and appropriate supervision (of whichever form) requires a clear understanding of its legal and policy contexts. However, while such an understanding may be a necessary condition of good practice, we suggested that it is certainly not sufficient. The technical-legal requirements of supervision, on which we focused in Chapter 5, should not operate separately from strategic, managerial, professional and administrative dimensions of supervision and case management. Mobilising self-efficacy and intrinsic motivation is crucial to changing the hearts and minds of individuals. To ensure ongoing reinforcement of learning from supervision, good strategic case management is essential with effective arrangements for ensuring active collaboration with other community agencies and protocols for partnership working. Effective supervision in the community relies on the quality of response. The trading standards definition of quality is 'fit for purpose' which implies there should be clear and stated purposes for intervention. The core purposes of community-based supervision are outlined in NOS (Scottish Executive 2004d, 2004e). However, considerations of quality and effectiveness must also recognise that there can be different purposes for different orders and that, at the individual level, supervisors have to match *individual* characteristics related to risks, needs and strengths (including gender, ethnicity, age and learning style) with the relevant mix of resources and skills to achieve the desired objectives.

We also noted in Chapter 5, in introducing the idea of restorative justice and the issue of supporting victims, that there is more to community supervision than 'just' reducing reoffending; it is also necessary for both ethical and practical reasons that community supervision itself involves fair and restorative processes that takes victims *and* offenders needs, rights and concerns seriously.

In Chapter 6 we suggested that, after many years of neglect, throughcare and resettlement again form a major part of government policy for promoting community safety. New organisational structures and requirements introduced by the 2005 Act place a greater corporate responsibility for the management of serious and violent offenders returning to the community on local authorities and the Scottish Prison Service as part of a wider community safety strategy. They set a new landscape for newly established dedicated social work throughcare teams and a challenge to provide meaningful and effective practices aimed both at offender management and positive integrative supervision. However, the measures contained in the Custodial Sentences and Weapons Bill, currently before the Scottish Parliament, by very significantly increasing the prison population, the numbers of prisoners subject to risk assessment procedures in custody and the numbers of ex-prisoners under supervision, represent major challenges for all parties involved. Unless the new measures are adequately resourced, particularly through the expansion and development of both the prison and social work workforces, there is a serious risk that the objectives of the Bill relating to public protection will not be achieved in practice.

Moving in Part III from the legal context towards thinking further about effective practice, we discussed offender management, case management and change management in Chapter 7. In exploring the process of supervision (whether in relation to community disposals or post-release work), we discussed the case manager's roles, tasks and skills in assessment, planning, delivery, monitoring and evaluation of change processes, concluding that effective relationships are at the crux of effective practice. The supervision process begins with the establishment of relationships, and the effectiveness of every subsequent part of the process will depend in part on the quality of relationships. More broadly, we suggested that the business of reducing reoffending by *supporting change* involves a range of skills that goes far beyond those involved in reducing reoffending by *imposing control*, monitoring or enforcement, important though these measures are. However, while there is much evidence that change-supporting relationships lie at the heart of effective practice and are a necessary condition of it, they are not sufficient. Those relationships must be purposive; they must be deployed in pursuit of positive changes in offenders' human and social capital.

In discussing the development of human capital in Chapter 8, we suggested that adopting social learning methods that help individuals acquire human capital or skills while providing assistance in applying these skills in real social situations looks the most promising approach to developing a strong sense of self-efficacy and supporting human agency and personal responsibility. However, we also noted that programmes for offenders make little coherent sense unless they are embedded within locally defined responses to individual need (Petersilia 1990; Rumgay 2000). We suggested therefore that the division between offence-focused, person-focused and community-focused approaches and priorities is often artificial and not necessarily helpful to practitioners. The expectation of a more dynamic and holistic approach to intervention is outlined in the Scottish standards. Offence-focused programmes should be located *alongside* other activities aimed at building the human capital necessary for offenders to participate effectively in programmes themselves, and located within a more integrated intervention plan which covers all the bases associated with both non-completion and reoffending. Rumgay (2000) cautions, however, that it is important to avoid the risk of utilising community-based services as forms of 'pseudo-penal' service or law enforcement rather than as agencies that can help individuals, in their own right, acquire both human and social capital and thus to move towards a better experience of community and social integration. By contrast, if the 'pro-social' world apparently has little to offer a person with a criminal record or with a long history of drug misuse, then its appeal will seem highly limited. It is for this reason that working to develop human capital must be connected to working to develop social capital.

In Chapter 9 we argued that social capital represents an important set of resources on which people draw in addressing all sorts of issues and problems. By contrast, a lack of social capital – or declining social capital – has been implicated not only in problems of community cohesion, collective efficacy, civic participation and the healthiness of democracy, but more specifically in terms of crime and disorder. At the individual level, for many offenders under supervision their access to the social capital that seems to be so critical in accessing new opportunities, new identities and social mobility will be highly limited. This suggested four main issues that criminal justice social work (and the new Community Justice Authorities) might productively strive to address. First, services need to find ways to engage effectively with reoffenders' families of origin (or other positive social networks) so as to enlist them, wherever possible, in supporting desistance. Second, the literature around generativity in particular suggests a productive focus for work around new and developing relationships and around parenting (and preparation for it). Moreover, it implies the need for individual workers and for local services to think creatively about other potentially generative activities, including paid employment, civic volunteering and other constructive, creative activities. Third, the evidence pointed to wider strategic priorities for the new Community Justice Authorities linked to community engagement and community development. Probation needs to engage communities because, in terms of desistance, while it may be necessary to prepare offenders for and assist them in accessing wider social networks, including through employment, such work is not sufficient. It is equally important to prepare communities (including employers and other agencies) for offenders and to support them in working with offenders.

This, in turn, led to the fourth, and most challenging, implication of our discussion. Developing the social capital of a vilified group is not easy in the context of insecure, late-modern societies like our own – societies that are more preoccupied with punishment of and protection from offenders than their reintegration. Clearly, this wider social context has profound implications for the work of the new Community Justice Authorities. Essentially we argued that the primary aim of CJAs should not be merely public protection through reduced reoffending but rather 'community justice' itself (Nellis 2001); meaning an enhanced sense that offending and reoffending were being dealt with not only *effectively*, but that they were being dealt with in ways that were procedurally and substantively *fair, proportionate, appropriate* and *proper* and that contribute meaningfully to the wider social well-being of the community. If desistance requires social capital, then services to support desistance need community planning and support – and that means engaging much more directly and meaningfully with communities and service providers than has hitherto been the case, despite community and locality being key themes of probation in Scotland since its inception.

Beyond reducing reoffending: victims and restorative justice

Our discussion of the significance of social capital in reducing reoffending provides empirical grounds for taking more seriously the irrefutable normative case for those working with offenders to take the needs of victims of crime more seriously (cf. Nellis 1995; Williams 2005) because unless victims are satisfied with the justice process, communities are unlikely to support the reintegration of offenders. In this respect, we realise that this book has reflected one of the major failures in the history of criminal justice social work to date: that is, its failure to develop an adequate understanding of, response to and engagement with victims. In some respects, Scotland has seen considerable progress in recent years on victims' issues, as we noted briefly in Chapter 5; for example, the Executive introduced its first Scottish Strategy for Victims in 2001 and has subsequently enacted a range of measures to enhance support for both victims and witnesses (Scottish Executive 2001). More recently, in 2005 the Executive published its *National Standards for Victims of Crime* (Scottish Executive 2005d) which aims to clarify what victims can expect of the justice system in terms of information, support and participation. Moreover, the new *National Strategy for Offender Management* makes improved victim satisfaction part of one of the required outcomes of such services and also stresses the need to provide better care for victims, to work with offenders to develop victim empathy and to communicate more effectively with victims about offender management (Scottish Executive 2006d).

Important though these measures are, they fall some way short of the kind of radical overhaul of approaches to working with offenders *and* victims that proponents of restorative justice advance. As we noted in Chapter 5, restorative justice is a response to crime that considers the needs of victims, those who offend and the community (Zehr 2002). It is an attempt to put into practice a set of ethical ideas about how human beings should relate to each other and, in particular, to those who cause harm and those who suffer harm, seeking to resolve and strengthen relationships where possible. Restorative practices are designed to give victims[1] of crime an opportunity to tell the offender about the impact of their actions on them and their families, to encourage acceptance of responsibility, to repair the harms caused and, where appropriate, to make amends. The general aim is to restore, to varying degrees, the relationship between the persons involved, to reduce reoffending and to improve their experience of the criminal justice system (Marshall 1999).

While active participation is a central aspect of restorative justice, none of these definitions stresses better social or community cohesion as an essential characteristic of restorative practice and the UN definition places little emphasis on mutually beneficial outcomes. Nonetheless, for many advocates, for justice to be restorative it must evidence the consistent involvement of all parties affected by the crime, and focus on the development, implementation and maintenance of mutual healing, reparation and satisfaction rather than retribution and punishment (Schiff 1998). Bazemore and Umbreit (1994) argue that the involvement of the person who causes harm and the person who suffers harm is essential and 'mutuality' needs to be maintained in any balanced system of restorative justice. Regrettably, these principles are seldom in operation in many Scottish practices incorporated into formal criminal legal processes discussed above.

Braithwaite's (1989) theory of 'reintegrative shaming' suggests that people are generally not deterred from committing crime by the threat of official punishment but by two informal processes of social control: fear of social disapproval and social conscience. Through restorative practice the offender can be made powerfully aware of the disapproval of their actions by significant others in their lives. The potentially alienating and stigmatising effects of shaming are overcome by reacceptance and affirmation of the person's value in the community. As a consequence, agreements reached by family members, friends, or other individuals important to the offender are likely to be more effective and lasting in their impact than those imposed by an impersonal legal institution. From this point of view, not only do restorative practices provide an opportunity for people to accept their share of responsibility for their actions, they also afford them the opportunity, where possible, to repair the harm they have caused with the support of their families while involving victims in the process, strengthening their sense of social cohesion, self-efficacy and responsibility.

Though the evidence about the impact of restorative practices on reoffending is still contestable, one authoritative recent review suggests grounds for cautious optimism (Hayes 2007). More generally, it is widely accepted that such practices are associated with improved victim *and* offender satisfaction with justice processes and (to a somewhat lesser extent) outcomes (see Daly 2002; Bazemore and Elis 2007). While it is beyond the scope of this book to explore the wide-ranging debates about restorative justice principles, practices and impacts (see Johnstone and Van Ness 2007), we have provided this brief account here because the emerging evidence from desistance studies (particularly about the significance of social capital and of offenders 'making good') suggests that the pursuit of reduced reoffending requires both policy-makers and practitioners in Scotland to give serious consideration to a much more radical engagement with victims and with restorative justice than has been the case hitherto.

Beyond reducing reoffending: social work and community justice

Given the evidence and arguments reviewed above both about desistance and about restorative justice, it seems to us that a brief discussion of the meaning and importance of 'community justice' is the natural place to end this book. It is likely that the naming of the new Community Justice Authorities was intended partly to offset dissent and anxiety in Scotland about the importation of more troubling correctional language around offender management. In this regard, it is interesting to note that the new National Advisory Body on Offender Management has quickly become known merely as the NAB. However, whether it was intended or not, the terminology of community justice connects Scottish developments to a much wider debate about the relationships between the courts, those organisations that administer court disposals (whether they are called corrections, probation, offender management or social work) and the communities from which offenders come, to which they belong and to which they return after sentencing or after release. Though the conclusion of this book is not the place for an in-depth discussion of community justice, it is worth noting that its evolution as a philosophy and a movement in North America owes much to the communitarian philosophy of Amitai Etzioni (1991), whose ideas briefly inspired aspects of New Labour's early programme of government.

However, the development of community justice in North America is best reflected in the work of Todd Clear and David Carp (Clear and Karp 1999; Karp 1998; Karp and Clear 2002). In the UK, Clear and Karp's ideas have been developed and discussed by Nellis (1995, 1998, 2000, 2002, 2005), Harding (2000, 2003) and others (see Winstone and Pakes, 2005).

While there is no standard or agreed formula (Clear and Karp 1999), Winstone and Pakes suggest that community justice reflects three key principles:

> First, the community is the ultimate consumer of criminal justice. Rather than offenders, or even victims, it is communities that the system ought to serve. Second, community justice is achieved in partnership at the local level. Third, it is problem focused: problems are addressed rather than cases processed. (Winstone and Pakes 2005: 2)

Clearly, these principles (especially the first and the third) are highly contestable and, in some respects, stand in opposition to, or at least in tension with, both traditional legal and criminal justice and more victim-centred perspectives, although as many advocates and commentators have suggested community justice is closely linked with the restorative justice movement. However, rather than engaging in detail with these normative debates here, we simply want to note that, at first sight, both these principles and some of the practical programmes through which they have been applied (see Karp and Clear 2002) resonate with certain aspects of Scotland's distinctive historical arrangements for the supervision of offenders. Most obviously, the current reforms represent merely the latest attempt to deliver services consistently across the country but without losing sight of the significance of the inescapably *local* contexts of *community*-based service delivery. The association of Scottish probation and latterly criminal justice social work with *local* authorities has always been based on recognition that services to reduce reoffending are *community* services committed to the promotion of social welfare. The fact that, despite the Morison Committee's (1962) recommendations, Scottish probation (and subsequently criminal justice social work) was never defined by its relations with the courts is a consequence of this tradition.

In some senses at least, community justice's problem focus is also consistent with the thinking behind the Kilbrandon reforms and the Social Work (Scotland) Act 1968. As we noted in the introduction to this book, Bruce (1975, 1985) suggested that the 1968 Act heralded a paradigm shift, transferring responsibility for community safety from the justice system directly to the community precisely because the Kilbrandon philosophy took a dim view of the comparative effectiveness of a *criminal justice paradigm* characterised by crime, conviction and punishment, and favoured instead a *social justice or social educational paradigm* characterised by prevention, change (or development) and inclusion (or integration).

A more recent development in the philosophy of punishment which resonates with some (but not all) aspects of the social, community and restorative justice agendas is Antony Duff's penal communications theory (Duff 2001, 2003). Duff (2003) has argued that probation can and should be considered a mode of punishment; indeed, he argues that it could be the model punishment. However, the notion of punishment that he advances is not 'merely punitive'; that is, it is not concerned simply with the infliction of pain as a form of retribution. Rather it is a form of 'constructive punishment' that inflicts pain only in so far as this is an inevitable (and intended) consequence of 'bringing offenders to face up to the effects and implications of their crimes, to rehabilitate them and to secure ... reparation and reconciliation' (Duff 2003: 181). The pains involved are akin to the unavoidable pains of repentance.

Duff's view is that while true repentance cannot be coerced, punishment (including the infliction of pain) is and should be communicative, encouraging repentance and forgiveness. The argument is that these processes are conducive to reconciliation and repairing harm – an obligation which ideally the offender imposes on himself or herself. That said, the kind of communicative punishment which Duff advocates is far removed from punishment as it is currently practised. In this regard, there is strong psychological evidence (Andrews and Bonta 2003) which suggests that punishment does not deter the most recalcitrant but simply gives the 'ordinary' person good reason for compliance. Punishment, at least as conventionally practised, is counter-productive; it tends to induce resistance, resentment and strategies to avoid pain not necessarily related to personal change. In this way punishment can inhibit learning rather than enhance it.

In some respects, aspects of Duff's philosophy resonate both with Bazemore's (1998) concept of 'earned redemption' and with Maruna's (2001) empirical findings about the significance for desisters of 'making good'. It seems significant that this 'making good' is productive rather than destructive; that is, the right to be rehabilitated or reintegrated is not the product of experiencing the pains of 'merely punitive' punishment, rather it is the result of evidencing change in practical ways. In working to support the reconstruction of identity involved in desistance, this seems to underline the relevance of the redemptive opportunities that both community and restorative justice approaches tend to offer. No less obvious, by contrast, are the futility and counter-productiveness of penal measures that label, exclude, and segregate and co-locate offenders as offenders. Such measures seem designed to confirm and cement 'condemnation scripts' and thus to frustrate desistance.

However, Duff's (2003) work also connects with social work's traditional pursuit of social justice (however defined) in arguing that the existence of social *injustice*, and in consequence the denial of citizenship to some, creates moral problems for the punishing polity. The response must be 'a genuine and visible attempt to remedy the injustices and exclusion that they [that is, some offenders] have suffered' (Duff 2003: 194). Duff suggests that this implies that:

> the probation officer ... will now have to help the offender negotiate his relationship with the polity against which he has offended, but by whom he has been treated unjustly and disrespectfully: she must speak for the polity to the offender in terms that are censorious but also apologetic – terms that seek both to bring him to recognise the wrong he has done and to express an apologetic recognition of the injustice he has suffered: *and she must speak to the polity for the offender*, explaining what is due to him as well as what is due for him. (Duff 2003: 194, emphasis added)

Thus it seems that help for and practical support to offenders can perhaps be relegitimated both empirically, in terms of the need to build social capital in supporting desistance, and normatively (even *within* a punishment discourse) as a prerequisite for making punishment both intelligible to and just for offenders and for communities.

Our ultimate conclusion, therefore, is that while reducing reoffending is a laudable and necessary aim, its effective pursuit requires much more than, and is in some sense at odds with, a narrowly correctionalist focus on managing offenders (McNeill 2004a). Indeed, it seems to us, particularly in the light of desistance research, that the current emphasis on reducing reoffending makes a necessity out of the virtues of Scotland's long-standing inclusive welfare traditions in terms of community justice. However, while these traditions are both laudable and long-standing, they have never come close to delivering on their full promise. To say that the conceptual and policy frameworks for criminal justice social work since before Kilbrandon have been broadly consistent with the *principles* of community justice is not to say that criminal justice social work has ever been able to deliver community justice *in practice*. Criminal justice social work's record in relation to both victims and restorative justice is even more questionable. Our view – as former practitioners, as interested observers and as committed advocates of criminal justice social work – is that it has never been *enabled* to fulfil its promise, for a variety of reasons too complex to review here. However, despite this sobering analysis of a history of (partly) lost opportunities, our view is that the new developments require not an abandonment of the past, but a fulfilment of it. This will necessitate careful analysis of how the new Community Justice Authorities and all their stakeholders can work together to progress, develop and better enact our traditions concerning locally responsive community services that promote social welfare and social justice for victims, offenders and communities. These are not mere aspirations; they are ultimately the only effective means by which we might progress, in the Executive's terms, towards 'A Safer Scotland'.

Note

1   The terms 'victim' and 'offender' are used hereafter for simplicity; this risks narrowly labelling them when it is their range of qualities and characteristics that are crucial to co-production in restorative practice.

Appendix: study guide

Introduction

This study guide is intended primarily for use by tutors and students involved in social work courses in Scotland, but it should also be of assistance to students on probation courses and on criminology courses further afield. For each chapter of the book we provide some advice and suggestions about further reading, as well as a set of study questions that can be used to focus reading and/or for seminar discussions.

For some chapters, we have provided case study questions to assist students in making connections between theory, research and practice. However, rather than using written case studies which tend to leave their characters lacking in depth and their lives lacking in detail, we suggest that students watch Ken Loach's (2002) film *Sweet Sixteen* and use its lead character, Liam, as the basis for case study discussions.

Sweet sixteen
Set in Greenock, the film tells the story of Liam (played by Martin Compston), a young man approaching his sixteenth birthday, whose mum Jean is in prison as a result of her relationship with Stan, her drug-dealing boyfriend. Liam is determined to help his mother escape both the relationship and her own drug problems. To do this he and his friend Pinball need to secure enough money to buy a caravan some miles outside of Greenock where Liam and Jean can live when she gets out of jail, away from the dealers, the police and all the other problems in their lives. Seeing no other way to earn the money they need, Liam's and Pinball's involvement with crime escalates from illicitly selling cigarettes to drug-dealing and this leads them into dangerous relationships and dangerous territory, as well as challenging their loyalty to each other. Liam's relationship with his sister Chantelle, who is determined to build a better life for herself and her son Callum, provides him with some respite from his struggles, but the relationship becomes strained after their mother's release from prison, as the film approaches its harrowing climax.

Under Ken Loach's faultless direction, the film's superb script (written by Paul Laverty) and the convincing portrayal of the main characters (by actors whose local roots and life experiences are evident in their performances) combine to produce a painfully realistic and moving account of one young man's struggle to cope with adversity, to save his family and to escape the personal and social problems that ensnare them. For our purposes, the film provides almost unique access to the process of 'coming of age' in desperate social circumstances, and to the part that crime sometimes plays in this process. For that reason, it provides a uniquely rich case study which locates reoffending (and indirectly locates the challenges of reducing reoffending) much more vividly and effectively than we can do in a book such as this. Further details of the film can be found at: http://www.imdb.com/title/tt0313670 (accessed 8 January 2007) and it can be rented or purchased from the usual sources.

That said, for students on placement or with relevant practice experience, the case study questions can also be adapted and applied to people with whom they are working or have worked.

Chapter I

Further reading
Regrettably, very little has been published about the history of social work with offenders in Scotland; most of what has been written is referenced in Chapter 1. Indeed, it might be argued that Scotland is still waiting for an authoritative and critical history of crime and punishment in general. Although it is not focused solely on Scotland, Linda Mahood's (1995) *Policing Gender, Class and Family* provides an excellent account of the period 1850–1950, focusing largely on child welfare but including some interesting material about the development of probation. A particular strength of Mahood's work is that she draws on the available accounts of early probation practitioners themselves (sometimes via their testimony to public inquiries) and on oral history interviews with some of the recipients of their services.

Though the quartet of essays on probation history in England and Wales by Bill McWilliams (1983, 1985, 1986, 1987) is unlikely ever to be surpassed both in scope and in the quality of analysis, Maurice Vanstone's (2004) book *Supervising Offenders in the Community* does an excellent job of revising 'official' probation histories (largely based on documentary analysis) in the light of original oral history work with probation managers and practitioners. For those in a hurry, Mike Nellis's (2001) chapter in Anthony Bottoms *et al.*'s *Community Penalties: Change and Challenges* provides a thoughtful overview, though his chapter in the forthcoming *Handbook of Probation* (2007) edited by Loraine Gelsthorpe and Rod Morgan, may be better still. In the same forthcoming edition, Gill McIvor and Fergus McNeill's chapter on 'Probation in Scotland' covers similar material to Chapter 1 of this book, but has much more to say about recent developments.

Though official documents necessarily have their limitations as historical sources, the reports of the Streatfeild (1961), Morison (1962) and Kilbrandon (1964) committees still provide very interesting reading, and some of the earlier Scottish documents referred to in Chapter 1 will reward those with the patience to track them down. For those considering a field trip or two, visits to Inveraray Jail (see http://www.inverarayjail.co.uk/) and to the Police Museum in Glasgow (see http://www.strathclyde.police.uk/index.asp?locID=434&docID=-1) provide excellent opportunities to place Scottish probation history in its wider context.

Study/seminar questions
1. What would you describe as the main features of practice in the different periods of probation history described in the chapter?
2. What do you think the impact might have been of the probation officer's role first being carried out by police officers?
3. What influence do you think the women probation officers might have had on the development of the service, particularly in the 1930s and 1940s?
4. Bearing in mind the discussion of the Morison Report in the chapter, do you think that it has been a strength or a weakness of probation in Scotland that it has typically been a local service as opposed to a court-based service?
5. To what extent do you think that the descriptions of probation practice drawn from early sources still reflect practice today? More generally, what would you identify as being the main continuities in the history of probation in Scotland?
6. What have been the most significant changes over the last 100 years?
7. Can you identify moments in the history of probation in Scotland when a significantly different path might have been taken?
8. Forty years on, just how significant have the Kilbrandon Report (1964) and Social Work (Scotland) Act 1968 been in both organisational and ideological terms?

Chapter 2

Further reading
In setting the contemporary agenda in Scotland, readers would be well advised to read the Scottish Executive (2004b, 2004c) publications associated with the 'Re:duce, Re:habilitate, Re:form' consultation and, perhaps most important, the recent National Strategy for Offender Management (Scottish Executive 2006d), as well as the Management of Offenders (Scotland) Act 2005.

In terms of assessing the effectiveness of criminal justice social work in Scotland, the series of evaluations published in the late 1990s and summarised in Paterson and Tombs (1998) still make interesting reading, though it is important to note that they relate to the period when the new arrangements (after the introduction of the national standards) were still bedding in. For wider discussions of methodological debates about the evaluation of community penalties, George Mair's (1997) edited collection *Evaluating the Effectiveness of Community Penalties* remains very useful, although Stephen Farrall's (2003a, 2003b) pair of articles in Volume 3 of *Criminology and Criminal Justice* has added new dimensions to these debates.

With regard to the backgrounds, characteristics and needs of reoffenders, though many of the studies mentioned in Chapter 2 would bear further study, the most accessible and most compelling read is probably the Social Exclusion Unit's (2002) report *Reducing Reoffending by Ex-prisoners*. More generally, in seeking to explain offending and reoffending, there is obviously a vast amount of relevant criminological material. In Chapter 2 we recommend overview chapters by Gelsthorpe (2003) and Whyte (2004), but perhaps the best advice is to delve into the excellent *Oxford Handbook of Criminology* edited by Mike Maguire, Rod Morgan and Rob Reiner. The third edition (where readers will find the chapters by David Farrington and David Smith referred to in Chapter 2) was published in 2002 but a new edition is expected soon.

Study/seminar questions

1. Why do you think reducing reoffending has become the key objective of criminal justice social work in Scotland? To what extent is the policy rhetoric about high reoffending rates justified, in your view?
2. How would you account for criminal justice social work's failure to impact on custodial sentencing, despite the increases in the use of community disposals?
3. What are the main implications of the 'dispersal of discipline' argument discussed in Chapter 2?
4. What do you find most striking about the backgrounds, characteristics and needs of reoffenders discussed in Chapter 2?
5. From Chapter 2 and from your own experience, to what extent do the backgrounds, characteristics and needs of male and female reoffenders differ and what are the implications of this in practice?
6. How would you explain offending and reoffending?
7. Are more persistent offenders somehow different from other offenders? If so, how?
8. What features or characteristics, if any, make probation practice distinctly a social work task as opposed to a correctional one?
9. How can Scottish social work justify its distinctive organisational approach and its service role within criminal justice provision?

Case study

1. Liam is a few months short of his sixteenth birthday when the film begins and is already subject to a supervision order from a Children's Hearing. List all of the offences that he commits during the film.
2. Which of the background features, characteristics and 'criminogenic needs' of reoffenders discussed in this chapter are evident in Liam's life?
3. How would you explain Liam's reoffending?

Chapter 3

Further reading

Readers would be well advised to start (or at least to develop) their thinking about desistance from offending by reading autobiographical accounts of the process. Fortunately for Scottish readers, some of the most compelling and acclaimed examples of such works are to be found in the two-volume autobiographies of Jimmy Boyle (1983, 1985) and Hugh Collins (1998, 2000). Given the contemporary focus on resettlement, Collins' second book, *Walking Away*, provides particularly interesting reading about his post-release experiences. Another excellent resource (providing accessible shorter accounts of the desistance process from a variety of ex-prisoners) is Angela Devlin and Bob Turney's (1999) collection *Going Straight: After Crime and Punishment*.

In terms of desistance research, Shadd Maruna's (2001) *Making Good: How Ex-convicts Reform and Rebuild Their Lives* (American Psychological Association), based on empirical research in Liverpool, provides a compelling and insightful study of the process which deserves to be read time and again. Stephen Farrall's (2002) *Rethinking What Works* is a different type of book; its emphasis on the relationships between desistance and probation supervision makes it essential reading for students of probation and social work. Stephen Farrall and Adam Calverley's (2006) recent *Understanding Desistance from Crime* updates and develops the 2002 book, as well as providing an excellent introduction to the latest developments in the study of desistance more generally. Ros Burnett's (1992) *Dynamics of Recidivism* study is due great credit for reinventing the study of desistance in the UK; both the original study and the more recent publications arising from it are equally rewarding. Monica Barry's (2006) excellent book *Youth Offending in Transition* reports the most in-depth study of desistance in Scotland to date.

Sue Rex's (1999) article in the *Howard Journal* on 'Desistance from offending: Experiences of probation' is a particularly important paper for probation and social work students and practitioners to read, given the messages that it conveys not only *about* supervision but *from* those subject to it. In attempting to develop a new paradigm for practice based on desistance research, McNeill's (2006) paper in a special issue of *Criminology and Criminal Justice* make a serious attempt to develop the implications of desistance research for probation practice; other papers in the same special edition are also well worth reading. A similar special edition of the *Howard Journal* in 2004 is also worth exploring.

Study/seminar questions

1. How would you define desistance from offending? Do you agree that desistance is the process that criminal justice social work exists to support?
2. Chapter 3 argues that for many reoffenders 'secondary desistance' will be an important part of their change process. What do you think? Is it a necessary and/or a sufficient part of the change process?
3. What kinds of life experiences have prompted you to reflect on and perhaps to alter or develop your own identity?
4. What motivates desistance?
5. On the basis of the evidence reviewed in this chapter and from your own experience, to what extent and in what ways is desistance significantly different for male and female offenders? How important are age differences? What impact might ethnicity have in the desistance process?
6. From your own experience, to what extent are Burnett's three types of desisters familiar to you? More generally, do Maruna's 'condemnation scripts' and 'redemption scripts' resonate with your professional experience?
7. Why do you think relationships might be so important in the process of desistance? What kinds of relationships seem most likely to support change?
8. How might social circumstances hinder or frustrate desistance?
9. To what extent do you think the 'desistance paradigm' outlined in Chapter 3 is consistent with Scottish policy and practice?

Case study

1. Despite the many risk factors and needs evident in his life, what strengths does Liam demonstrate and what positive resources does he have around him?
2. What kind of values and moral qualities does he demonstrate?
3. Reflecting on the film, does Liam's path towards serious offending seem inevitable, or are there points in the story where alternative pathways might have been possible? What are these potential 'turning points'?
4. What seems to be central to Liam's identity? To what extent does he identify himself as an offender? What kind of life script is he enacting?
5. Discuss the relationship between Liam and Pinball. What role does it play in Liam's life and in his offending?
6. To what extent is Liam motivated to offend and to desist, at different points in the story?
7. Which of his relationships seem likely to support offending and which seem likely to support desistance? Does this differ at different points in the story?

8. How do his social circumstances prompt and sustain his offending? How would his circumstances need to change to prompt and sustain desistance?

Chapter 4

Further reading

There is very little literature on writing or presenting reports for courts in Scotland. In addition to the material available in this chapter, Social Work Inspection reports such as *Helping the Court Decide* (SWSI 1996) and current Performance Inspections of Criminal Justice Social Work Services (available at: www.swia.gov.uk) provide a contemporary picture. In terms of recent research, McNeill and Burns's (2005) paper reporting the ESRC study mentioned in the chapter is available as an audio recording at: http://www.sieswe.org/node/130. Whyte *et al.*'s (1995) *Social Work in the Criminal Justice System in Scotland* provides further relevant reading. There are also some interesting observations in Creamer's (2000) paper 'Reporting to the Scottish Courts: The quality of social enquiry reports and custody' in the *International Journal of the Sociology of Law*.

There are a number of useful publications from England and Wales: Bottoms and Stelman's (1988) *Social Inquiry Reports: A Framework for Practice Development*, though now somewhat dated, still provides useful insights. Other interesting contributions include Raynor *et al.*'s (1995) 'Quality assurance, pre-sentence reports and the Probation Service' in *British Journal of Social Work*, and Downing and Lynch (1997), 'Pre-sentence reports: Does quality matter?' in *Social Policy and Administration*. For interesting discussions of gender and ethnicity see Horn and Evans (2000) 'The effect of gender on pre-sentence reports', in the *Howard Journal*, and Hudson and Bramhall (2005) 'Assessing the other: Constructions of "Asianness" in risk assessments by probation officers', *British Journal of Criminology*.

Study/seminar questions

There is no practical substitute for observation and participation in writing and presenting an SER in court. Enquiry Action Learning is used in many fields of professional development including social work (see, e.g. Burgess and Jackson 1990; Baldwin and Burgess 1992). All social work students completing their education and training at the University of Edinburgh have the opportunity to complete an SER through simulation which concludes in the presentation of an 'aggregated' version in a mock hearing in Edinburgh Sheriff Court. Students have the opportunity to question the sheriff, fiscal, defence agent and social worker on the use made of the mock report by them. A video of a summary court hearing involving a mock SER compiled by students can be viewed at: http://webhelp.ucs.ed.ac.uk/domsdemo/wmedia/v2003-2.wvx

An EAL study unit is designed to enhance students' problem-solving skills and their ability to relate relevant theories to social work practice. Students work in small groups with a facilitator on case scenarios drawn ideally from current social work practice. The work of an EAL study unit is normally spread over four weeks. Individual and group activities take place, as well as weekly meetings with a facilitator and 'consultant' professionals. While an EAL unit may not be possible for all courses, elements of the exercise outlined below can be explored by students and teachers.

Group tasks
1. Observe court proceedings for half a day at a sheriff court.
2. In your group discuss the process you observed:
    (a) Personal feelings raised by being in court.
    (b) Roles of the people working in court.
    (c) Role of the criminal justice social worker.
    (d) How s/he presented SERs or other information to the court.
    (e) Use made of SERs in sentencing.
    (f) Sentences imposed by the sheriff.
    (g) Function of the sheriff clerk.
3. In a skills session, role play an interview with 'Liam' (at some specific point in the film) or another prepared case, for the purpose of an SER. Use National Objectives and Standards for SERs and Related Reports as a guide for preparing for and conducting the interview. Keep notes throughout. It is important that the 'client' should not make life too difficult or too easy for the interviewer.
4. From your notes prepare an 'aggregate' SER (some imagination will be required to sort out anomalies, etc.) and discuss in pairs or fours:
    (a) Your assessment of the situation and formulation.
    (b) Your proposal (or recommendation) and initial action plan, giving your reasons for this plan.
    (c) What effect do you think your gender/class/race may have had on the mock interview?
    (d) Consider the report in the context of anti-discriminatory practice, for example in relation to issues of language, values, culture and power.
    (e) What differences would have arisen if the client had been female, or over 50, or from an ethnic minority background?

SER – Assessing risk and planning intervention
Risk assessment is now expected to be an integral part of the SER process. There is a growing body of literature on risk assessment (see Chapter 7). If unfamiliar with it, then Kemshall (2002) is probably the place to start

(http://www.scotland.gov.uk/cru/kd01/green/raam-00.asp). National Standards (NOS) identify some key 'static factors' that can assist reoffending prediction: age at first conviction; number of custodial sentences under age 21; number of custodial sentences over age 21; number of previous convictions; offence type and gender.

Community Justice Authorities in Scotland are likely to expect or require the use of standardised assessment tools such as Level of Service Inventory – Revised (LSI-R) or a development of it (LS/CMI) (Andrews and Bonta 2001) to assist assessment and planning based on 'dynamic' factors (see Raynor *et al.* 2000). While standardised risk assessment tools such as LSI-R can assist locate an individual on a population distribution to indicate 'high', 'medium' or 'low' risk of reoffending, these tools have not been validated in Scotland. Raynor's excellent paper (2006) 'Risk and need in British probation: The contribution of LSI-R', *Psychology, Crime and Law*, provides a balanced critique and suggests that scores may vary from jurisdiction to jurisdiction and so should be used with caution for the purposes of risk prediction. The great strength of a standardised inventory is the explicit identification of 'need/risk' variables considered to be associated with sustaining and supporting criminality which can or should then be a priority focus of planned intervention.

Practitioners and students in placements using standardised tools should find the table below a helpful aid in compiling a summary action plan based on assessment evidence. The table is adapted from a more detailed pro-forma included in OASys (Home Office 2003).

The Risk Management Authority has produced a Risk Assessment Tools Evaluation Directory (2006) (http://www.rmascotland.gov.uk/home.aspx) with which Scottish readers should be familiar. The Scottish Office *Management and Assessment of Risk in Social Work Services Manual* (SWSI 1998), although somewhat dated, still has a wealth of information, guidance, literature and exercises for practitioners and students alike.

Chapter 5

Further reading
In relation to the legal and policy contexts, readers would be well advised to read the National Standards in relation to probation (Scottish Executive 2004d) and community service (Scottish Executive 2004e), as well as the primary and secondary legislation discussed in the chapter (much of which can be located at: http://www.opsi.gov.uk/).

Concerning wider debates about probation practice, the following books provide excellent learning resources: Chui and Nellis's (2003) edited collection *Moving Probation Forward: Evidence, Arguments and Practice*; Raynor and Vanstone's *Understanding Community Penalties: Probation, Policy and Social Change* (2002); and Ward *et al.*'s collection (2002) *Probation: Working for Justice*;

Objectives and summary action plan

Priorities: Reducing risk to others/self/Reducing reoffending

Relevant domain and score	SMART objective. What are you trying to do?	How will you measure any progress?	What work will be done to achieve the objectives?	Who will do the work?	What is the timescale for the work and for review?	What are the gaps?	What evidence will be required for the next review?

Worrall and Hoy's (2005) *Punishment in the Community: Managing Offenders, Making Choices*. For a very useful recent collection on issues of 'race' in probation work, see Lewis *et al*.'s (2006) *Race and Probation*.

Suitability – A twin track approach
The chapter discusses the 'twin track' approach to criminal justice social work disposals distinguishing between community disposals for non-violent offenders likely to be facing short prison sentences and alternatives to custody for violent offenders who can be maintained in the community. The framework, however, is a conceptual 'aid' rather than an empirically based one when considering who may be suitable, in policy terms, for community-based social work disposals. Using the following brief case examples 'locate' them in the 'twin track' table below, identifying whether, in principle, a community disposal or alternative to custody should be offered in an SER. How would you match to or target them against available social work disposals?

1. John is 24. He spent some time in care in a residential school. He has a history of drug misuse dating back to using solvents as a 14 year old. He says he is no longer 'doing drugs' and that they are no longer a problem in his life. He has numerous previous conviction for offences of dishonesty and has had two short periods of custody. He was placed on probation when he was 18 but his response was poor. He is currently facing 19 charges of theft.
2. Janet (20) is a single parent with one child aged two and a half. She lives in public sector housing (a former council flat) and is in receipt of Income Support and Housing Benefit. She is struggling to make ends meet and has no family supports nearby. She has few close friends other than her companions in the local pub where she has been known to become aggressive after consuming alcohol. She claims she is in control of her drinking. She has had no previous social work contact of any sort. She has seven previous convictions for offences of dishonesty, mainly theft from shops, and is currently appearing on a charge of serious assault.
3. Steven Smith is sixteen and a half. Most of his companions are involved in offending. He is a first offender charged with two 'THBs' (theft by house breaking). He lives with his mother and her partner. Steven's drinking and misuse of alcohol has created difficulties throughout his late childhood, particularly at school. He is unemployed and having exhausted his entitlement to bridging allowance has no income. He tends to sleep all day and go out with his friends at night.
4. Thomas Green is 34 and single. He is unemployed and has recently moved into a bed and breakfast within your area. He has been convicted of Breach of the Peace. The offence involved following an eight-year-old girl home from school and indecently exposing himself to her. He has two previous offences of a similar nature within the last four years.

5. James Jones is 45. He has been found guilty of sexually assaulting his 14-year-old daughter. He has no previous convictions. He lives with his wife.

6. Andrew McCall is 20. He has been convicted of theft of goods valued at £1,000 from two houses. He has two previous convictions for which he was fined.

Seriousness/persistence

Risk level	Non-violent offence	Violent offence
High		
Medium		
Low		

Study/seminar questions

1. NOS distinguish between standard probation, probation with conditions and intensive probation. What should be the distinguishing characteristics of the range of social work community disposals?

2. What part should level of restriction and the 'time demand' on offenders play when considering options?

3. How well does probation perform in comparison with other disposals in reducing reoffending and risk of harm to others?

4. What evidence is there that the attitudes/behaviours/circumstances of offenders can be changed for the better as a consequence of being on probation?

5. What are the implications of the 'twin track' policy and the National Objectives for planning and delivering supervision services?

6. Using the crude distinction between violent and non-violent offenders, what is the case for suitability for probation or other social work disposals?

7. What 'types' of offences are likely to fall into each track and which are likely to overlap the two tracks?

8. Which groups of offenders are a priority for community-based social work irrespective of their offence?

9. What is required from management structures to provide practitioners with authority, professional and structural, clear service targets and objectives and a well-articulated portfolio of provision to build 'human capital'?

10. What range of provision is likely to be required for those presenting low, medium and high risk of reoffending?

11. What kinds of services are likely to be best located within a framework of local services, CJA provision and national provision?

Chapter 6

Further reading

Practice in prison throughcare has been relatively under-researched but is again becoming the focus of political and professional concern. Probably among the best studies on outcomes, though a little dated, remain Zamble and Porporino (1988) *Coping Behaviour and Adaptation in Prison Inmates* and Zamble and Quinsey (1997) *The Criminal Recidivism Process*. Recent and notable research discussed in this chapter relates to the evaluation of the Resettlement Pathfinders in England and Wales which has generated a plethora of papers on the subject, including Lewis *et al.*'s (2003a, 2003b) *The Resettlement of Short-term Prisoners: An Evaluation of Seven Pathfinder Schemes* Home Office Research Findings and Occasional Paper; Clancy *et al.*'s (2006) *Getting Out and Staying Out: Results of the Prisoner Resettlement Pathfinders*; Lewis's (2004) 'What Works in the Resettlement of Short-Term Prisoners?' in *VISTA*; Maguire and Raynor's (2006) 'How the resettlement of prisoners promotes desistance from crime: Or does it?', *Criminology and Criminal Justice*; and Raynor's (2004b) 'Opportunity, Motivation and Change: Some Findings from Research on Resettlement', in *What Works in Probation and Youth Justice*, edited by Burnett and Roberts.

Some recent studies have focused specifically on challenging issues of working with people with drug problems, including Burke *et al.*'s (2006) 'An evaluation of service provision for short-term and remand prisoners with drug problems' in *Probation Journal*; Fox *et al.*'s (2005) *Throughcare and Aftercare: Approaches and Promising Practice in Service Delivery for Clients Released from Prison or Leaving Residential Rehabilitation*; Mitchell and Mc-Carthy's (2001) 'What happens to drug misusers on release from prison? An observational study at two London prisons', in *Drugs Education Prevention and Policy*.

A web-based learning object on Throughcare in Scotland has been designed and produced by the Criminal Justice Social Work Development Centre and the Learning Exchange, and will be available early in 2007 online at: http://www.cjsw.ac.uk/throughcaremap. The throughcare map is intended to guide social workers through the various stages involved in the provision of a throughcare service to prisoners from the point of sentence to release and supervision in the community. It contains fragments from three fictional case studies with videos of interviews with prisoners, examples of reports, risk assessments, and optional exercises to help you think about how you would contribute to the delivery of a throughcare service.

Study/seminar questions

1. Why did the Scottish Executive decide, in 2006, to end automatic unconditional early release and what are the practice implications of the main proposals in the Custodial Sentences and Weapons Bill?
2. What are the two main interrelated elements of throughcare?
3. What is the rationale for integrated case management (ICM) and on what model is it predicated?
4. What is the purpose of community integration plans?
5. What is the purpose of a home background report (HBR) and what factors are likely to influence the resettlement prospects of the prisoner on his release?
6. Why do NOS stress the importance of providing available information on the attitude of victims and/or the local community?
7. Do you think there should still be a place for voluntary throughcare and who should be a priority?
8. Discuss the role of the Risk Management Authority (RMA) in setting standards for risk assessment/management and lifelong restriction.
9. Discuss the role and purpose of Multi-Agency Public Protection Arrangements (MAPPA).

Chapter 7

Further reading

Though there is a burgeoning literature on risk and needs assessment in probation and social work (which can be accessed via some of the references in this chapter), surprisingly little has been written specifically about case management in probation, perhaps because of the focus (until recently) on programmes. Notable exceptions include the work of Paul Holt; his (2000) monograph provides a very useful overview. Partridge's (2004) more recent review of case management practices in England and Wales includes some very interesting material and Gwen Robinson's (2005) paper 'What works in offender management?' in the *Howard Journal* provides an excellent critical perspective.

Ros Burnett and Fergus McNeill's (2005) paper in the *Probation Journal* helpfully re-examines the evidence about the significance of relationships and one-to-one work in supporting desistance; a theme which also emerges strongly from McNeill *et al.*'s (2005) literature review exploring the professional skills required to support desistance and reduce reoffending. This review is available online at: http://www.scotland.gov.uk/Resource/Doc/37432/0011296.pdf. Some similar messages emerge from Dowden and Andrews' (2004) paper in the *International Journal of Offender Therapy and Comparative Criminology*. Some of the most useful and usable work on the skills and styles of probation officers has been done by the Chris Trotter in the context of his work on pro-social modelling. Trotter's excellent book *Working with Involuntary Clients* was republished in its second edition in 2006.

In relation to the important issue of compliance specifically, Tony Bottoms' chapter in Bottoms *et al.*'s (2001) collection *Community Penalties*, provides the most insightful, thought-provoking and practical paper on this subject to date. That said, in the context of a wider discussion of electronic monitoring, Mike Nellis's (2004) chapter in Bottoms *et al.*'s (2004) collection *Alternatives to Prison* takes the discussion on usefully.

Study/seminar questions

1. What are your views about the use of the terms 'offender management', 'case management' and 'change management'? Which of these terms best describes what criminal justice social workers or probation officers do?
2. To what extent do you think that findings from research on psychotherapy and counselling *in general* has relevance for work with offenders? What might be some of the problems in reading across from one area to another?
3. Why is legitimacy so important in work with offenders? In practical terms, what can practitioners do to enhance the legitimacy of their work?
4. Why is respecting diversity so important in assessing risk and needs?
5. In discussing 'research-based planning' of interventions, the authors argue in Chapter 7 that practitioners need to develop clear and explicit theories of change, i.e. articulating why they think that doing what they propose to do will bring about the right results. From your experience, to what extent are such theories of change apparent in practice, either implicitly or explicitly? Can you articulate a theory of change in relation to someone with whom you have worked?
6. Summarise the strengths and weaknesses of specialist, generic and hybrid models of case management, as outlined by Partridge (2004).
7. To what extent do you agree that Holt's (2000) four 'C's sum up the key issues in case management?
8. Reviewing Bottoms (2001) typology of compliance mechanisms, which mechanisms do you think tend to be most relied upon in probation work? Which mechanisms are likely to matter most in supporting desistance?

Case study

1. How would you go about developing a working relationship with Liam? What might make this difficult? (Bear in mind that you would not know anything near as much about his life in the real world as the film enables you to see.)
2. What would respecting diversity in assessing risks and needs mean in Liam's case?
3. Assume that Liam is two years older (i.e. 17/18) at the start of the film and that he is successfully prosecuted for drug-dealing at an early stage in the film (before his involvement with Scullion). He is placed on intensive

probation (with conditions requiring him to undertake community service and attend intensive groupwork). Bearing in mind the risks, needs and strengths that you have already discussed in relation to previous chapters, what kind of supervision plan would you develop with Liam?

4. What is your rationale for this plan? Why do you think that doing what you propose to do will bring about the results that you are after?

5. What would Holt's (2000) four 'C's require in this case?

6. What kinds of approaches to compliance do you think might work best in Liam's case? What do you think would not work?

Chapter 8

Further reading

As the chapter highlights, there is an abundance of literature examining supervision and change which brings together material from criminology, social work, social education and psychology and person-centred approaches. In relation to the development of the 'what works?' agenda and the distillation of the principles of effective practice, the books by McGuire (1995) and Chapman and Hough (1998) are key texts. Mair's (2004) edited collection provides the best collection of critical essays, both on the evidence base itself and on the way it was subsequently implemented in England and Wales.

Measured analyses of these debates in the light of emerging evidence from the pathfinders in England and Wales (summarised in Hollin *et al.*, 2004) is provided by Raynor (2004a, 2004b) and in Burnett and Roberts' (2004) collection. On motivational interviewing the key source is Miller and Rollnick (2002) and on pro-social modelling see Trotter (2006).

Study/seminar questions

1. Discuss Coleman's definition of capital as a 'productive' investment and its implication for service approaches?

2. What are the advantages, disadvantages, challenges and tensions as practice adopts more accredited structured programmes?

3. Why are we unlikely to see the major impact on reoffending rates suggested by the 'what works?' literature from structured programmes alone?

4. What other approaches can be used to help people acquire understanding and skills?

5. How can non-accredited practice make use of the principles of effective practice?

6. What factors in research seem to distinguish completers from non-completers and non-starters?

7. What are the key features of building a meaningful and effective working alliance between social worker and client?

8. Examine Prochaska and DiClemente's model of change and discuss its implications for different stages of intervention.
9. Discuss the key aspects of motivational interviewing (MI) and readiness to change.
10. Much of the evidence surrounding MI suggests it is effective because it is person-centred and reflective. Discuss aspects of the criminal justice culture that may help or hinder the motivation of offenders to change.
11. What part can person centred methods play in supervision in the community?

Case study
1. What types of human capital does Liam evidence in the film?
2. To what extent do you think his offending is a result of a lack of human capital, or a lack of skills and abilities?
3. Where would you place Liam on Prochaska and DiClemente's model of change at different stages in the film? Does he seem motivated to change his behaviour at any stage? If not, why not? What might generate such motivation in him?
4. To what extent do you think that accredited programmes would be (a) necessary and (b) sufficient to address Liam's offending?
5. How do you think Liam might get on in a groupwork context?
6. What would it mean to be person-centred in working with Liam?

Chapter 9

Further reading
John Field's (2003) excellent book *Social Capital* provides a very accessible and authoritative introduction to the subject of social capital and to the rapidly increasing literature about it. From there, or from the entries in the References related to Chapter 9, readers will be able to access a much wider range of sources.

In relation to social capital and crime, Bottoms and Wiles' (2002) chapter in the third edition of the *Oxford Handbook of Criminology* provides an excellent overview of related discussions in environmental criminology, although it is safe to assume that the equivalent chapter in the forthcoming fourth edition will have more to say about social capital. Monica Barry's (2006) *Youth Offending in Transition* discusses different forms of capital accumulation and expenditure and their significance in relation to the onset, maintenance and ending of criminal careers. The article by Webster *et al.* (2006) referenced in the chapter is also well worth reading.

Stephen Farrall's (2002) book and his (2004b) chapter in Maruna *et al.*'s (2004) collection entitled *After Crime and Punishment* provide the only developed consideration of the potential role that probation staff could play in developing offenders' social capital and are well worth reading for that reason. McNeill and Maruna's (2007) forthcoming chapter on issues around generativity and desistance (in Gill McIvor and Peter Raynor's collection *Developments in Work with Offenders*) provides a helpful discussion of the significance of generative activities in the desistance process.

Study/seminar questions

1. Identify the main differences in the concepts of social capital deployed by Bourdieu, Coleman and Putnam.
2. Is there more to social capital than just networks and contacts?
3. Thinking about your own experiences of growing up, to what extent do you find Barry's (2006) arguments about the links between liminality, capital, offending and desistance convincing?
4. Do Webster *et al.*'s (2006) findings about the damaged and disrupted social capital of persistent offenders and drug users concur with your own practice experience?
5. Outline ways in which you think probation and social work staff could develop social capital in their work with offenders through:
    (a) Working with families of origin.
    (b) Working with families of formation.
    (c) Working with communities.
6. What are some of the difficulties that practitioners might face in seeking to develop offenders' social capital?
7. What kinds of 'generative activities' might probation and community service provide for offenders or enable them to access?
8. How might the Community Justice Authorities develop community support for ex-offender reintegration?

Case study

1. Describe the types of social capital that Liam does and does not have access to.
2. To what extent do Barry's (2006) and Webster *et al.*'s (2006) analyses of the links between social capital, offending and desistance make sense in Liam's case?
3. Discuss the role of family issues in Liam's offending.
4. If you were Liam's supervising officer, what work might you attempt to undertake with his family? Specifically, to what extent and in what ways might you seek to engage with his mum and with his sister Chantelle?
5. Which of the relationships that matter most to Liam are most likely to support desistance and why? Can he and should he be expected or enabled to withdraw from relationships that seem to be associated with his offending? Bear in mind that this might mean distancing himself from Pinball and from his mum.
6. In terms of his role in his wider community, what difficulties might you face in seeking to develop positive social capital for and with Liam?

7. What kinds of generative roles and activities are available to him? How might his strengths be developed and redeployed in this regard?

Conclusion

Further reading

In relation to restorative justice, a great wealth of up-to-date material is provided in Gerry Johnstone and Daniel Van Ness's (2006) *Handbook of Restorative Justice*. Specifically in connection with links between restorative justice and work with offenders, the work of Gordon Bazemore on 'earned redemption' is particularly interesting. His 1998 paper 'Restorative justice and earned redemption' in *American Behavioural Scientist* and his chapter 'After Shaming' in the 1999 collection on *Restorative Juvenile Justice* which he edited with Lode Walgrave are obvious places to start.

In connection with the ideals and practices of community justice, the concluding chapter refers to a number of publications by David Karp and Todd Clear. Their edited collection *What is Community Justice? Case Studies of Restorative Justice and Community Supervision* (2002) is a useful introduction containing some interesting case studies. Mike Nellis and John Harding have been the main proponents of community justice in the UK; their various papers referred to in the Conclusion are well worth exploring. Brian Williams' (2005) recent book *Victims of Crime and Community Justice* provides a useful counter-balance for anyone at risk of becoming solely offender-focused.

The work of Antony Duff on penal communication is also well worth examining in detail. Though his 2001 book *Punishment, Communication and Community* provides the most comprehensive account of his views, his 2003 article 'Probation, punishment and restorative justice: Should Al Truism be engaged in punishment?' in the *Howard Journal* is essential reading for students of probation and social work.

Study/seminar questions

1. To what extent have probation and social work policy and practice to date paid adequate attention to the needs and rights of victims of crime?
2. If there has been a neglect of victims' needs and rights in probation and social work, what are the implications of this for:
    (a) The moral legitimacy of probation and social work.
    (b) Public support for probation and social work.
3. If there has been a neglect of victims' needs and rights in probation and social work, to what extent do you think that restorative justice provides appropriate responses to this neglect?
4. What might be the benefits and costs of probation and social work services developing more restorative approaches? To what extent are such approaches consistent with Scottish traditions in this field?

5. To what extent do you agree with the three principles of community justice discussed in the Conclusion? To what extent are such approaches consistent with Scottish traditions in this field?
6. Summarise Duff's account of penal communication. To what extent do you agree with his position?
7. To what extent are you persuaded by Duff's vision of the probation officer as the conduit of communicative punishment?
8. Reread the final paragraph of the conclusion. Do you agree that:
   (a) Scotland has never lived up to the promise of its inclusive welfare traditions in this field.
   (b) Reducing reoffending requires it to do so.

Case study
1. Who are the victims of Liam's offending and what are their needs and rights? To what extent does the film blur the victim/offender dichotomy?
2. At what points in the film do you think that restorative justice processes might have been usefully applied?
3. Think again about the three principles of community justice outlined in the Conclusion. What might the application of these principles have meant in Liam's case – especially if, as we assumed in relation to Chapter 7, he had been caught before the seriousness of his offending escalated?
4. Could Duff's account of penal communication be applied in this case? If so, what would it mean for Liam and for the community?
5. To what extent is Liam's reoffending the product of a lack of social or community justice in his own life?

References

ADSW (Association of Directors of Social Work) (1996) *Policy on Victims*. Glasgow: Association of Directors of Social Work.

ADSW (2005) *Changing Lives: A Response to the 21st Century Social Work Review*. At: http://www.adsw.org.uk/documents/ADSW.21CSW.ChangingLives.brief.doc

Anderson, S., Kinsey, R., Loader, I. and Smith, C. (1994) *Cautionary Tales: Young People, Crime and Policing in Edinburgh*. Avebury: Ashgate.

Andrews, D. and Bonta, J. (1998) *The Psychology of Criminal Conduct*. Cincinnati, OH: Anderson Publishing.

Andrews, D. A. and Bonta, J. (2001) *LSI-R User's Manual*. Toronto: Multi-Health Systems, Inc.

Andrews, D. and Bonta, J. (2003) *The Psychology of Criminal Conduct*, 3rd edn. Cincinnati, OH: Anderson Publishing.

Andrews, D. and Kiessling, J. (1980) 'Program structure and effective correctional practices: A summary of the CaVIC research', in R. Ross and P. Gendreau (eds) *Effective Correctional Treatment*. Toronto: Butterworth.

Andrews, D., Zinger, I., Hoge, R., Bonta, J., Gendreau, P. and Cullen, F. (1990) 'Does correctional treatment work? A clinically relevant and psychologically informed meta-analysis', *Criminology*, 28: 369–404.

Annison, J. (2006) 'Style over substance? A review of the evidence base for the use of learning styles in probation', *Criminology and Criminal Justice*, 6(2): 239–57.

Audit Commission (1990) *The Probation Service: Providing Value for Money*. London: HMSO.

Baldwin, M. and Burgess, H. (1992) 'Enquiry and action learning in practice placements', *Social Work Education*, 11(3): 36–44.

Barber, J. (1991) *Beyond Casework*. Basingstoke: Macmillan.

Barry, M. (2000) 'The mentor/monitor debate in criminal justice: What works for offenders', *British Journal of Social Work*, 30(5): 575–95.

Barry, M. (2004) 'Understanding Youth Offending: In Search of "Social Recognition"', PhD dissertation, University of Stirling.

Barry, M. (2006) *Youth Offending in Transition: The Search for Social Recognition*. London: Routledge.

Bateman, T. and Pitts, J. (2005) 'Conclusion: What the Evidence Tells Us', in T. Bateman and J. Pitts (eds) *The RHP Companion to Youth Justice*. Lyme Regis: Russell House Publishing.

Bauman, Z. (1997) *Postmodernity and its Discontents*. Cambridge: Polity Press.

Bazemore, G. (1998) 'Restorative justice and earned redemption: Communities, victims and offender reintegration', *American Behavioural Scientist*, 41(6): 768–813.

Bazemore, G. (1999) 'After Shaming, Whither Reintegration: Restorative Justice and Relational Rehabilitation', in G. Bazemore and L. Walgrave (eds) *Restorative Juvenile Justice: Repairing the Harm of Youth Crime*. Monsey, NY: Criminal Justice Press.

Bazemore, G. and Elis (2007) 'Evaluation of Restorative Justice', in G. Johnstone and D. Van Ness (eds) *Handbook of Restorative Justice*. Cullompton: Willan Publishing.

Bazemore, G. and Umbreit, M. (1994) *Balanced and Restorative Justice*. Washington, DC: Department of Justice, Office of Justice Programs.

Bergman, A. H. (2002) *Teaching a New Way of Thinking: An Evaluation of the Cognitive Skills Programme in the Prison and Probation Service 1995–2000*. Stockholm: National Council for Crime Prevention, Sweden.

Biestek, F. P. (1961) *The Casework Relationship*. London: Unwin University Books.

Boeck, T., Fleming, J. and Kemshall, H. (2004) 'Young People, Social Capital and the Negotiation of Risk', paper presented at the European Society of Criminology Annual Conference, Amsterdam.

Bonta, J., Rugge, T., Sedo, B. and Coles, R. (2004) *Case Management in Manitoba Probation*. Manitoba, Canada: Manitoba Department of Corrections.

Bordin, E. (1979) 'The generalizability of the psychoanalytic concept of the working alliance', *Psychotherapy*, 16: 252–60.

Bottoms, A. (1983) 'Neglected Features of Contemporary Penal Systems', in D. Garland and P. Young (eds) *The Power to Punish: Contemporary Penality and Social Analysis*. London: Heinemann.

Bottoms, A. (2001) 'Compliance and Community Penalties', in A. Bottoms, L. Gelsthorpe and S. Rex (eds) *Community Penalties: Changes and Challenges*. Cullompton: Willan Publishing.

Bottoms, A. and McWilliams, W. (1979) 'A non-treatment paradigm for probation practice', *British Journal of Social Work*, 9(2): 160–201.

Bottoms, A. and Stelman, A. (1988) *Social Inquiry Reports: A Framework for Practice Development*. London: Wildwood House.

Bottoms, A. and Wiles, P. (2002) 'Environmental Criminology' in M. Maguire, R. Morgan and R. Reiner (eds) *The Oxford Handbook of Criminology*, 3rd edn. Oxford: Oxford University Press.

Bottoms, A. and Wilson, A. (2004) 'Attitudes to Punishment in Two High-crime Communities', in A. Bottoms, S. Rex and G. Robinson (eds) *Alternatives to Prison: Options for an Insecure Society*. Cullompton: Willan Publishing.

Bottoms, A., Shapland, J., Costello, A., Holmes, D. and Muir, G. (2004) 'Towards desistance: Theoretical underpinnings for an empirical study', *Howard Journal*, 43(4): 368–89.

Bourdieu, P. and Wacquant, L. (1992) *An Invitation to Reflexive Sociology*. Cambridge: Polity Press.

Boyle, J. (1983) *A Sense of Freedom*. London: Pan Books.

Boyle, J. (1985) *The Pain of Confinement: Prison Diaries*. London: Pan Books.

Braithwaite, J. (1989) *Crime, Shame and Reintegration*. Cambridge: Cambridge University Press.

Braithwaite, J. (1999) 'Restorative Justice: Assessing Optimistic and Pessimistic Accounts', in M. Tonry (ed.) *Crime and Justice: A Review of Research*. Chicago: University of Chicago Press.

Bruce, N. (1975) 'Children's Hearings: A retrospect', *British Journal of Criminology* 15(4): 333–44.

Bruce, N. (1985) 'Juvenile Justice in Scotland: A Historical Perspective', paper presented at a Franco-British workshop, 'The Best Interests of the Child', Edinburgh, April.

Burgess, H. and Jackson, S. (1990) 'Enquiry and action learning: A new approach to social work education', *Social Work Education*, 9(3): 3–19.

Burke, L., Mair, G. and Ragonese, E. (2006) 'An evaluation of service provision for short-term and remand prisoners with drug problems', *Probation Journal*, 53(2): 109–23.

Burnett, R. (1992) *The Dynamics of Recidivism.* Oxford: University of Oxford Centre for Criminological Research.

Burnett, R. (1996) *Fitting Supervision to Offenders: Assessment and Allocation in the Probation Service*, Research Study 153. London: Home Office.

Burnett, R. (2000) 'Understanding criminal careers through a series of in-depth interviews', *Offender Programs Report*, 4(1): 1–16.

Burnett, R. (2004) 'One-to-one Ways of promoting Desistance: In Search of an Evidence Base', in R. Burnett and C. Roberts (eds) *What Works in Probation and Youth Justice.* Cullompton: Willan Publishing.

Burnett, R. and McNeill, F. (2005) 'The place of the officer–offender relationship in assisting offenders to desist from crime', *Probation Journal*, 52(3): 247–68.

Burnett, R. and Maruna, S. (2004) 'So "prison works" does it? The criminal careers of 130 men released from prison under Home Secretary, Michael Howard', *Howard Journal*, 43(4): 390–404.

Burnett, R. and Roberts, C. (eds) (2004) *What Works in Probation and Youth Justice.* Cullompton: Willan Publishing.

Caddick, B. (1994) 'The "New Careers" experiment in rehabilitating offenders: Last messages from a fading star', *British Journal of Social Work*, 24: 449–60.

Carlen, P. (2002) *Women and Punishment: The Struggle for Justice.* Cullompton: Willan Publishing.

Carter, P. (2004) *Managing Offenders, Reducing Crime: A New Approach.* London: Home Office, Strategy Unit.

Chapman, T. and Hough, M. (1998) *Evidence Based Practice: A Guide to Effective Practice.* London: Home Office.

Chui, W.-H. and Nellis, M. (eds) (2003) *Moving Probation Forward: Evidence, Arguments and Practice.* London: Longman.

City of Glasgow (1955) *Probation: A Brief Survey of Fifty Years of the Probation Service of the City of Glasgow 1905–1955.* Glasgow: City of Glasgow Probation Area Committee.

City of Glasgow (1968) *Annual Report 1968.* Glasgow: City of Glasgow Probation Area Committee.

Clancy, A., Hudson, K., Maguire, M., Peake, R., Raynor, P., Vanstone M. and Kynch, J. (2006) *Getting Out and Staying Out: Results of the Prisoner Resettlement Pathfinders.* Bristol: Policy Press.

Clear, T. and Karp, D. (1999) *The Community Justice Ideal: Preventing Crime and Achieving Justice.* Oxford: Westview Press.

Coffield, F., Moseley, D., Hall, E. and Ecclestone, K. (2004) *Learning Styles and Pedagogy in Post-16 Learning.* London: Learning and Skills Research Centre.

Cohen, S. (1985) *Visions of Social Control: Crime, Punishment and Classification.* Cambridge: Polity Press/Blackwell.

Coleman, J. (1990) *Equality and Achievement in Education*. Boulder, CO: Westview Press.

Coleman, J. (1994) *Foundations of Social Theory*. Cambridge, MA: Harvard University Press.

Collins, H. (1998) *Autobiography of a Murderer*. London: Pan Books.

Collins, H. (2000) *Walking Away*. Edinburgh: Canongate.

Cooper, M. (2004) *Person-Centred Therapy: Myth and Reality*. Available online at: www.strath.ac.uk/counsunit/features-articles.htm

Coyle, A. (2003) 'Joining up Criminal Justice Services: Scotland in an International Context', unpublished speech to ADSW conference, Dunblane, 20 November 2003.

Creamer, A. (2000) 'Reporting to the Scottish Courts: The quality of social enquiry reports and custody', *International Journal of the Sociology of Law*, 28: 1–13.

Croall, H. (2006) 'Criminal justice policy in post-devolutionary Scotland', *Critical Social Policy*, 26(3) 587–607.

Daly, K. (2002) 'Restorative justice: The real story', *Punishment and Society*, 4(1): 55–79.

Daly, K. and Hayes, H. (2001) *Restorative Justice and Conferencing in Australia. Trends and Issues in Crime and Criminal Justice No. 186*. Canberra: Australian Institute of Criminology.

Davies, M. (1978) 'Social Inquiry for the Courts', in J. Baldwin and K. Bottomley (eds) *Criminal Justice: Selected Readings*. London: Martin Robertson.

Devlin, A. and Turney, B. (1999) *Going Straight: After Crime and Punishment*. Winchester: Waterside Press.

Dowden, C., and Andrews, D. A. (1999) 'What works for female offenders: A meta-analytic review', *Crime and Delinquency*, 45: 438–52.

Dowden, C. and Andrews, D. (2004) 'The importance of staff practice in delivering effective correctional treatment: A meta-analytic review of core correctional practice', *International Journal of Offender Therapy and Comparative Criminology*, 48(2): 203–14.

Downing, K. and Lynch, R. (1997) 'Pre-sentence reports: Does quality matter?' *Social Policy and Administration*, 31(2): 173–90.

Drakeford, M. and Vanstone, M. (eds) (1996) *Beyond Offending Behaviour*. Aldershot: Arena/Ashgate.

Duff, A. (2001) *Punishment, Communication and Community*. New York: Oxford University Press.

Duff, A. (2003) 'Probation, punishment and restorative justice: Should Al Truism be engaged in punishment?', *Howard Journal*, 42(2): 181–97.

Duff, P. and Burman, M. (1994) *Diversion from Prosecution to Psychiatric Care*. Edinburgh: Scottish Office Central Research Unit.

Duncan, B. L., Hubble, M. A. and Miller, S. D. (1997) *Psychotherapy with Impossible Cases: The Efficient Treatment of Therapy Veterans*. New York: Norton.

Dutton, K. and Whyte, B. (2006) *Implementing Restorative Justice within an Integrated Welfare System: The Evaluation of Glasgow's Restorative Justice Service, Interim Summary Report*. Edinburgh: Criminal Justice Social Work Development Centre for Scotland.

Eley, S., McIvor, G., Malloch, M. and Munro, B. (2005) *A Comparative Review of Alternatives to Custody: Lessons from Finland, Sweden and Western Australia*, Final Report commissioned by the Scottish Parliament Information Centre for the Justice 1 Committee. Edinburgh: Scottish Parliament.

Etzioni, A. (1991) *A Responsive Society: Collected Essays on Guiding Deliberate Social Change*. San Francisco, CA: Jossey-Bass.

European Union (2001) *Framework on the Standing of Victims in Criminal Proceedings*. Strasbourg: European Union.

Farrall, S. (2002) *Rethinking What Works with Offenders: Probation, Social Context and Desistance from Crime*. Cullompton: Willan Publishing.

Farrall, S. (2003a) 'J'accuse: Probation evaluation-research epistemologies: Part 1: The critique', *Criminology and Criminal Justice*, 3: 161–79.

Farrall, S. (2003b) 'J'accuse: Probation evaluation-research epistemologies: Part 2: This time it's personal and social factors', *Criminology and Criminal Justice*, 3: 249–68.

Farrall, S. (2004a) 'Supervision, Motivation and Social Context: What Matters Most When Probationers Desist?', in G. Mair (ed.) *What Matters in Probation*. Cullompton: Willan Publishing.

Farrall, S. (2004b) 'Social Capital, Probation Supervision and Desistance from Crime', in S. Maruna and R. Immarigeon (eds) *After Crime and Punishment: Ex-Offender Reintegration and Desistance from Crime*. Cullompton: Willan Publishing.

Farrall, S. and Bowling, B. (1999) 'Structuration, human development and desistance from crime', *British Journal of Criminology*, 17(2): 252–67.

Farrall, S. and Calverley, A. (2006) *Understanding Desistance from Crime: Theoretical Directions in Rehabilitation and Resettlement*. Maidenhead: Open University Press.

Farrington, D. (1996) *Understanding and Preventing Youth Crime*. York: Joseph Rowntree Foundation.

Farrington, D. (1997) 'Human Development and Criminal Careers', in M. Maguire, R. Morgan and R. Reiner (eds) *The Oxford Handbook of Criminology*, 2nd edn. Oxford: Oxford University Press.

Farrington, D. (2002) 'Developmental Criminology and Risk-focussed Prevention', in M. Maguire, R. Morgan and R. Reiner (eds) *The Oxford Handbook of Criminology*, 3rd edn. Oxford: Oxford University Press.

Feeley, M. and Simon, J. (1992) 'The new penology: Notes on the emerging strategy of corrections and its implications', *Criminology*, 30(4): 449–74.

Feeley, M. and Simon, J. (1994) 'Actuarial Justice: The Emerging New Criminal Law', in D. Nelken (ed.) *The Futures of Criminology*. London: Sage.

Field, J. (2003) *Social Capital*. London: Routledge.

Flood-Page, C., Campbell, S., Harrington, V. and Miller, J. (2000) *Youth Crime: Findings from the 1998/99 Youth Lifestyles Survey*, Home Office Research Study 209. London: Home Office.

Fox, A., Khan, L., Briggs, D., Rees-Jones, N., Thompson, Z. and Owens, J. (2005) *Throughcare and Aftercare: Approaches and Promising Practice in Service Delivery for Clients Released from Prison or Leaving Residential Rehabilitation*, online report 01/05. London: Home Office.

Garland, D. (2001) *The Culture of Control: Crime and Social Order in Contemporary Society*. Oxford: Oxford University Press.

Garrett, C. (1985) 'Effects of residential treatment on adjudicated delinquents: A meta-analysis', *Journal of Research in Crime and Delinquency*, 22: 287–308.

Gelsthorpe, L. (2003) 'Theories of Crime' in W.-H. Chui and M. Nellis (eds) *Moving Probation Forward: Evidence, Arguments and Practice*. Harlow: Pearson Education.

Gelsthorpe, L. and Morgan, R. (2007) *Handbook of Probation*. Cullompton: Willan Publishing.

Gendreau (1996) 'The Principles of Effective Intervention with Offenders', in A. T. Harland (ed.) *Choosing Correctional Options that Work: Defining the Demand and Evaluating the Supply*. Thousand Oaks, CA: Sage.

Gendreau, P. and Ross, R. (1979) 'Effective correctional treatment: Bibliotherapy for cynics', *Crime and Delinquency*, 25: 463–489.

Gendreau, P. and Ross, R. (1981) 'Offender rehabilitation: The appeal of success', *Federal Probation*, 45(4): 45–8.

Gendreau, P. and Ross, R. (1987) 'Revivification or rehabilitation: Evidence from the 1980s', *Justice Quarterly*, 4: 349–407.

Gendreau, P., Cullen, F. T. and Bonta, J. (1994) 'Intensive rehabilitation services: The next generation in community corrections', *Federal Probation*, 58: 72–8.

Gendreau, P., Little, T. and Goggin, G. (1996) 'A meta-analysis of the predictors of adult offender recidivism: What works!', *Criminology*, 34(4): 575–607.

Giordano, P., Cernkovich, S. and Rudolph, J. (2002) 'Gender, crime and desistance: Towards a theory of cognitive transformation', *American Journal of Sociology*, 107: 990–1064.

Graham, J. and Bowling, B. (1995) *Young People and Crime*, Home Office Research Study 145. London: Home Office.

Hagan, J. (1993) 'The social embeddedness of crime and unemployment', *Criminology*, 31(4): 465–91.

Halpern, D. (2001) 'Moral values, social trust and inequality: Can values explain crime', *British Journal of Criminology*, 41(2): 236–51.

Hannah-Moffat, K. (2006) 'Pandora's box: Risk/need and gender-responsive corrections', *Criminology and Public Policy*, 5(1): 183–92.

Harding, J. (2000) 'A community justice dimension to effective probation practice', *Howard Journal*, 39(2): 132–49.

Harding, J. (2003) 'Which way probation: A correctional or community justice service?', *Probation Journal*, 50(4): 369–73.

Harper, G. and Chitty, C. (2004) *The Impact of Corrections on Re-Offending: A Review of 'What Works'*, Home Office Research Study 291. London: Home Office.

Harper, R. and Hardy, S. (2000) 'An evaluation of motivational interviewing as a method of intervention with clients in a probation setting', *British Journal of Social Work*, 30: 393–400.

Harper, G., Taylor, S., Man, L. and Niven, S. (2004) 'Factors Associated with Offending', in G. Harper and C. Chitty (eds) *The Impact of Corrections on Re-Offending: A Review of 'What Works'*, Home Office Research Study 291. London: Home Office.

Harris, R. (1992) *Crime, Criminal Justice and the Probation Service*. London: Routledge.

Hayes, H. (2007) 'Reoffending and Restorative Justice', in G. Johnstone and D. Van Ness (eds) *The Handbook of Restorative Justice*. Cullompton: Willan Publishing.

Hill, M. (1999) 'What's the problem? Who can help? The perspectives of children and young people on their well-being and on helping professionals', *Journal of Social Work Practice*, 13(2): 135–45.

HMIP (Her Majesty's Inspectorate of Prisons) (2001) *Through the Prison Gate: A Joint Thematic Review by HM Inspectorates of Prisons and Probation*. London: HMSO.

HMSO (1970) *Report of the Advisory Council on the Penal System: Non-Custodial and Semi-Custodial Penalties* (Wootton Report). London: HMSO.

HMSO (1983) *Report of the Committee on Keeping Offenders Out of Court: Further Alternatives to Prosecution* (Stewart Report), Cmnd 8958. Edinburgh: HMSO.

HMSO (1989) *Report of the Review Committee on Parole and Related Issues in Scotland* (Kincraig Report), Cm 598. Edinburgh: HMSO.

Hollin C., McGuire, J. and Palmer, E. (2002) *Introducing Pathfinder Programmes into the Probation Service: An Interim Report*. London: Home Office Research ESD.

Hollin C., McGuire, J. and Palmer, E. (2004) *Pathfinder Programmes in the Probation Service: A Retrospective Analysis*. London: Home Office Research ESD.

Holt, P. (2000) *Case Management: Context for Supervision: Community and Criminal Justice Monograph 2*. Leicester: De Montfort University.

Home Office (2000) *Think First: Programme Outline*. London: Home Office.

Home Office (2003) *OASys (Offender Assessment System) Manual*, version 2. London: Home Office.

Honey, P. and Mumford, A. (2000) *The Learning Styles Helper's Guide*. Maidenhead: Peter Honey Publications.

Hopkinson, J. and Rex, S. (2003) 'Essential Skills in Working with Offenders', in W.-H. Chui and M. Nellis (eds) *Moving Probation Forward: Evidence, Arguments and Practice*. Harlow: Pearson Education.

Horn, R. and Evans, M. (2000) 'The effect of gender on pre-sentence reports', *Howard Journal*, 39(2): 184–97.

Houchin, R. (2005) *Social Exclusion and Imprisonment in Scotland: A Report*. Glasgow: Glasgow Caledonian University.

Hoyle, C. and Young, R. (2002) 'Restorative Justice: Assessing the Prospects and Pitfalls', in M. McConville and G. Wilson (eds) *The Handbook of the Criminal Justice Process*. Oxford: Oxford University Press.

Hubble, M. A., Duncan, B. L. and Miller, S. D. (eds) (1999) *The Heart and Soul of Change: What Works in Therapy*. Washington, DC: American Psychological Association.

Hudson, B. and Bramhall, G. (2005) 'Assessing the other: Constructions of "Asianness" in risk assessments by probation officers', *British Journal of Criminology*, 45: 721–40.

Hugo, V. (1862/1982) *Les Miserables*. London: Penguin.

Huntingford, T. (1992) 'The introduction of 100 per cent central government funding for social work with offenders', *Local Government Policy Making*, 19: 36–43.

Hutchinson, S. (2006) 'Countering catastrophic criminology: Reform, punishment and the modern liberal compromise', *Punishment and Society*, 8(4): 443–67.

Hutton, N. (1999) 'Sentencing in Scotland', in P. Duff and N. Hutton (eds) *Criminal Justice in Scotland*. Aldershot: Ashgate/Dartmouth.

Innes, M. (2004) 'Reinventing tradition? Reassurance, neighbourhood security and policing', *Criminal Justice*, 4(2): 151–71.

Jamieson, J., McIvor, G. and Murray, C. (1999) *Understanding Offending Among Young People*. Edinburgh: Scottish Executive.

Jenkins, R. (1992) *Pierre Bourdieu*. London: Routledge.

Johnstone, G. and Van Ness, D. (eds) (2007) *Handbook of Restorative Justice*. Cullompton: Willan Publishing.

Justice Department (2001) *Criminal Justice Social Work Services: National Priorities for 2001–2002 and onwards*. Edinburgh: Scottish Executive.

Karp, D. (ed.) (1998) *Community Justice: An Emerging Field*. Oxford: Rowan and Littlefield.

Karp, D. and Clear, T. (eds) (2002) *What is Community Justice? Case Studies of Restorative Justice and Community Supervision*. Thousand Oaks, CA: Sage.

Kawachi, I., Kennedy, B. P. and Lochner, K. (1997) 'Long live community: Social capital as public health', *American Prospect* (Nov/Dec): 56–9.

Kemshall, H. (2002) *Risk Assessment and Management of Serious and Violent Sexual Offenders: A Review of Current Issues*. Edinburgh: The Stationery Office.

Kendall, K. (2004) 'Dangerous Thinking: A Critical History of Correctional Cognitive Behaviouralism', in G. Mair (ed.) *What Matters in Probation?* Cullompton: Willan Publishing.

Kilbrandon Report (1964) *Children and Young Persons (Scotland)*, Cmnd 2306. Edinburgh: HMSO.

Klein, P. D. (2003) 'Rethinking the multiplicity of cognitive resources and curricular representations: Alternative to "learning styles" and "multiple intelligences"', *Journal of Curriculum Studies*, 35(1): 45–81.

Kolb, D. A. (1984) *Experiential Learning: Experience as the Source of Learning and Development*. New Jersey: Prentice Hall.

Lab, S. and Whitehead, J. (1990) 'From "nothing works" to the "appropriate works": The latest step in the search for the secular grail', *Criminology*, 28, 405–17.

Lambert, M. J. and Ogles, B. M. (2004) 'The Efficacy and Effectiveness of Psychotherapy', in M. J. Lambert (ed.) *Bergin & Garfield's Handbook of Psychotherapy and Behavior Change*, 5th edn. New York: John Wiley.

Laub, J. and Sampson, R. (2003) *Shared Beginnings, Divergent Lives: Delinquent Boys to Age Seventy*. Cambridge, MA: Harvard University Press.

Laub, J., Sampson, R., Corbett, R. and Smith, J. (1995) 'The Public Policy Implications of a Life-course Perspective on Crime', in H. Barlow (ed.) *Crime and Public Policy*. Oxford: Westview Press.

Lewis, S. (2004) 'What works in the resettlement of short-term prisoners?' *VISTA*, 8(3): 163–70.

Lewis, S., Maguire, M., Raynor, P., Vanstone, M. and Vennard, J. (2003a) *The Resettlement of Short-term Prisoners: An Evaluation of Seven Pathfinder Programmes*, Home Office Research Findings 200, London: Home Office.

Lewis, S., Raynor, P., Smith, D. and Wardak, A. (2006) *Race and Probation*. Cullompton: Willan Publishing.

Lewis, S., Vennard, J. Maguire, M. Raynor, P., Vanstone, M., Raybould S. and Rix, A. (2003b) *The Resettlement of Short-Term Prisoners: An Evaluation of Seven Pathfinders*, RDS Occasional Paper 83. London: Home Office.

Lin, N. (2001) *Social Capital: A Theory of Social Structure and Action*. Cambridge: Cambridge University Press.

Lipsey, M. (1992) 'Juvenile Delinquency Treatment: A Meta-analytic Inquiry into the Viability of Effects', in T. Cook, H. Cooper, D. Cordray, H. Hartmann, L. V. Hedges, R. J. Light, T. A. Louis and F. Mosteller (eds), *Meta-analysis for Explanation*. New York: Sage.

Lipsey, M. (1995) 'What Do We Learn from 400 Research Studies on the Effectiveness of Treatment with Juvenile Delinquents?', in J. McGuire (ed.) *What Works: Reducing Reoffending: Guidelines from Research and Practice*. Chichester: John Wiley.

Lipton, D. S., Martinson, R. and Wilks, J. (1975) *The Effectiveness of Correctional Treatment: A Survey of Treatment Evaluation Studies*. New York: Praeger.

Lloyd, C., Hough, J. M. and Mair, G. (1994) *Explaining Reconviction Rates: A Critical Analysis*. London: HMSO.

McAdams, D. P. and de St Aubin, E. (1998) 'Introduction', in D. P. McAdams and E. de St Aubin (eds), *Generativity and Adult Development: How and Why We Care for the Next Generation*. Washington, DC: American Psychological Association, pp. xix–xxiv.

McAra, L. (1998) *Social Work and Criminal Justice, Vol. 5: Parole Board Decision-Making*. Edinburgh: The Stationery Office.

McAra, L. and McVie, S. (2005) 'The usual suspects? Street life, young people and the Police', *Criminology and Criminal Justice*, 5(1): 5–36.

McConnell, J. (2003) 'Respect, Responsibility and Rehabilitation in Modern Scotland', Apex Lecture 1, September, Edinburgh: Scottish Executive.

McCulloch, P. (2005) 'Probation, social context and desistance: Retracing the relationship', *Probation Journal*, 52(1): 8–22.

McCulloch, P. and McNeill, F. (2007, forthcoming) 'Consumer society, commodification and offender management', *Criminology and Criminal Justice*.

McGuire, J. (ed.) (1995) *What Works: Reducing Reoffending*. Chichester: John Wiley.

McGuire, J. and Priestley, P. (1995) 'Reviewing "What Works": Past, Present and Future', in McGuire, J. (ed.) (1995) *What Works: Reducing Reoffending*. Chichester: John Wiley.

McIvor, G. (1990) *Sanctions for Serious and Persistent Offenders: A Review of the Literature*. Stirling: University of Stirling Social Work Research Centre.

McIvor, G. (1992) *Sentenced to Serve: The Operation and Impact of Community Service by Offenders*. Aldershot: Avebury Press.

McIvor, G. (ed.) (2004) *Women Who Offend*. London: Jessica Kingsley.

McIvor, G. and Barry, M. (1998a) *Social Work and Criminal Justice, Volume 6: Probation*. Edinburgh: The Stationery Office.

McIvor, G. and Barry, M. (1998b) *Social Work and Criminal Justice, Volume 7: Community-based Throughcare*. Edinburgh: The Stationery Office.

McIvor, G. and McNeill, F. (2007) 'Probation in Scotland: Past, Present and Future', in L. Gelsthorpe and R. Morgan (eds) *The Probation Handbook*. Cullompton: Willan Publishing.

McIvor, G. and Williams, B. (1999) 'Community-based Disposals', in P. Duff, and N. Hutton (eds) *Criminal Justice in Scotland*. Aldershot: Ashgate/Dartmouth.

McIvor, G., Jamieson, J. and Murray, C. (2000) 'Study examines gender differences in desistance from crime', *Offender Programs Report*, 4(1): 5–9.

McMahon, G., Hall, A., Hayward, G., Judson, C., Roberts, C., Fernandez, R. and Burnett, R. (2004) *Basic Skills Programmes in the Probation Service Evaluation of the Basic Skills Pathfinder*, Report 14/04. London: Home Office.

McMurran, M. (ed.) (2004) *Motivating Offenders to Change*. London: John Wiley.

McNeill, F. (2000) 'Defining effective probation: Frontline perspectives', *Howard Journal*, 39(4): 382–97.

McNeill, F. (2001) 'Developing effectiveness: frontline perspectives', *Social Work Education*, 20(6): 671–87.

McNeill, F. (2002) 'Assisting Sentencing, Promoting Justice?', in C. Tata and N. Hutton (eds) *Sentencing and Society: International Perspectives*. Aldershot: Ashgate.

McNeill, F. (2003) 'Desistance Based Practice', in W.-H. Chui and M. Nellis (eds) *Moving Probation Forward: Evidence, Arguments and Practice*. Harlow: Pearson Education.

McNeill, F. (2004a) 'Desistance, rehabilitation and correctionalism: Developments and prospects in Scotland', *Howard Journal*, 43(4): 420–36.

McNeill, F. (2004b) 'Supporting desistance in probation practice: A response to Maruna, Porter and Carvalho', *Probation Journal*, 51(3): 241–7.

McNeill, F. (2006) 'A desistance paradigm for offender management', *Criminology and Criminal Justice*, 6(1): 39–62.

McNeill, F. and Batchelor, S. (2002) 'Chaos, containment and change: Undertaking a local analysis of the problems of persistent offending by young people', *Youth Justice*, 2(1): 27–43.

McNeill, F. and Batchelor, S. (2004) 'Persistent offending by young people: Developing practice', *Issues in Community and Criminal Justice*, Monograph Number 3.

McNeill, F. and Burns, N. (2005) 'Redemption and Risk: Social Enquiry and the New Penology', paper presented at the Glasgow School of Social Work Seminar Series on 6 December (audio recording available at: http://www.sieswe.org/node/130).

McNeill, F. and Maruna, S. (2007, forthcoming) 'Giving Up and Giving Back: Desistance, Generativity and Social Work with Offenders', in G. McIvor and P. Raynor (eds) *Developments in Work with Offenders*. London: Routledge.

McNeill, F., Batchelor, S., Burnett, R. and Knox J. (2005) *21st Century Social Work. Reducing Re-offending: Key Practice Skills*. Edinburgh: Scottish Executive.

McWilliams, W. (1983) 'The mission to the English police courts 1876–1936', *Howard Journal*, 22: 129–47.

McWilliams, W. (1985) 'The mission transformed: Professionalisation of probation between the wars', *Howard Journal*, 24(4): 257–74.

McWilliams, W. (1986) 'The English probation system and the diagnostic ideal', *Howard Journal*, 25(4): 241–60.

McWilliams, W. (1987) 'Probation, pragmatism and policy', *Howard Journal*, 26(2): 97–121.

Maguire, M. and Raynor, P. (2006) 'How the resettlement of prisoners promotes desistance from crime: Or does it?', *Criminology and Criminal Justice* 6(1): 19–38.

Mahood, L. (1995) *Policing Gender, Class and Family: Britain, 1850–1940*. London: UCL Press.

Mahood, L. (2002) ' "Give him a doing": The birching of young offenders in Scotland', *Canadian Journal of History*, 37(3): 439–58.

Mair, G. (ed.) (1997) *Evaluating the Effectiveness of Community Penalties*. Aldershot: Avebury.

Mair, G. (ed.) (2004) *What Matters in Probation*. Cullompton: Willan Publishing.

Mair, G. and May, T. (1997) *Offenders on Probation*, Home Office Research Study 167. London: Home Office.

Marshall, T. (1999) *Restorative Justice: An Overview*. London: Home Office Research Development and Statistics Directorate.

Marshall, W. L. and Serran, G. A. (2004) 'The role of therapist in offender treatment', *Psychology, Crime and Law*, 10(3): 309–20.

Marsland, M. (1977) 'The decline of probation in Scotland', *Social Work Today*, 8(23): 17–18.

Martinson, R (1974) 'What works? – Questions and answers about prison reform', *The Public Interest*, 10: 22–54.

Martinson, R. (1979) 'New findings, new views: A note of caution regarding sentencing reform', *Hofstra Law Review*, 7: 243–58.

Maruna, S. (2000) 'Desistance from crime and offender rehabilitation: A tale of two research literatures', *Offender Programs Report*, 4(1): 1–13.

Maruna, S. (2001) *Making Good*. Washington, DC: American Psychological Association.

Maruna, S. and Farrall, S. (2004) 'Desistance from crime: A theoretical reformulation', *Kvlner Zeitschrift fur Soziologie und Sozialpsychologie*, 43: 171–94.

Maruna, S. and LeBel, T. (2003) 'Welcome home? Examining the "re-entry court" concept from a strengths-based perspective', *Western Criminology Review*, 4(2): 91–107.

Maruna, S., Immarigeon, R. and LeBel, T. (2004) 'Ex-offender Reintegration: Theory and Practice', in S. Maruna and R. Immarigeon (eds) *After Crime and Punishment: Pathways to Offender Reintegration*. Cullompton: Willan Publishing, pp. 3–26.

May, T. (1999) *Explaining Reconviction Following a Community Sentence: The Role of Social Factors*, Home Office Research Study 192. London: Home Office.

Mearns, D. (2003) *Developing Person-Centred Counselling*, 2nd edn. London: Sage.

Merrington, S. and Stanley, S. (2004) 'What works?: Revisiting the evidence in England and Wales', *Probation Journal*, 51(1): 7–20.

Miller, W. (1983) 'Motivational interviewing with problem drinkers', *Behavioural Psychotherapy*, 11: 147–72.

Miller, W. R. (1998) 'Toward a motivational definition and understanding of addiction', *Motivational Interviewing Newsletter for Trainers*, 5(3): 2–6.

Miller, W. R. and Rollnick, S. (eds) (2002) *Motivational Interviewing: Preparing People to Change*, 3rd edn. New York: Guilford Press.

Millham, S. (1993) Speech to the Association of Chief Probation Officers, AGM, March, as cited in J. Harding, 'Youth Crime: A Relational Perspective', in J. Burnside and N. Barker (eds), *Relational Justice*. Winchester: Waterside Press.

Mitchell, D. and McCarthy, M. (2001) 'What happens to drug misusers on release from prison? An observational study at two London prisons', *Drugs Education Prevention and Policy*, 8(3): 203–17.

Moffitt, T. (1993) '"Life-course-persistent" and "adolescence-limited" anti-social behaviour: A developmental taxonomy', *Psychological Review*, 100: 674–701.

Moffitt, T. (1997) 'Adolescence-limited and Life-course-persistent Offending: A Complementary Pair of Developmental Theories', in T. P. Thornberry (ed.) *Advances in Criminological Theory, 7: Developmental Theories of Crime and Delinquency*. New Brunswick and London: Transaction.

Moore, G. (1978) 'Crisis in Scotland', *Howard Journal*, 17(1): 32–40.

Moore, G. and Whyte, B. (1998) *Moore and Wood's Social Work and Criminal Law in Scotland*, 3rd edn. Edinburgh: Mercat Press.

Moore, G. and Wood, C. (1992) *Social Work and Criminal Law in Scotland*, 2nd edn. Edinburgh: Mercat Press.

Morgan, R. (2003) 'Foreword', in *Her Majesty's Inspectorate of Probation Annual Report 2002/03*. London: Home Office.

Morison Report (1962) *Report of the Departmental Committee on the Probation Service*, Cmnd 1650. London: HMSO.

MRUK (2004) *Research on Community Involvement and Alternatives to Prosecution*. Edinburgh: Scottish Executive. Available at: www.scotland.gov.uk/Topics/Justice/19008/MRUKreport

Murphy, J. (1992) *British Social Services: The Scottish Dimension*. Edinburgh: Scottish Academic Press.

Nellis, M. (1995) 'Probation values for the 1990s', *Howard Journal*, 34(1): 19–44.

Nellis, M. (1998) 'Community justice: A new name for the probation dervice?', *Justice of the Peace*, 25 April, 162: 17.

Nellis, M. (2000) 'Creating Community Justice', in S. Ballantyne, K. Pease and V. McClaren (eds) *Secure Foundations: Key Issues in Crime Prevention, Crime Reduction and Community Safety*. London: Institute for Public Policy Research.

Nellis, M. (2001) 'Community Penalties in Historical Perspective', in A. Bottoms, L.

Gelsthorpe and S. Rex (eds) *Community Penalties: Change and Challenges*. Cullompton: Willan Publishing.

Nellis, M. (2002) 'Community justice, time and the new national probation service', *Howard Journal*, 41(1): 59–86.

Nellis, M. (2004) 'Electronic Monitoring and the Community Supervision of Offenders', in A. Bottoms, S. Rex and G. Robinson (eds) *Alternatives to Prison: Options for an Insecure Society*. Cullompton: Willan Publishing.

Nellis, M. (2005) 'Dim Prospects: Humanistic Values and the Fate of Community Justice', in J. Winstone and F. Pakes (eds) *Community Justice: Issues for Probation and Criminal Justice*. Cullompton: Willan Publishing.

Nelson, S. (1977) 'Why Scotland's after-care is lagging', *Community Care*, 14(12): 87.

Newburn, T. and Shiner, M. (2005) *Dealing with Disaffection: Young People, Mentoring and Social Inclusion*. Cullompton: Willan Publishing.

NOMS (2005) *Working Together to Reduce Reoffending: The NOMS Offender Management Model Version II*. London: National Offender Management System.

Norcross, J. C. (ed.) (2002) *Psychotherapy Relationships that Work: Therapist Contributions and Responsiveness to Patients*. New York: Oxford University Press.

O'Malley, P. (2004) 'The uncertain promise of risk', *Australian and New Zealand Journal of Criminology*, 37(3): 323–43.

Ostrom, E. (1997) 'Crossing the Great Divide: Co-production, Synergy, and Development', in P. Evans (ed.) *State–Society Synergy: Government and Social Capital in Development*. Berkeley, CA: International and Area Studies, University of California.

Palmer, T. (1992) *The Re-Emergence of Correctional Intervention*. Newbury Park, Sage.

Parsloe, P. (1976) 'Social work and the justice model', *British Journal of Social Work*, 6: 71–89.

Partridge, S. (2004) *Examining Case Management Models for Community Sentences*, Home Office Online Report 17–04. London: Home Office.

Paterson, F. and Tombs, J. (1998) *Social Work and Criminal Justice, Volume 1: The Impact of Policy*. Edinburgh: Scottish Office Central Research Unit.

Patterson, G. A. and Forgatch, M. S. (1985) 'Therapist behaviour as a determinant for client non-compliance: A paradox for the behavior modifier', *Journal of Consulting and Clinical Psychology*, 53: 846–51.

Pease, K. (1999) 'The probation career of Al Truism', *Howard Journal*, 38(1): 2–16.

Petersilia, J. (1990) 'Conditions that permit intensive supervision programs to survive', *Crime and Delinquency*, 36(1): 126–45.

Petersilia, J. and Turner, S. (1990) 'Comparing intensive and regular supervision for high-risk probationers: Early results from an experiment in California', *Crime and Delinquency*, 36(1): 87–111.

Pratt, J. (2000) 'Emotive and ostentatious punishment: Its decline and resurgence in modern society', *Punishment and Society*, 2(4): 417–40.

Pratt, J., Brown, D., Brown, M., Hallsworth, S. and Morrison, W. (2004) *The New Punitiveness: Trends, Theories, Perspectives*. Cullompton: Willan Publishing.

Prins, H. (1999) *Will They Do It Again?* London: Routledge.

Prochaska, J. and DiClemente, C. (1982) 'Trans-theoretical therapy: Toward a more integrative model of change', *Psychotherapy, Theory, Research and Practice*, 19(3): 276–88.

Prochaska, J., DiClemente, C. and Norcross, J. (1992) 'In search of how people change: Applications to addictive behaviours', *American Pychologist*, 47: 1102–4.

Prouty, G., Pörtner, M. and Van Werde, D. (2002) *Pre-Therapy: Reaching Contact Impaired Clients*. Ross-on-Wye: PCCS Books.

Putnam, R. D. (1993) *Making Democracy Work: Civic Traditions in Modern Italy*. Princeton, NJ: Princeton University Press.

Putnam, R. D. (2000) *Bowling Alone: The Collapse and Revival of American Community*. New York: Simon and Schuster.

Raynor, P. (1985) *Social Work, Justice and Control*. Oxford: Blackwell.

Raynor, P. (2004a) 'Rehabilitative and Reintegrative Approaches', in A. Bottoms, S. Rex and G. Robinson (eds) *Alternatives to Prison: Options for an Insecure Society*. Cullompton: Willan Publishing.

Raynor, P. (2004b) 'Opportunity, Motivation and Change: Some Findings from Research on Resettlement', in R. Burnett and C. Roberts (eds) *What Works in Probation and Youth Justice*. Cullompton: Willan Publishing.

Raynor, P. (2006) 'Risk and need in British probation: The contribution of LSI-R', *Psychology, Crime and Law*, published online: DOI: 10.1080/10683160500337592.

Raynor, P. and Vanstone, M. (1994) 'Probation practice, effectiveness and the non-treatment paradigm', *British Journal of Social Work*, 24(4): 387–404.

Raynor, P. and Vanstone, M. (2002) *Understanding Community Penalties: Probation, Policy and Social Change*. Buckingham: Open University Press.

Raynor, P., Gelsthorpe, L. and Tisi, A. (1995) 'Quality assurance, pre-sentence reports and the Probation Service', *British Journal of Social Work*, 25: 477–88.

Raynor, P., Kynch, J., Roberts, C. and Merrington, S. (2000) *Risk and Need Assessment in Probation Services: An Evaluation*, Home Office Research Study 211. London: Home Office.

Raynor, P., Smith, D. and Vanstone, M. (1994) *Effective Probation Practice*. Basingstoke: Macmillan.

Rex, S. (1999) 'Desistance from offending: Experiences of probation', *Howard Journal*, 36(4): 366–83.

Rex, S. (2004) 'Beyond Cognitive Behaviouralism? Reflections on the Effectiveness Literature', in A. Bottoms, L. Gelsthorpe and S. Rex (eds) *Community Penalities: Changes and Challenges*. Cullompton: Willan Publishing.

Rex, S. (2005) *Reforming Community Penalties*. Cullompton: Willan Publishing.

Rex, S., Gelsthorpe, L., Roberts, C. and Jordan, P. (2004) *Crime Reduction Programme: An Evaluation of Community Service Pathfinder*. London: Home Office.

Rifkind, M. (1989) 'Penal policy: The way ahead', *Howard* Journal, 28(2): 81–90.

Ripple, L., Alexander, E. and Polemis, B. W. (1964) *Motivation, Capacity and Opportunity: Studies in Casework Theory and Practice*. Chicago: School of Social Service Administration, University of Chicago.

Roberts, C. (2004) 'Offending Behaviour Programmes: Emerging Evidence and Implications for Practice', in R. Burnett and C. Roberts (eds) *What Works in Probation and Youth Justice*. Cullompton: Willan Publishing.

Robinson, G. (2003) 'Risk Assessment', in W.-H. Chui and M. Nellis (eds) *Moving Probation Forward: Evidence, Arguments and Practice*. Harlow: Pearson Education.

Robinson, G. (2005) 'What works in offender management?', *Howard Journal*, 44(3): 307–18.

Robinson, G. and Dignan, J. (2004) 'Sentence Management', in A. Bottoms, S. Rex and G. Robinson (eds) *Alternatives to Prison: Options for an Insecure Society*. Cullompton: Willan Publishing.

Robinson, G. and McNeill, F. (2004) 'Purposes Matter: Examining the "Ends" of Probation', in G. Mair (ed.) *What Matters in Probation*. Cullompton: Willan Publishing.

Rollnick, S. and Miller, W. R. (1995) 'What is motivational interviewing?', *Behavioural and Cognitive Psychotherapy*, 23: 325–34.

Rose, N. (1985) *The Psychological Complex: Psychology, Politics and Society in England 1869–1939*. London: Routledge and Kegan Paul.

Rose, N. (1996) 'Psychiatry as a political science: Advanced liberalism and the administration of risk', *History of the Human Sciences*, 9(2): 1–23.

Rumgay, J. (2000) 'Policies of Neglect : Female Offenders and the Probation Service', in H. Kemshall and R. Littlechild (eds) *User Involvement and Participation in Social Care: Research Informing Practice*. London: Jessica Kingsley.

Rumgay, J. (2004) 'Scripts for safer survival: Pathways out of female crime', *Howard Journal*, 43(4): 405–19.

Rutter, M., Giller, H. and Hagell, A. (1998) *Anti Social Behaviour by Young People*. Cambridge: Cambridge University Press.

Saleebey, D. (ed.) (1997) *The Strengths Perspective in Social Work Practice*, 2nd edn. New York: Longman.

Sampson, R. and Raudenbush, S. (1999) 'Systematic social observation of public spaces: A new look at disorder in urban neighborhoods', *American Journal of Sociology*, 105(3): 603–51.

Sarno, C., Hearnden, I., Hedderman, C., Hugh, M., Nee, C. and Herrington, V. (2000) *Working their Way out of Offending*, Home Office Research Study 218. London: Home Office.

SCCCJ (Scottish Consortium on Crime and Criminal Justice) (2005) *Reducing the Prison Population: Penal Policy and Social Choices*. Edinburgh: SCCCJ.

Schiff, M. F. (1998) 'Restorative justice interventions for juvenile offenders: A research agenda for the next decade', *Western Criminology Review*, 1(1) (June).

Schoon, I. J. and Bynner, H. (2003) 'Risk and resilience in the life course: Implications for interventions and social policies', *Journal of Youth Studies*, 6(1): 21–31.

Scottish Executive (2000a) *National Standards for Social Enquiry and Related Reports and Court Based Social Work Services*. Edinburgh: Social Work Services Group.

Scottish Executive (2000b) *Scottish Strategy for Victims: Scottish Executive Justice Department Action Plan*. Edinburgh: Scottish Executive.

Scottish Executive (2001) *Scottish Strategy for Victims*. Edinburgh: Scottish Executive.

Scottish Executive (2002) *Victims in the Scottish Criminal Justice System*. Edinburgh: Scottish Executive.

Scottish Executive (2003a) *A Partnership for a Better Scotland*. Available online at: http://www.scotland.gov.uk/library5/government/pfbs.pdf

Scottish Executive (2003b) *Developing the Service: Report of the Tripartite Group on Throughcare Issues*. Edinburgh: Scottish Executive. Available online at: http://www.scotland.gov.uk/Publications/2003/01/16093/16159

Scottish Executive (2004a) *Supporting Safer, Stronger Communities: Scotland's Criminal Justice Plan*. Edinburgh: Scottish Executive.

Scottish Executive (2004b) *Re:duce, Re:habilitate, Re:form: A Consultation on Reducing Reoffending in Scotland*. Edinburgh: Scottish Executive.

Scottish Executive (2004c) *Consultation on Reducing Reoffending in Scotland: Analysis of Responses*. Edinburgh: Scottish Executive.

Scottish Executive (2004d) *National Objectives and Standards for Social Work Services in the Criminal Justice System: Standards – Probation.* Published online at: http://www.scotland.gov.uk/Publications/2004/12/20473/49294

Scottish Executive (2004e) *National Objectives and Standards for Social Work Services in the Criminal Justice System: Standards – Community Service.* Published online at: http://www.scotland.gov.uk/Publications/2004/12/20475/49356

Scottish Executive (2004f) *Victim Notification Scheme – Guidance for Victims.* Edinburgh: Scottish Executive.

Scottish Executive (2004g) *National Objectives and Standards for Social Work Services in the Criminal Justice System: Standards – Throughcare.* Published online at: http://www.scotland.gov.uk/Publications/2004/12/20473/49294

Scottish Executive (2004h) *The Summary Justice Review Committee: Report to Ministers* (McInnes Report). Edinburgh: Scottish Executive.

Scottish Executive (2005a) *Supporting Safer, Stronger Communities: Consultation on Community Justice Authorities.* Edinburgh: Scottish Executive.

Scottish Executive (2005b) *Statistical Bulletin CrJ/2005/07: Reconvictions of Offenders Discharged from Custody or Given Non-Custodial Sentences in 1999, Scotland.* Edinburgh: Scottish Executive.

Scottish Executive (2005c) *Smarter Justice, Safer Communities.* Edinburgh: Scottish Executive.

Scottish Executive (2005d) *National Standards for Victims of Crime.* Edinburgh: Scottish Executive.

Scottish Executive (2005e) *Registering the Risks: Review of Notification Requirements, Risk Assessment and Risk Management of Sex Offenders* (Irving Report). Edinburgh: Scottish Executive.

Scottish Executive (2005f) *Statistical Bulletin CrJ/2005/8: Prison Statistics Scotland, 2004/05.* Edinburgh: Scottish Executive.

Scottish Executive (2005g) *Guidance for Phase 2 in Implementing the Enhanced Throughcare Strategy (Revised): Incorporating the New Throughcare Addiction Service.* Edinburgh: Scottish Executive.

Scottish Executive (2006a) *Changing Lives: Report of the 21st Century Review Group.* Edinburgh: Scottish Executive.

Scottish Executive (2006b) *Community Justice Authorities.* Available online at: http://www.scotland.gov.uk/News/Releases/2006/04/03081953

Scottish Executive (2006c) *National Advisory Body on Offender Management.* Available online at: http://www.scotland.gov.uk/News/Releases/2006/03/20150733

Scottish Executive (2006d) *Reducing Reoffending: National Strategy for Offender Management.* Edinburgh: Scottish Executive.

Scottish Executive (2006e) *Statistical Bulletin CrJ/2006/3: Criminal Proceedings in Scottish Courts, 2004/05.* Edinburgh: Scottish Executive.

Scottish Executive (2006f) *Reconvictions of Offenders Discharged from Custody or Given Non-Custodial Sentences in 2002/03, Scotland.* Edinburgh: Scottish Executive.

Scottish Executive (2006g) *Statistical Bulletin CrJ/2006/01: Criminal Justice Social Work Statistics, 2004/05.* Edinburgh: Scottish Executive.

Scottish Executive (2006h) *Costs, Sentencing Profiles and the Scottish Criminal Justice System, 2004/05.* Edinburgh: Scottish Executive.

Scottish Executive (2006i) *Release and Post Custodial Management of Offenders.* Edinburgh: Scottish Executive.

Scottish Labour (2003), Scottish Labour Manifesto 2003: *On Your Side.* Available online at: http://www.scottishlabour.org.uk/manifesto/

Scottish Office (1947) *The Probation Service in Scotland: Its Objects and its Organisation.* Edinburgh: HMSO.

Scottish Office (1955) *The Probation Service in Scotland.* Edinburgh: HMSO.

Scottish Office (1961) *The Probation Service in Scotland.* Edinburgh: HMSO.

Scottish Office (1998) *Community Sentencing: The Tough Option – Review of Criminal Justice Social Work Services.* Edinburgh: Scottish Office.

Sentencing Commission for Scotland (2006) *Early Release from Prison and Supervision of Prisoners on their Release.* Edinburgh: Sentencing Commission for Scotland.

Shaw, M. and Hannah-Moffat, K. (2004) 'How Cognitive Skills Forgot About Gender and Diversity', in G. Mair (ed.) *What Matters in Probation.* Cullompton: Willan Publishing.

Sherman, L., Gottfredson, D., MacKenzie, D., Eck, J., Reuter, P. and Bushway, S. (1997) *Preventing Crime: What Works, What Doesn't, What's Promising,* Report to the United States Congress. Available online at: http://www.ncjrs.org

Simon, J. and Feeley, M. (1995) 'True Crime: The New Penology and Public Discourse on Crime', in T. Blomberg and S. Cohen (eds) *Punishment and Social Control: Essays in Honor of Sheldon L. Messinger.* New York: Aldine de Gruyter.

Smith, D. J. (2002) 'Crime and the Life Course', in M. Maguire, R. Morgan and R. Reiner (eds) *The Oxford Handbook of Criminology,* 3rd edn. Oxford: Oxford University Press.

Smith, M. and Whyte, B. (forthcoming) 'Social education and social pedagogy: Reclaiming a Scottish tradition in social work', *European Journal of Social Work.*

Social Exclusion Unit (2002) *Reducing Reoffending by Ex-prisoners.* London: Office of the Deputy Prime Minister.

Social Work Inspection Agency/Her Majesty's Inspectorate of Constabulary (2005) *Review of the Management Arrangements of Colyn Evans by Fife Constabulary and Fife Council.* Edinburgh: Scottish Executive.

Spencer, J. and Deakin, J. (2004) 'Community Re-integration for Whom?', in G. Mair (ed.) *What Matters in Probation.* Cullompton: Willan Publishing.

Streatfeild Report (1961) *Report of the Interdepartmental Committee on the Business of the Higher Criminal Courts,* Cmnd 1289. London: HMSO.

Stone, N. (1992) 'Pre-sentence reports, culpability and the 1991 Act', *Criminal Law Review,* August: 558–67.

SWSG (Social Work Services Group) (1989) *National Objectives and Standards for the Operation of the Community Service by Offenders Schemes in Scotland.* Edinburgh: Scottish Office.

SWSG (1991a) *National Objectives and Standards for Social Work Services in the Criminal Justice System.* Edinburgh: Social Work Services Group.

SWSG (1991b) *Social Work Supervision: Towards Effective Policy and Practice – A Supplement to the National Objectives and Standards for Social Work Services in the Criminal Justice System.* Edinburgh: Social Work Services Group.

SWSG (1996) *Part 2 – Service Standards: Throughcare.* Edinburgh: Social Work Services Group.

SWSI (Social Work Services Inspectorate) (1996) *Helping the Court Decide.* Edinburgh: Scottish Office.

SWSI (1997) *A Commitment to Protect – Supervising Sex Offenders: Proposals for More Effective Practice.* Edinburgh: The Stationery Office.

SWSI (1998) *Management and Assessment of Risk in Social Work Services.* Edinburgh: Scottish Office.

Thornton, D., Mann, R., Webster, S., Blud, L., Travers, R., Friendship, C. and Erikson, M. (2003) 'Distinguishing and combining risks for sexual and violent recidivism', *Annals of the New York Academy of Science*, 98(9): 225–35.

Tombs, J. (2004) *A Unique Punishment: Sentencing and the Prison Population in Scotland.* Edinburgh: Scottish Consortium on Crime and Criminal Justice.

Tombs, J. and Jagger, E. (2006) 'Denying responsibility: Sentencers' accounts of their decisions to imprison', *British Journal of Criminology*, 46(5): 803–21.

Tonry, M. and Bottoms, A. (2004) *Youth Crime and Youth Justice.* Chicago: University of Chicago.

Trotter, C. (1993) *The Supervision of Offenders: What Works.* Sydney: Victorian Office of Corrections.

Trotter, C. (1996) 'The impact of different supervision practices on in community corrections', *Australian and New Zealand Journal of Criminology*, 28(2): 29–46.

Trotter, C. (1999) *Working with Involuntary Clients: A Guide to Practice.* London: Sage.

Trotter, C. (2000) 'Social work education, pro-social orientation and effective probation practice', *Probation Journal*, 47(4): 256–61.

Trotter, C. (2006) *Working with Involuntary Clients: A Guide to Practice*, 2nd edn. London: Sage.

Tuddenham, R. (2000) 'Beyond defensible decision-making: Towards reflexive assessment of risk and dangerousness', *Probation Journal*, 47(3): 173–83.

Uggen, C. and Janikula, J. (1999) 'Volunteerism and arrest in the transition to adulthood', *Social Forces*, 78: 331–62.

Uggen, C. and Kruttschnitt, K. (1998) 'Crime in the breaking: Gender differences in desistance', *Law and Society Review*, 32(2): 339–66.

Uggen, C., Manza, J. and Thompson, M. (2006) 'Citizenship, democracy and the civic reintegration of criminal offenders', *Annals of the American Academy of Political and Social Science*, 605 (May): 281–310.

Underdown, A. (1998) *Strategies for Effective Supervision: Report of the HMIP What Works Project.* London: Home Office.

United Nations (2000) *Declaration on Basic Principles on the Use of Restorative Justice Programmes in Criminal Matters.* Vienna: UN Economic and Social Council.

Vanstone, M. (2000) 'Cognitive-behavioural work with offenders in the UK: A history of influential endeavour', *Howard Journal*, 39(2): 171–83.

Vanstone, M. (2004) *Supervising Offenders in the Community: A History of Probation Theory and Practice.* Aldershot: Ashgate.

Vaughan, B. (2000) 'Punishment and conditional citizenship', *Punishment and Society*, 2(1): 23–39.

Vaughan, B. (2006) 'The internal narrative of desistance', *British Journal of Criminology*, Advance Access: doi:10.1093/bjc/azl083

Ward, D., Scott, J. and Lacey, M. (eds) (2002) *Probation: Working for Justice.* Oxford: Oxford University Press.

Warner, S. (1992) *Making Amends: Justice for Victims and Offenders.* Aldershot: Avebury.

Warner, S. and Knapp, M. (1992) *Making Amends: Justice for Victims and Offenders – An Evaluation of the Sacro Reparation and Mediation Project.* Aldershot: Avebury.

Webster, C., MacDonald, R. and Simpson, M. (2006) 'Predicting criminality? Risk factors, neighbourhood influence and desistance', *Youth Justice*, 6(1): 7–22.

Wenger, E. (1998) *Communities of Practice: Learning, Meaning, and Identity*. Cambridge: Cambridge University Press.

White, W. (2000) 'Toward a New Recovery Movement: Historical Reflections on Recovery, Treatment and Advocacy', paper presented at the Center for Substance Abuse Treatment, Recovery Community Support Program Conference, Alexandria, Virginia, April.

Whyte, B. (2004) 'Understanding Youth Crime', in J. McGhee, M. Mellon and B. Whyte (eds) *Meeting Needs, Addressing Deeds: Working with Young People who Offend*. Glasgow: NCH Scotland.

Whyte, B. (forthcoming) 'Restoring "Stakeholder" Involvement in Justice', in P. Richie and S. Hunter (eds) *Co-production in Social Work: Research Highlights*. London: Jessica Kingsley.

Whyte, B., Ramsay, J., Clark, C. and Waterhouse, L. (1995) *Social Work in the Criminal Justice System*. Edinburgh: Scottish Office.

Williams, B. (2005) *Victims of Crime and Community Justice*. London: Jessica Kingsley.

Winstone, J. and Pakes, F. (eds) (2005) *Community Justice: Issues for Probation and Criminal Justice*. Cullompton: Willan Publishing.

Woolcock, M. (2001) 'The Place of Social Capital in Understanding Social and Economic Outcomes', in J. F. Helliwell (ed.) *The Contribution of Human and Social Capital to Sustained Economic Growth and Well-Being*. Ottawa: HDRC.

Worrall, A. and Hoy, C. (2005) *Punishment in the Community: Managing Offenders, Making Choices*. Cullompton: Willan Publishing.

Young, J. (1999) *The Exclusive Society*. London: Sage.

Young, P. (1976) 'A sociological analysis of the early history of probation', *British Journal of Law and Society*, 3: 44–58.

Young, P. (1997) *Crime and Criminal Justice in Scotland*. Edinburgh: Scottish Office.

Zamble, E. and Porporino, F. J. (1988) *Coping Behaviour and Adaptation in Prison Inmates*. New York: Springer-Verlag.

Zamble, E. and Quinsey, V. (1997) *The Criminal Recidivism Process*. Cambridge: Cambridge University Press.

Zaplin, R. (ed.) (1998) *Female Offenders: Critical Perspectives and Effective Interventions*. Gaithersburg: Aspen.

Zehr, H. (2002) *The Little Book of Restorative Justice*. Intercourse, PA: Good Books.

Index